CHILDREN'S
PLAY

The Roots of Reading

EDITED BY
EDWARD F. ZIGLER
YALE UNIVERSITY, CENTER IN CHILD DEVELOPMENT AND SOCIAL POLICY
DOROTHY G. SINGER
YALE UNIVERSITY, DEPARTMENT OF PSYCHOLOGY
SANDRA J. BISHOP-JOSEF
YALE UNIVERSITY, CENTER IN CHILD DEVELOPMENT AND SOCIAL POLICY

ZERO TO THREE
PRESS
WASHINGTON, DC

Published by

 ZERO TO THREE
PRESS

ZERO TO THREE
2000 M St., NW, Suite 200, Washington, DC 20036-3307
(202) 638-1144; Fax: (202) 638-0851
Toll-free orders (800) 899-4301
Web: http://www.zerotothree.org

Cover design: Kirk DouPonce, UDG Designworks
Text design and composition: PreMediaOne, A Black Dot Group Company

Library of Congress Cataloging-in-Publication Data

Children's play : the roots of reading / edited by Edward F. Zigler, Dorothy G. Singer, Sandra
J. Bishop-Josef.—1st ed.
          p. cm.
   Includes bibliographical references.
   ISBN 0-943657-75-X
   1. Play—United States. 2. Early childhood education—United States. I. Zigler, Edward,
1930– II. Singer, Dorothy G. III. Bishop-Josef, Sandra J.
   LB1139.35.P55C48 2004
   155—dc22   2003027631

First Edition Third Printing August 2006
ISBN 0-943657-75-X
Printed in the United States of America

Suggested citations:
Book citation: Zigler, E. F., Singer, D. G., & Bishop-Josef, S. J. (Eds.). (2004). *Children's
play: The roots of reading*. Washington, DC: ZERO TO THREE Press.
Chapter citation: Thompson, R. A. (2004). Development in the first years of life. In E. F.
Zigler, D. G. Singer, & S. J. Bishop-Josef (Eds.), *Children's play: The roots of reading* (pp.
15–31). Washington, DC: ZERO TO THREE Press.

Table of Contents

Foreword

THE PROMISE OF PLAY FOR HUMAN DEVELOPMENT

The following pages, chapter after chapter, study upon study, make clear the connection between healthy early childhood play experiences and outcomes most of us would want for children: verbal and mathematical literacy, organizational skills, intrinsic excitement about learning, school readiness, creativity, and more. The evidence is powerful and holds great promise for children. Play is the natural way for children to explore, learn, and build skills.

Many voices and viewpoints have shaped our culture's parenting and educational philosophies over past generations, as they will for generations to come. Paradigms of good practice are created, debated, embraced, shifted, and discarded. Yet one constant remains—the child's natural tendency to play, no matter what age, gender, cultural background, socioeconomic circumstances, abilities, or level of development. Self-directed play is a deeply satisfying emotional, cognitive, and physical experience for most children and one from which they draw an intrinsic motivation to learn about and engage with the world. This connection has been true since time immemorial; indeed, anthropologists will point out that it is true for the young in almost every mammal species.

It can be argued that today's prevailing paradigm is based on the view of the child as a future producer who must learn certain specific skills—primarily, cognitive and physical—to fulfill that role. Child-rearing and pedagogical trends imply that this view has been embraced by many, and its effects range from the explosion of overscheduled children in organized activities and lessons (at the expense of free playtime) to the adoption of structured, goal-oriented, adult-directed classroom instruction for younger and younger children (at the expense of learning through developmentally appropriate play).

It is tempting to frame a debate about these choices as play-based, open-ended learning on the one hand versus more academically oriented, focused teaching with more easily measurable outcomes on the other hand. That debate may be a worthy discussion, though the likely conclusion is that many children (though not all) can learn certain well-defined competencies like literacy either way, and the differences center on pace and process—and the amount of stress experienced by the child.

The more compelling issue, however, is what play-based learning can offer children that formal classroom instruction cannot. Mastering specific skills is one benefit derived from play. But the promise of play—and its many other well-documented benefits—extends significantly beyond the development of literacy, arithmetic, and science skills so spotlighted in today's early childhood classrooms. Play contributes to the emotional, intellectual, physical, social, and spiritual development of the child in ways that cannot be taught through instruction. They must be experienced, and play is the natural, built-in way children accumulate that experience.

What is so important about play? It helps children develop the capacity to understand themselves and others; solve problems; be flexible and self-motivated; learn to regulate their own emotions and behavior; have resiliency and confidence; and develop a strong, usable set of personal ethics. Indeed, how else could very young children, including infants, develop these qualities without self-directed exploration of and experimentation with objects, places, and relationships, free from the possibility of failure? For many, that description could serve as a working definition of healthy play. Worth underscoring is that these very aspects of a child's "infrastructure" developed through play will also help her or him master the more narrow cognitive skills that many classrooms set as the goal.

Our children will soon be adults, shaped by their own inchoate abilities plus the effect of parenting, community influences, and our educational system. The decisions we make today on their behalf will affect our culture for generations. Implicit in our choices—whether or not it is ever articulated—is a vision for them, ideally one of hope. What kind of people do we hope our children will be?

If we make it available, play can be an effective, equal-access way to contribute to more children becoming creative, compassionate, competent thinkers and capable problem solvers—and to give them the magic of childhood at the same time.

Susan J. Oliver

Executive Director, Playing for Keeps[1]

---

[1]Playing for Keeps is a national not-for-profit organization that contributes to better outcomes and higher quality of life for children through increasing their access to healthy, constructive play.

Acknowledgments

We have been encouraged in developing this volume by a number of child-oriented, play-promoting nonprofit organizations. We thank Susan Oliver, Executive Director of one such organization, Playing for Keeps, for writing the eloquent Foreword to this book. We would like to thank Sara MacLeman for her help with preparing the manuscript and Sally J. Styfco for editorial assistance. We are also grateful to Emily Fenichel and Nancy Guadagno at ZERO TO THREE for their assistance with this project.

Introduction

Edward F. Zigler, Dorothy G. Singer, and Sandra J. Bishop-Josef

Louis and Jarrett are sitting in a large box. They are playing "fishing" and the box has become their "boat." They decorated this box with magic markers, using many colors. With their teacher's help, they fashioned a fishing pole, using Legos™ and a long string attached to one end. The boys "sail" out to sea and take turns catching the fish. When a storm comes, we hear much giggling and silly noises as their "boat" begins to rock back and forth.

These friends are having fun doing what seems to come naturally to most children. They are playing make-believe. In the course of their play, they cooperate, share, take turns, talk to each other when they disagree, but most of all, they are having fun. Unfortunately, many children do not play as imaginatively as these boys. However, with the help of teachers, parents, or other caregivers, children can learn how to play and, as they engage in their pretend games, develop many of the skills they will need for entry into kindergarten.

What do we mean by *pretend play* and why is this concept so important? Jean Piaget, the prominent Swiss psychologist, defined the various kinds of play in his classic book, *Play, Dreams and Imitation in Childhood* (1962). Play, according to Piaget, takes many forms. Symbolic play, the kind of play we allude to in this book, refers to play during which the child may be using objects in the environment in a way that is quite different from the actual purpose of the object. A broom becomes a horse, a banana becomes a telephone, and clay becomes a cookie. These objects are used with no other purpose than to evoke a new organized memory structure, which psychologists call a schema or idea. Symbolic play can be a familiar activity that is performed in a different situation but without the right equipment or tools. It can involve something illogical and impossible—pirates who sail away after their boat sinks, or it can involve simply feeding a doll with a little stick as the spoon, or role-playing a princess or an astronaut.

The peak period for symbolic play is between the ages of 3 and 5 years when children are heavily involved in pretend games and when many of these children are either in day care centers or with homecare providers. Symbolic play continues until approximately 7 years of age when the demands of school begin to replace the pretend-play periods in a child's life. Fortunately, play can continue beyond the set stages discussed by Piaget and can be practiced throughout the lifespan.

Sensory-motor play, which precedes this stage of symbolic play, starts at birth and persists to about 24 months. During this period, infants repetitively imitate the sounds and actions of people around them. The smiles of the caregiver serve to reinforce the child's behavior, even when the imitated acts have no real meaning for the child. The child who waves and says "bye-bye" as someone enters a room may seem quaint to us, but only later as the toddler reaches the symbolic stage of play will the words and movements match appropriately.

The last period of play that Piaget describes is the period from the age of about 7 years until age 15 when games with rules predominate. These include board games (e.g., checkers and chess) or other games that require a partner and that entail some competition and adherence to the rules.

This book was written in response to the apparent policies of the George W. Bush administration, that play is no longer a viable means for learning and that time spent in free play could be used to study phonics. As the readers will discover in the following chapters, the writers present both theoretical and practical aspects of play. A strong case is made for the continued encouragement of imaginative play in preschool because of the many benefits derived from that play and the relationship of those benefits to school readiness skills.

This book's opening chapter by Edward Zigler and Sandra Bishop-Josef reviews the policies of the George W. Bush administration and the administration's emphasis on cognitive development and literacy, which neglect the importance of play as a major contributor to a child's intellectual, social, emotional, and physical development. The authors indicate that this narrow emphasis on cognitive development, as opposed to the whole child approach, has serious implications for early childhood centers, including those supported by the private sector and those such as Head Start that are funded by the government.

The Zigler and Bishop-Josef chapter discusses the No Child Left Behind Act of 2001 and its thrust toward literacy training as well as the introduction of phonics in the early grades. Head Start, for example, is requiring that directors no longer use free play periods in the traditional manner of allowing children simply to choose the toys and activities they prefer. Instead, as many of the other authors in this book have noted, the focus has shifted to a strong emphasis on preliteracy, encouraging children through formal instruction to learn their letters and to use phonics as part of reading readiness. A House bill reauthorizing Head Start (H.R. 2210) includes provisions for assessments that will determine whether children meet specified goals on preliteracy and pre-math tests. The chapter authors deem the current attack on play as a "step backward" in our nation's history.

Ross Thompson's chapter 2 introduces the notion of the growth of the brain from the first month after conception ("experience-expectant") and its continuous development throughout our lives ("experience-dependant"). Many researchers finally are acknowledging the fact that substantial changes occur in the human brain well beyond early childhood and that this information about brain plasticity needs to be made available to parents and teachers in a more accessible format. Thompson describes and gives examples of the "growth of the body (physical size, motor coordination, health); the growth of the mind (thinking, language, concepts and problem solving); the growth of the person (relationships, social understanding, emotions); and the growth of the brain (development of neurons, synapses, and the influence of experience on brain growth)."

Sensitive periods do exist for the development of sensory or motor systems such as vision and first-language acquisition, but the stimulation children need for this development is generally present in most reasonable human environments. Therefore, it is important to ascertain through early physical examinations that children's eyes and ears are functioning in a normal way, one of the benefits provided poor children participating in the Head Start program.

Thompson is a strong advocate of the need for caregivers to interact with children to provide the cognitive, physical, social, and emotional support they need. He advocates affordable and desirable child-care arrangements and decent wage policies. Parents need to obtain both prenatal and postnatal health care to screen children for developmental difficulties. Finally, Thompson points out that school readiness not only is a matter of promoting literacy and number skills but also is an issue of paramount importance for preschool teachers as they help children gain self-confidence, self-control, the ability to cooperate and to foster curiosity, and the eagerness to learn.

In chapter 3, Marilyn Segal sets the scene for the numerous definitions of play that are discussed by other authors in this book and discusses the value of play for learning. She offers the reader a clear description of the kinds of environments that are developmentally appropriate for infants, toddlers, and preschoolers and that are conducive to play. These young children need to form secure attachments in their early years, but in addition, the adults in their lives need to be continuously nurturing and interactive to encourage play. By outlining examples of simple games and suggestions for play scripts, she presents some practical tips on how the parent and teacher can extend and enrich children's play. The vivid vignettes she presents for the various kinds of play emphasize the important role that language takes in fostering thematic play and in the expanding complexity of role play wherein children enact a familiar or imaginary theme and sustain this theme for long periods.

Play, as Segal postulates, provides opportunities for children not only to feel good about themselves, but also to handle fears, anxieties, and unpleasant experiences. Her examples clarify for the reader how play is vital for helping children deal with the negative emotions. Segal stresses the fact that play affords children a sense of power when they reverse the roles of parent and child in their pretend games.

Brian Vandenberg, in chapter 4, reviews some of the reasons proposed by Piaget and Freud for why children play and the assumptions of these two men that the growth of reason results in the disappearance of play as an important factor in thought. Although Freud believed that play is a mastery of past traumatic events,

Vandenberg suggests that children's fantasy play is an expression of the human capacity to create imaginary worlds that "structure, energize, and give meaning to experience." He claims that children are capable of distinguishing what is play from what is not play but that they may have more difficulty than a sophisticated adult in their interpretation of what is real and not real. Not until adolescence can the child truly understand the difference between reality and fantasy, and only then does play become "more realistic, rule-bound, and rational."

Play is also shaped by cultural factors. As mothers move into the workplace, the demand is increasing for younger children to be "subjected to rigorous tutoring" to prepare them for the necessary skills of "academic survival." According to Vandenberg, play is an attractive solution to this dilemma. He calls attention to the "play curriculum" concept involving toys that are carefully selected, activities that are planned, and adult tutoring and guidance that have specific goals. Vandenberg, however, warns of the danger that concern for imparting educational lessons in play "destroys the child's freedom, joy, and passion realized at the boundary of real and not real."

Chapter 5 by Sharon Kagan and Amy Lowenstein begins with a discussion of two constructs, readiness for learning and readiness for school. The former notion applies to children at all ages and the latter to young children at the preschool or kindergarten level. The former approach views the content of early education as fluid and evolving and the latter as more static and fixed. The authors discuss maturational readiness, acknowledging that all children do not develop at the same pace and that all will not attain school readiness at the same time. Recently, the authors claim this concept has been criticized for its influence in preventing many needy children from enrolling in kindergartens that might foster, rather than deter, their development.

Kagan and Lowenstein continue their chapter with a discussion of the goals of the National Education Goals Panel and the Technical Planning Group's report in 1995, which outline the five dimensions of readiness that evolved from the input of many scholars and from decades of research. The five dimensions include (a) physical well-being and motor development, (b) social and emotional development, (c) approaches toward learning, (d) language development, and (e) cognition and general knowledge. The authors also relate research to these dimensions. Included in their chapter is a brief historical and theoretical perspective on play. The chapter ends with an interesting question, which asks whether or not play is the preferred or the exclusive pedagogy to accelerate children's learning.

Jerome Singer and Mawiyah Lythcott begin chapter 6 with an attempt to place symbolic and sociodramatic play into a more basic framework within general psychology. They draw upon the analyses of learning by renowned cognitive psychologists John Anderson, Lynn Reder, and the Nobelist Herbert Simon, who have examined the relative values of formal drill compared with a more constructivist, "whole child" orientation in literacy acquisition. Without denying the usefulness of repetition and rote memory for some phases of early learning, modern cognition research also points to the value of symbolic representations and schema or script formations in the development of efficient retrievable knowledge. Singer and Lythcott then proceed to show how both spontaneous and guided play activities fostered by teachers can fulfill a valuable role in developing schemas and scripts as organized mental structures for early literacy, emotional readiness, and Robert Sternberg's research-based conception of effective intelligence.

Children's eagerness for storytelling makes it possible for teachers and parents to tell tales, read, or foster playlets to help children acquire a variety of new schemas and to motivate them to play and replay new vocabulary, counting opportunities, and new kinds of social interaction. The fun of playing leads children to engage in spontaneous "drill" activities that can provide the repetitive practice that learning research also suggests is necessary for forming associative mental structures. The authors review in detail actual research studies that provide evidence that classroom sociodramatic play can foster impulse control, self-regulatory skills, and curiosity for new knowledge. The authors review the findings of Sternberg who has proposed that effective school or day-to-day intelligence involves not only the analytic skills of traditional IQ measures but also practical and creative abilities. Imaginative play is especially relevant to foster the more creative facets of intelligence.

Chapter 7 by Kathleen Roskos and James Christie analyzed 20 investigations of the relationship between play and literacy, examining how the problem was formed, what path the solution took, what claims were made, and what evidence supports these claims. Before they describe their analyses in detail, the authors review the research on play and literacy. They comment on the notion that emergent reading is predicted by children's ability to talk about language using metalinguistic verbs such as *talk*, *write*, and *read*. They also accept Vygotsky's construct of the zone of proximal development and the idea that adults or older siblings who are involved with young children as mediators can foster the amount of literacy-related play.

Rather than use a technical explanation that focuses on the integrity of the research design, the validity of statistical findings, and the effect sizes, Roskos and Christie emphasize first analyzing the definitions, explanations, and solutions put forth as conceptualizations and then challenging them. They judged that only 12 of the 20 studies demonstrated sound research. These particular studies supplied evidence that play can be an aid to literacy in the following ways: (a) providing settings that promote literacy activity, skills, and strategies; (b) serving as a language experience that can build connections between oral and written modes of expression; and (c) providing opportunities to teach and learn literacy.

Table 1 in the chapter presents a good summary of the characteristics of the 20 reports. The authors indicate that, for most of the research reports they reviewed, play is a "fuzzy' construct with varying definitions. The research reports were more explicit in their definitions of literacy. Literacy is confined to a "narrower strip of activity" that involves primarily reading and writing where children scribble, they pretend to read and respond to books read to them, and they print. Literacy is confined by these researchers to print-based experiences. A general consensus suggests that the "play environment can be engineered to enhance the literacy experiences of young children." Sociodramatic play was found to be particularly useful for more advanced syntactic utterances and sentence expansions that are linked to reading success. The authors conclude their chapter with suggestions for future research on play and literacy, and they offer ideas of how educators and parents can help to promote this connection.

Play, according to Barbara Bowman in chapter 8, consists of personal characteristics, intelligence, and social components. Play helps children to cope with feelings and to make sense of what they know and what they are trying to know. Bowman traces the development of play from infants' exploration of their own and of their caregivers' bodies to repetitive games, then to manipulative games, and eventually to social dramatic play followed by games of rules. Bowman is sensitive to the cultural aspects of play and reveals that, despite the diversity of cultures, play is quite similar across cultures. Bowman suggests that children in many cultures, "chase, roughhouse, explore, fantasize, practice, create, play games with rules." Nevertheless, we must be cautious in interpreting the play behavior in different cultures. The strategies used by parents in their encouragement of their children's play may vary, as can the form of play, the amount of time spent on play, and what actually is called play in an authoritarian culture or in a democratic culture.

Bowman describes and gives examples of five psychological perspectives that have influenced programs for young children's care and education: maturation-oriented, behavioral, constructivist, psychodynamic, and sociocultural. She then reviews how numerous preschools have moved away from the play tradition, increasing didactic instruction or eliminating or reducing free play. Many of these programs originally were designed for low-income children but gradually infiltrated to other programs for children regardless of socioeconomic class. Bowman cites the stand taken by the National Association for the Education of Young Children opposing the programs that are laden with direct instruction to the detriment of play. At the end of her chapter, Bowman makes a strong case for the education of teachers. A relationship is evident not only between a mother's education and a child's achievement but also between the teacher's education and a child's achievement in school.

An important contribution to this book is made in chapter 9 by Carollee Howes and Alison Wishard in their discussion of culture and shared pretend play. By *shared play*, the authors mean the mutual understanding of the goals and the sequence of behaviors within an action sequence as well as the social skills that are needed to reverse the actions of the partner while establishing mutual gaze. Shared meaning play is also called complementary and reciprocal play. Social pretend play involves the idea of pretend within the shared meaning. To develop shared fantasy or shared pretend play, the children who are play partners must integrate their emerging understanding of pretend and their emerging social interaction. According to the authors, social pretend play is easier to achieve if a more knowledgeable partner such as a mother, teacher, or older sibling plays along with the toddler or young preschooler.

Howes and Wishard discuss the meaning of proto-narratives, the very short stories, sometimes only two utterances long, about children's routine experiences. Children who are just learning to talk produce proto-narratives. Social pretend play and proto-narratives offer children opportunities to discuss meaning with a partner. Although cooperative social pretend play can be enacted without any verbal exchanges, pretend play that involves verbal negotiation offers children the opportunity to jointly construct narratives. Narrative development is consistent in structure with written stories and helps children move toward reading comprehension and later literacy development. Early childhood teachers have encouraged children to make and illustrate their own books based on the stories they enact in their social pretend play. The teachers, of course, write down the stories, read them to the children, and encourage the parents to read these books at home. An alternative, which also can be an addition to this approach, is for teachers to provide more encouragement to engage the children in social pretend play. Nevertheless, the authors have found that social pretend play in community-based child-care centers in the Los Angeles area has decreased between 1982 and 2002. This decrease is consistent with anecdotal reports indicating that other early child-care centers are providing little unstructured time for children to play. The chapter includes a description of cases involving three different centers serving (a) Mexican children, (b) African-American children, and (c) Spanish-speaking and Chinese children.

In summary, the authors suggest that narratives and proto-narratives as well as social pretend play with peers are important factors in emergent literacy. Cultural practices suggest that pretending occurs outside of the home, with older children being responsible for the toddlers. They contend that community cultural practices must be considered with respect to shared meanings, whether in narratives or in social pretend play.

Sue Bredekamp's chapter 10 outlines the brief history of the concept of school readiness, which first reached national prominence in 1990 when President George H. W. Bush and the 50 governors established the National Education Goals Panel. In the following year, five dimensions related to "ready to learn" were identified: (a) language use, (b) cognition and general knowledge, (c) physical health and well-being, (d) social and emotional development, and (e) approaches to learning. In 2001, Head Start expanded these dimensions to include mathematics, science, and creative arts.

Kindergarten teachers generally were in agreement with these goals as documented in a survey conducted by the U.S. Department of Education. Fewer than 20% of kindergarten teachers, however, believed that it was essential for children entering kindergarten to count to 20, have good problem solving skills, use a pencil, or know letters of the alphabet. They were in favor of children possessing language abilities, being eager to learn, and regulating their behaviors in group settings as the major determinants of school readiness. The research indicates that, contrary to what teachers believe is most important for children entering kindergarten, those children who have skills in letter recognition, phonological awareness, and overall language ability are more likely to succeed later on.

Bredekamp continues her discussion with a definition of play, stating that the most effective kind of play for enhancing school readiness is sociodramatic play that is also imaginative or pretend play. The teacher is an important facilitator of sociodramatic play. Teachers can provide time, space, and props for play. They act as observers, stage managers, and co-players, but they must be careful not to intervene unnecessarily. They can provide a theme for the play, and as co-player, the teacher can scaffold language and intervene to support and extend the play. The author cites numerous studies detailing the relationship between play and specific school readiness factors such as self-regulation, social skills, and language development.

The final chapter, 11, by Dorothy Singer and Jerome Singer reviews their play research carried out over a 5-year period with inner-city parents, teachers, and homecare providers. The studies were in response to surveys indicating that more than one third of American children were entering school ill prepared. Another motive for developing training procedures for adults stemmed from the indications received in meeting with groups of inner-city parents that they were somewhat at a loss about engaging in pretend play with their preschoolers. Many parents reported that no one had played with them in this fashion and that they needed to be convinced that make-believe play could be useful in helping their children prepare for school entry.

The authors developed a series of make-believe games that were then produced on a video with printed manuals to accompany them. Embedded in these games were social behaviors such as sharing, taking turns, cooperating, and using manners; cognitive skills such as recognizing numbers, colors, and shapes; and language skills such as gaining new vocabulary, recognizing letters and their sounds, and using language to express ideas.

An important feature of this series of studies was the involvement of the parents and other adults as participants in the actual development of the videotapes. Although these parents were generally not highly educated, they became involved quite readily in providing feedback on issues they thought would help other caregivers in using play to enhance school readiness. In some cases, through the focus groups that met with the producers and researchers, new suggestions emerged for story content that would be valuable in the videotapes. The caregivers rated the materials as not only useful but also fun for them and the children and described them as leading to meaningful bonding experiences. Replication of the studies in various sites around the country supported the findings. Results of the studies described in this chapter indicated that a guided play approach led to improvements in an array of cognitive and social skills in preschoolers. This chapter offers evidence that supports the suggestions made by the previous authors in this book concerning how important an adult mediator can be as a partner in play.

Reference

Piaget, J. (1962). *Play, dreams and imitation in childhood*. New York: W. W. Norton & Co.

PLAY UNDER SIEGE:
A Historical Overview

Edward F. Zigler and Sandra J. Bishop-Josef[1]

The Current Attack on Play

In recent years, children's play has come under serious attack. Many preschools and elementary schools have reduced or even eliminated playtime from their schedules (Bodrova & Leong, 2003; Brandon, 2002; Johnson, 1998; Murline, 2000). For example, in some places, dress-up areas are being removed from preschool classrooms and recess periods in elementary schools are being shortened or omitted. Play is being replaced by lessons targeting cognitive development and the content of standardized testing, especially in the area of literacy and reading (Brandon, 2002; Fromberg, 1990; Johnson, 1998). This policy change resulted partially from findings showing the poor academic performance of many American children, particularly in comparison to students from other nations (Elkind, 2001). The change also reflects an attempt to eliminate the well-documented gap in achievement between children from low socioeconomic backgrounds and minority families and those from higher income, nonminority backgrounds (Raver & Zigler, in press).

The policies of the George W. Bush administration did much to fuel the latest attack on play. The president spoke often about reforming education (including preschool education) with curricula focused on cognitive development, literacy, and "numeracy." Mrs. Bush, a former librarian, met the tradition of holding White House conferences on children's issues with the White House Summit on Early Childhood Cognitive Development—not child development nor actually the whole of cognitive development. The focus was on literacy, one cognitive skill out of many related to success in school. The Elementary and Secondary Education Act, first passed in 1965, was renamed The No Child Left Behind Act when it was reauthorized in 2001.

---

[1]The authors would like to thank Sally J. Styfco for her assistance with this chapter.

The new law added the President's initiative that all children be able to read by third grade (Bush, 2003). The reading mandate and accompanying testing resulted in further emphasis on literacy training, particularly phonics, in the early elementary grades.

The spotlight on cognition also found its way into policies and proposals for preschool services, most notably Head Start. The Bush administration initially wanted to change Head Start from a comprehensive intervention to a literacy program (Raver & Zigler, in press; Steinberg, 2002; Strauss, 2003; Zigler, in press). This sort of change could be made only by changing the law governing Head Start—a time-consuming process. To move the program in the direction it wanted more quickly, the administration imposed new protocols on how the program should be run (decisions that are within its power). For example, training and technical assistance was diverted from its usual function of helping programs meet quality standards to training teachers in literacy instruction. A new reporting system was instituted that imposes standardized testing of Head Start preschoolers twice a year to assess their cognitive development (language, preliteracy, and pre-math skills). The results of the testing will be used to determine whether centers are performing adequately; one fear is that funding decisions may be based on children's test scores.

In 2003, Congress began work to reauthorize Head Start. The reauthorization process typically adjusts program details to keep budgets and services current. This time, however, Congress sought to redesign Head Start. Among other things, a version of a bill later passed in the House (H.R. 2210) removed language in the law relating to what has always been one focus of Head Start, social and emotional development. Most occurrences of these words were replaced with one word, "literacy." This version also stopped assessments of children's social and emotional functioning in ongoing national evaluations of Head Start (Schumacher, Greenberg, & Mezey, 2003). Instead, representatives wanted assessments of whether children meet specified goals on preliteracy and pre-math tests. (These goals prevailed in the bill that eventually passed, although the obliteration of language pertaining to social and emotional competence and evaluations did not.)

Many experts vocally criticized these policy changes, arguing that the overemphasis on cognitive development and standardized testing was inappropriate (Steinberg, 2002; Strauss, 2003). Elkind (2001), in a piece titled, "Young Einsteins: Much Too Early," argued that young children learn best through direct interaction with the environment. Before a certain age, they simply are not capable of the level of reasoning necessary for formal instruction in reading and mathematics. Elkind believed this fact of development explained why the pioneers of early childhood education developed hands-on models of learning. A counterpoint by Whitehurst (2001) titled, "Young Einsteins: Much Too Late" appeared in the same journal issue. Whitehurst, who was subsequently appointed director of the Institute of Education Sciences at the U.S. Department of Education by President Bush, claimed that "content-centered" approaches (i.e., academically oriented) are more likely to facilitate children's literacy learning. Raver and Zigler (in press) disagreed, criticizing the emphasis on cognitive development and standardized testing as being far too narrow and unsupported by scientific evidence on how children learn. They advocated for continued attention to and assessment of children's social and emotional development, viewing this domain as synergistic with intellectual development. Without taking sides on whether emotion or cognition should be primary, more than 300 scholars signed a letter protesting the plan to carry out standardized testing in Head Start, questioning the validity of the proposed assessments (Raver & Zigler, in press). Related data have shown that many children are failing to meet the inappropriate demands placed on them. For example, the number of children held back in kindergarten in Chicago quadrupled from 1992 to 2001 (Brandon, 2002).

A Historical Perspective

A similar repudiation of play and overemphasis on cognitive skills occurred in the late 1950s when American attitudes toward education were seriously affected by the Russians' launching of Sputnik in 1957 (Zigler, 1984). This focus on cognitive skills had nothing to do with new knowledge about child development or education. The Russians' beating the United States into space was traumatic for Americans, representing a clear case of not "keeping up with the Joneskis" and injuring our pride. The Russians' feat was perceived by many as evidence that the more rigorous Soviet education system was more effective than ours. A return to the "3 Rs" was touted as the way to build American superiority in the global arena.

A prominent spokesperson for this point of view was not an eminent early childhood educator, but an admiral in the U.S. Navy. At this time in history, America was deep into the cold war, and the debate about schooling was seen as a matter of such national concern that it seemed appropriate for military leadership to get involved. A key participant was Admiral Hyman G. Rickover, who made the provocative assertion that young children in Russia were being trained in mathematics while America's young children were busy finger painting. The first author of this chapter (Zigler) was trying to forge a middle ground, writing and speaking of the need to nurture all aspects of early development, including the physical, socioemotional, and cognitive systems. He remembers vividly getting a call from Admiral Rickover, whom he had never met. The purpose of the call was to castigate Dr. Zigler for championing a whole child approach instead of encouraging attention to cognition. Thus, the battle line was clearly drawn between "academic" pursuits and play.

By the 1960s, the emphasis on cognition was accompanied by a facile and overstated environmentalism or "environmental mystique" (Zigler, 1970). This view held that minimal environmental interventions during the preschool years could yield dramatic increases in children's cognitive functioning. A book by Joseph McVicker Hunt, *Intelligence and Experience* (1961), was the bible of this point of view and had an immense effect. Hunt argued that the right environmental input could raise children's IQs by as much as 30 to 70 points. Given that IQ is among the most stable of all psychological measures, this promise was completely unrealistic. However, the environmental theory was glorified through the popular press, and bookstores filled with titles such as "How to Give Your Child A Superior Mind." Academic prescriptions for infants appeared, grounded in the argument that, if one started cognitive training early enough, remedial efforts would not be necessary later on. Play, which previously had been considered as the real work of children, became suspect. Instead, drill and exposure to educational gadgetry were seen as the activities worthy of children's time and attention.

Another guiding principle of this environmental theory was that intervention programs are most effective if they are administered during a critical period—the earlier the better. This "critical period" concept was popularized in Benjamin Bloom's (1964) book, *Stability and Change in Human Characteristics.* Bloom pointed out that IQ scores at age 4 years account for half of the variance in adult IQ scores. Bloom's claim was misinterpreted by the popular media to mean that half of the child's learning is over by age 4. This questionable argument further fueled the infatuation with cognitive development and compelled parents and educators to feverishly teach children as much as possible, as early as possible.

Even Head Start fell victim to the excessive focus on cognitive skills and naïve environmentalism (Zigler, 1970). From its inception in 1965, Head Start has been a comprehensive program, with components to support physical health, nutrition, social and emotional development, education, services for children's families, and community and parental involvement. The founders of Head Start believed that preparing children who live in poverty for school requires meeting all of their needs, not just focusing on their academic skills. However, when researchers began to evaluate early intervention programs, they were drawn to assessments of cognitive functioning, particularly IQ test scores (Zigler & Trickett, 1978). Part of the reason was the zeitgeist of the time (e.g., the work of Hunt and Bloom).

Evaluators also became enthralled with the results: Relatively minor interventions—even 6 to 8 weeks of a preschool program—seemed to produce large increases in children's IQs. These gains were soon found to be caused by improvements in motivation rather than cognitive functioning (Zigler & Butterfield, 1968). Yet findings such as these did not (and still do not) deter the use of IQ as a primary measure of Head Start's effectiveness (Raver & Zigler, 1991; Zigler & Trickett, 1978). This practice is understandable in that measures of IQ were readily available, easy to administer and score, and deemed reliable and valid, whereas measures of socioemotional constructs were less developed. Also, IQ was a construct that policymakers and the public could easily understand, and it was known to be related to many other behaviors, particularly school performance.

Before long, however, researchers lost faith in IQ as a measure of Head Start's success (Raver & Zigler, 1991). In 1969, the Westinghouse Report found that Head Start children failed to sustain their IQ advantage once they moved through elementary school. Investigators began to understand that Head Start children's rapid IQ gains could be explained by motivational factors (e.g., less fear of the test and tester, more self-confidence), rather than by true improvement in cognitive ability (Zigler & Trickett, 1978). Experts also pointed out the numerous difficulties and biases in using IQ to evaluate comprehensive intervention programs (e.g., Zigler & Trickett, 1978).

In the early 1970s, the Office of Child Development (OCD; now the Administration on Children, Youth, and Families) articulated social competence as the overriding goal of Head Start and encouraged broader evaluations to measure more accurately the program's effectiveness (Raver & Zigler, 1991). However, no accepted definition was available of social competence, much less established measures. Therefore, OCD funded the Measures Project in 1977, a multisite study to develop a battery of measures of the factors making up social competence, including but not limited to appropriate cognitive measures. Zigler and Trickett (1978) also suggested approaches to assessing social competence, arguing that measures of motivational and emotional variables, physical health and well-being, achievement, and formal cognitive ability must all be included.

Thus, by the late 1970s to early 1980s, the naïve cognitive-environmental view had largely been rejected, and a renewed appreciation of the whole child was becoming evident. The first author of this chapter (Zigler) wrote optimistically in 1984, "I am happy to report that the view of the child as only a cognitive system is now defunct" (Zigler, 1984, p. x). He cited as evidence the Head Start program, which had always addressed all aspects of the child's development, despite the missteps in evaluation. Books by David Elkind, *The Hurried Child* (1981) and *Miseducation: Preschoolers at Risk* (1987), argued that children were being pushed too hard, too early and were being driven to grow up quickly, especially with respect to intellectual tasks. Children were being rushed through childhood, Elkind stated, with little time allowed for being a child and experiencing age-appropriate activities, including play. He saw the consequences of this pressure as severe, ranging from stress to behavior problems and even to suicide. Elkind's books were very popular and were important in moving both professionals and the general public toward a view that social and emotional development is a valuable part of child development and strongly affects intellectual growth.

However, the pendulum had already started to swing back in the opposite direction. In 1982, the Reagan administration cut most of the funding for the Measures Project, supporting only the site that was developing measures of cognitive functioning. In 1991, Raver and Zigler, in an article titled "Three Steps Forward, Two Steps Back," described how, during the Reagan and George H. W. Bush years, the Head Start administration was again focusing almost exclusively on cognitive measures to assess the program's effectiveness. Further, the cognitive measurement system that emanated from the Measures Project (Head Start Measures Battery) was accompanied by a curriculum, which led to concerns about "teaching to the test."

The tide began to shift yet again during the next decade (Zigler, 1994). For example, in 1995, the National Educational Goals Panel, a semigovernmental group composed of federal and state policymakers, officially defined school readiness as consisting of five dimensions: (a) physical well-being and motor development, (b) social and emotional development, (c) approaches to learning, (d) language development, and (e) cognition and general knowledge (Bredekamp, chapter 10, and Kagan & Lowenstein, chapter 5, of this volume; Kagan, Moore, & Bredekamp, 1995). This definition emphasized that these dimensions are inextricably linked and must be considered in their totality as indicators of school readiness. The 1998 reauthorization of Head Start explicitly stated that the goal of the program is "school readiness," similarly defining readiness in terms of physical and mental health, social and emotional development, as well as parental involvement and pre-academic skills (Raver & Zigler, in press). Finally, a sensible middle ground seemed to have been reached, a consensus that learning is fostered by more than cognitive training. However, the tide turned again shortly thereafter, culminating in the recent attack on play and the prescribed focus on academics described early in this chapter. Once again, the emphasis on cognition was accompanied by a simplistic environmentalism, as when mothers were given Mozart CDs in the hospital, with the prescription to play them for their infants to increase their intelligence (Jones & Zigler, 2002).

The foregoing narrative demonstrates that the current disenchantment with play is a step backward in our nation's history. It is also a clear illustration of the swinging pendulum that is often evident in American education, where prevailing political winds allow one extreme view to quickly rise to ascendancy, only to be replaced by another view. Clearly, what is needed is a balanced approach that is based on knowledge derived from the best child development research and sound educational practice.

The Whole Child Approach

Adherents of the whole child approach do not devalue the importance of cognitive skills, including literacy. No reasonable person would argue against the merits of literacy. President George W. Bush's initiative to ensure that every child in America will be a proficient reader is laudable. However, reading is only one aspect of cognitive development, and cognitive development is only one aspect of human development. Cognitive skills are very important, but they are so intertwined with the physical, social, and emotional systems that it is myopic, if not futile, to dwell on the intellect and exclude its partners.

Consider what goes into literacy. It involves mastery of the alphabet, phonemes, and other basic word skills, for certain. But a prerequisite to achieving literacy is good physical health. The child who is frequently absent from school because of illness or who has vision or hearing problems will have difficulty learning to read. So will children who suffer emotional problems such as depression or post-traumatic stress disorder. By the same token, a child who begins kindergarten knowing letters and sounds may be cognitively prepared, but if he or she does not understand how to listen, share, take turns, and get along with teachers and classmates, this lack of socialization will hinder further learning. To succeed in reading and at school, a child must receive appropriate education, of course, but he or she must also be physically and mentally healthy, have reasonable social skills, and have curiosity, confidence, and motivation to succeed. This broader view was endorsed in the authoritative book

Neurons to Neighborhoods (Shonkoff & Phillips, 2000) in which the finest child development thinkers in the nation pointed out the importance of emotional and motivational factors in human development and learning.

The position that social and emotional factors are essential for cognitive development, including literacy, is not new. The founders of Head Start recognized the importance of these factors when they designed the program in 1965. Since that time, a body of research has demonstrated the importance of emotional and social factors for school readiness (Raver, 2002; Shonkoff & Phillips, 2000). For example, emotional self-regulation has been found to be an especially important component of learning (Raver & Zigler, 1991). Children must be able to focus their attention to the task at hand, filtering out distractions. They must be able to control their emotions when in the classroom, both during individual and group activities. They must be able to organize their behavior and listen to the teacher. All of these are essentially noncognitive factors that foster learning. Further, as discussed in this volume (see Bredekamp, chapter 10), this type of emotional self-regulation can be developed through play when children take turns, regulate one another's behavior, and learn to cooperate. Play also provides opportunities for acquiring many cognitive skills. Through play, children learn vocabulary, concepts, a variety of abilities, self-confidence, motivation, and an awareness of the needs of others. These factors are just as important in learning to read as the ability to recognize letters or sounds.

Play and Development: Theory

The current attack on play contradicts sound developmental theory. The two preeminent theorists of cognitive development of the 20th century, Jean Piaget and Lev Vygotsky, both stressed the essential role of play in cognitive development.

Jean Piaget (1896–1980) was a Swiss psychologist who wrote on cognitive development for more than 50 years, beginning in the 1920s, although his work did not come to prominence in the United States until the 1960s and 1970s (Zigler & Finn-Stevenson, 1993). Piaget developed his theory of cognitive development after making extensive observations of his own three children, including their play. He argued that all knowledge comes from action and that children actively acquire knowledge through interacting with the physical environment. In particular, cognitive development occurs through the complementary processes of assimilation and accommodation. In assimilation, the child interprets the environment in terms of his or her present way of thinking. For example, a child using a box as if it were a car is assimilating the box to his or her mental concept of what a car is. Accommodation, in contrast, consists of the child changing and expanding on what he or she already knows. When the child encounters something in the environment that he or she does not understand, the child has to expand, through accommodation, his or her view of the world and thereby restore equilibrium. Play, according to Piaget (1932), provides the child with a multitude of opportunities to interact with materials in the environment and construct his or her own knowledge about the world. Thus, play is one of the primary contexts of cognitive development.

Lev Vygotsky (1896–1934) was a Russian psychologist and theorist of cognitive development as well as a contemporary of Piaget. Like Piaget, Vygotsky's work was not widely known in the United States until years later (in the 1980s). Vygotsky emphasized sociocultural influences on development, particularly how interactions with people—parents, teachers, peers—foster cognitive development. He argued that development occurs within the "zone of proximal development," when tasks that are difficult for the child to learn alone can be mastered if the child is guided by someone who is skilled at the task. The zone of proximal development was conceptualized as having a lower limit (what the child can do alone) and an upper limit (what the child is capable of with guided instruction). In interacting with more skilled partners, the child can be taught the upper limit of the zone. Vygotsky (1978a, 1978b) claimed that play serves as the primary context for cognitive development: "Play is the source of development and creates the zone of proximal development" (1978a, p. 138). In play, the child interacts with others (more skilled peers, teachers, parents) and can learn from them. Further, Vygotsky argued, when children use objects to represent other objects in play (e.g., using a block as a telephone), they inadvertently set the stage for abstract thought. Once the child has developed representational abilities through play, he or she is able to use these abilities to develop reading and writing. In addition, following the rules inherent in all play leads children to develop self-regulation, an ability important for success in the structured environment of the school classroom.

Play and Development: Empirical Research

Decades of empirical research clearly demonstrate the benefits of play for children's cognitive, social, and physical development. Several of the chapters in this volume review this research, so only a very brief summary of major findings is presented here:

- *Cognitive development*—A body of research has demonstrated the beneficial effects of play for cognitive development, including language skills, problem solving, perspective taking, representational skills, memory, and creativity (e.g., Davidson, 1998; Newman, 1990; Russ, Robins, & Christiano, 1999; Singer, Singer, Plaskon, & Schweder, 2003).

- *Social development*—Play has been shown to contribute to the development of social skills such as turn taking, collaboration and following rules, empathy, self-regulation, impulse control, and motivation (e.g., Corsaro, 1988; Klugman & Smilansky, 1990; Krafft & Berk, 1998).

■ *Physical development*—Studies have found the positive effects of play on children's physical development, including muscle development, coordination, and obesity prevention (Council on Physical Education for Children, 2001; Marcon, 2003).

Play and Development: Practice

Recognizing the vital importance of play for children's development, experts have designed curricula using play to enhance cognitive development as well as teach preliteracy and literacy skills (e.g., Bodrova & Leong, 2001, 2003; Bruce, 2001; Gronlund, 2001; Owocki, 1999; Sawyers & Rogers, 1988; Singer et al., 2003). For example, Bodrova and Leong's (2001, 2003) "Tools of the Mind" preschool and kindergarten classrooms, based on Vygotsky's theory of cognitive development and the work of his student, Elkonin, use sociodramatic play to foster literacy. These classrooms contain dramatic play areas where children spend a substantial amount of time daily, and dramatic play permeates many classroom activities. Teachers support children's play by helping them create imaginary situations, providing props and expanding possible play roles. Children, with the teacher's assistance, develop written play plans, including the theme, the roles, and the rules that will govern the play. Preliminary evaluations of the Tools of the Mind curriculum support its effectiveness (Bodrova & Leong, 2001; Bodrova, Leong, Norford, & Paynter, 2003). In one study, children who spent 50 to 60 minutes of a 2 1/2-hour program engaging in supported sociodramatic play scored higher on literacy skills than did children in control classrooms (Bodrova & Leong, 2001). Thus, play, rather than detracting from academic learning, actually supported it.

Conclusion

The current volume offers unequivocal evidence for the critical importance of play for children's development. Play has been found to contribute to development in several domains, including social, emotional, and, most relevant to this volume, cognitive development, including literacy. Thus, the current attack on play defies the evidence and appears to be misguided.

In response to the renewed focus on cognitive skills, many organizations have advocated for the vital importance of play for children's development. For example, the National Association for the Education of Young Children (NAEYC), the leading organization of early childhood educators, has developed a position statement on "principles of child development and learning that inform developmentally appropriate practice." The statement includes the item: "Play is an important vehicle for children's social, emotional, and cognitive development, as well as a reflection of their development" (NAEYC, 1996). Articles in NAEYC's professional journal also promote the benefits of play (e.g., Stone, 1995). In addition, several organizations have been founded to advocate for the importance of play. These include Playing for Keeps (www.playingforkeeps.org); Alliance for Childhood (www.allianceforchildhood.net); American Association for the Child's Right to Play (www.ipausa.org); and Play Matters (www.playmatters.net), founded by Dorcia Zavitkovsky, a former president of NAEYC.

Really, the need to defend play should not be necessary, just as the need to muster support for cognitive training should not be required. The chapters in this book demonstrate the two-way relationship between the two, which leads back to the position explained earlier in this chapter and, in fact, back to the time before any formal study of child development: To foster learning, parents, educators, and policymakers must focus on the whole child. An important point to emphasize is that those who espouse the whole child approach do not reject the value of promoting cognitive development. Instead, they view all systems of development as synergistic and, in that perspective, as the proper focus of child rearing and education. In contrast, those who believe that the cognitive system merits the most attention of parents and educators are essentially rejecting the needs of the rest of the child. By ignoring the contributions of the physical and psychological systems to learning, they promote an educational system designed to fail. To be fair, their extreme view that only cognitive skills are important may be simply a backlash reaction to extreme views that only socioemotional health is important. Both extremes are unfounded and likely detrimental to children learning all that they can.

References

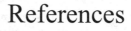

Bloom, B. S. (1964). *Stability and change in human characteristics*. New York: Wiley.

Bodrova, E., & Leong, D. J. (2001). *Tools of the mind: A case study implementing the Vygotskian approach in American early childhood and primary classrooms*. Geneva, Switzerland: International Bureau of Education.

Bodrova, E., & Leong, D. J. (2003). Chopsticks and counting chips: Do play and foundational skills need to compete for the teacher's attention in an early childhood classroom? *Young Children, 58,* 10–17.

Bodrova, E., Leong, D. J., Norford, J. S., & Paynter, D. E. (2003). It only looks like child's play. *Journal of Staff Development, 24,* 47–51.

Brandon, K. (2002, October 20). Kindergarten less playful as pressure to achieve grows. *Chicago Tribune*, p.1.

Bruce, T. (2001). *Learning through play: Babies, toddlers, and the foundation years*. London: Hodder & Stoughton.

Bush, G. W. (2003, January 8). *Remarks by the president on the first anniversary of the No Child Left Behind Act*. Retrieved September 10, 2003 from http://www.whitehouse.gov/news/releases/2003/01/20030108-4.html

Corsaro, W. A. (1988). Peer culture in the preschool. *Theory into Practice, 27,* 19–24.

Council on Physical Education for Children. (2001). Recess in elementary schools: A position paper from the National Association for Sport and Physical Education. Retrieved September 10, 2003 from http://www.aahperd.org/naspe/pdf_files/pos_papers/current_res.pdf

Davidson, J. I. F. (1998). Language and play: Natural partners. In E. P. Fromberg & D. Bergen (Eds.), *Play from birth to twelve and beyond: Contexts, perspectives, and meaning* (pp. 175–183). New York: Garland.

Elkind, D. (1981). *The hurried child: Growing up too fast, too soon.* Reading, MA: Addison-Wesley.

Elkind, D. (1987). *Miseducation: Preschoolers at risk.* New York: Knopf.

Elkind, D. (2001). Young Einsteins: Much too early. *Education Matters, 1*(2), pp.9–15.

Fromberg, D. P. (1990). An agenda for research on play in early childhood education. In E. Klugman & S. Smilanksy (Eds.), *Children's play and learning: Perspectives and policy implications* (pp. 235–249). New York: Teacher's College Press.

Gronlund, G. (2001). Rigorous academics in preschool and kindergarten? Yes! Let me tell you how. *Young Children, 56,* 42–43.

Hunt, J. M. (1961). *Intelligence and experience.* New York: Ronald Press.

Johnson, D. (1998, April 7). Many schools putting an end to child's play. *New York Times,* pp. A1, A16.

Jones, S. M., & Zigler, E. (2002). The Mozart effect: Not learning from history. *Journal of Applied Developmental Psychology, 23,* 355–372.

Kagan, S. L., Moore, E., & Bredekamp, S. (Eds.). (1995). *Reconsidering children's early development and learning: Toward common views and vocabulary* (GPO 1995-396-664). National Education Goals Panel, Goal 1 Technical Planning Group. Washington, DC: U.S. Government Printing Office.

Klugman E., & Smilansky, S. (1990). *Children's play and learning: Perspectives and policy implications.* New York: Teachers College Press.

Krafft, K. C., & Berk, L. E. (1998). Private speech in two preschools: Significance of open-ended activities and make-believe play for verbal self-regulation. *Early Childhood Research Quarterly, 13,* 637–658.

Marcon, R. (2003). Research in review: Growing children: The physical side of development. *Young Children, 58,* 80–87.

Murline, A. (2000, May). What's your favorite class? Most kids would say recess. Yet many schools are cutting back on unstructured schoolyard play. *U.S. News and World Report, 128*(17), 50–52.

National Association for the Education of Young Children (NAEYC). (1996). Position statement: Principles of child development and learning that inform developmentally appropriate practice. Retrieved September 18, 2003 from http://www.naeyc.org/resrouces/position_statements/dap3.htm

Newman, L. S. (1990). Intentional and unintentional memory in young children: Remembering vs. playing. *Journal of Experimental Child Psychology, 50,* 243–258.

No Child Left Behind Act of 2001, Pub. L. No. 107-110, 115 Stat 1535, 20 USC 6361, Part B, Subpart 1, Sec. 1201.

Owocki, G. (1999). *Literacy through play.* Portsmouth, NH: Heinemann.

Piaget, J. (1932). *Play, dreams, and imitation.* New York: Norton.

Raver, C. C. (2002). Emotions matter: Making the case for the role of young children's emotional development for early school readiness. *Social Policy Report, XVI*(3).

Raver, C. C., & Zigler, E. F. (1991). Three steps forward, two steps back: Head Start and the measurement of social competence. *Young Children, 46,* 3–8.

Raver, C. C., & Zigler, E. F. (in press). Another step back? Cognitively oriented assessments will hurt rather than help Head Start preschoolers.

Russ, S. W., Robins, A. L., & Christiano, B. A. (1999). Pretend play: Longitudinal prediction of creativity and affect in fantasy in children. *Creativity Research Journal, 12,* 129–139.

Sawyers, J. K., & Rogers, C. S. (1988). *Helping young children develop through play: A practical guide for parents, caregivers, and teachers.* Washington, DC: National Association for the Education of Young Children.

Schumacher, R., Greenberg, M., & Mezey, J. (2003, June 2). *Head Start reauthorization: A preliminary analysis of H.R. 2210, the "School Readiness Act of 2003."* Washington, DC: Center for Law and Social Policy.

Shonkoff, J. P., & Phillips, D. A. (Eds.). (2000). *From neurons to neighborhoods: The science of early childhood development.* Washington, DC: National Academy Press.

Singer, D. G., Singer, J. L. Plaskon, S. L.,& Schweder, A. E. (2003). A role for play in the preschool curriculum. In S. Olfman (Ed.), *All work and no play: How educational reforms are harming our preschoolers* (pp. 59–101). Westport, CT: Greenwood Publishing Group.

Steinberg, J. (2002, December 4). For Head Start children, taking a turn at testing. *New York Times*, p. B10.

Stone, S. J. (1995). Wanted: Advocates for play in the primary grades. *Young Children, 50,* 45–54.

Strauss, V. (2003, January 17). U.S. to review Head Start program: Bush plan to assess 4-year-olds' progress stirs criticism. *Washington Post*, p. A1.

Vygotsky, L. (1978a). Play and its role in the mental development of the child. In J. K. Gardner (Ed.), *Readings in developmental psychology* (pp. 130–139). Boston, MA: Little Brown.

Vygotsky, L. (1978b). The role of play in development. *Mind in society.* Cambridge, MA: Harvard University Press.

Whitehurst, G. J. (2001). Young Einsteins: Much too late. *Education Matters, 1*(2), 9, 16–19.

Zigler, E. (1970). The environmental mystique: Training the intellect versus development of the child. *Childhood Education, 46,* 402–412.

Zigler, E. (1984). Foreword. In B. Biber, *Education and psychological development* (pp.ix–xi). New Haven, CT: Yale University Press.

Zigler, E. F. (1994). Foreword. In M. Hyson, *The emotional development of young children: Building a emotion-centered curriculum* (pp. ix–x). New York: Teachers College Press.

Zigler, E. F. (in press). Foreword. In M. Hyson, *The emotional development of young children: Building an emotion-centered curriculum* (2nd ed.). New York: Teachers College Press.

Zigler, E., & Butterfield, E. C. (1968). Motivational aspects of changes in IQ test performance of culturally deprived nursery school children. *Child Development, 39,* 1–14.

Zigler, E. F., & Finn-Stevenson, M. (1993). *Children in a changing world: Development and social issues.* Pacific Grove, CA: Brooks/Cole.

Zigler, E., & Trickett, P. (1978). IQ, social competence, and evaluation of early childhood intervention programs. *American Psychologist, 33,* 789–798.

DEVELOPMENT IN
THE FIRST YEARS OF LIFE[1]

Ross A. Thompson

Any discussion on how we care for infants and toddlers must begin with the interests and needs of the children themselves. Therefore, this issue opens with an overview of the dramatic development that takes place during the first 3 years of life, which turns the dependent human newborn into a sophisticated 3-year-old who walks, talks, solves problems, and manages relationships with adults and other children.

This article explains the new understanding of brain development that has captured public attention in recent years, and links it to developments in infant behavior that are equally impressive and influential: the growth of the body (size and coordination), the growth of the mind (language and problem-solving abilities), and the growth of the person (emotional and social mastery). It emphasizes how much early experiences and relationships matter.

The article highlights themes that resonate across these aspects of development:

■ *A drive to development is inborn, propelling the human infant toward learning and mastery.*

■ *People (especially parents and other caregivers) are the essence of the infant's environment, and their protection, nurturing, and stimulation shape early development.*

The author envisions a society that stands beside the families and caregivers who nurture young children, equipping them with knowledge and resources and surrounding them with supportive workplaces, welfare policies, and child care systems.

The mind and heart of the young child have captivated adults for centuries. Young children have been represented as many things: pure innocents, balls of clay, self-entered egoists, confused dependents, a cauldron of impulses, and more recently, information-processing machines and beloved suitors for affection. In their efforts to understand early development, scientists and parents alike have asked: Do early experiences leave an enduring impression on young minds and personalities? Do the first relationships—with parents and other caregivers—shape life-long self-understanding and social relationships? Is the infant's world a "blooming, buzzing confusion" for which adults must provide clarity and organization? Are there truly windows of opportunity in the early years when critical environmental catalysts are required for healthy development? These questions endure because the behavior of young children is hard to interpret. What do the apparently aimless gazing of a newborn, the squeals of a baby's delight or distress, or the casual play of a toddler reveal about the workings of the mind?

The answers to these questions are important because they define the nature of early development and the responsibilities of adults. After all, the obligations of caregivers are established by the needs of young children. Thus, it is important to know if early relationships are formative or peripheral because the answer has implications for how much society values those who care for young children. It makes a difference if young minds are malleable and how they are shaped because therein lies the importance to children of what happens at home and in child care.

Fortunately, developmental psychologists have devoted concerted research efforts to answering these questions about development in the first years of life. Recently, their efforts have been aided by developmental neuroscientists whose initial conclusions about brain growth complement the findings of behavioral scientists. Here is what they have learned (Shonkoff & Phillips, 2000). The early years are important. Early relationships matter. Even in infancy, children are active participants in their own development, together with the adults who care for them. Experience can elucidate, or diminish, inborn potential. The early years are a period of considerable opportunity for growth and vulnerability to harm.

This article explores these questions and answers by considering growth in the early years in four domains:

1. the growth of the *body* (physical size, motor coordination, health);

2. the growth of the *mind* (thinking, language, concepts, problem solving);

3. the growth of the *person* (relationships, social understanding, emotions); and

4. the growth of the *brain* (development of neurons, synapses, and the influence of experience on brain growth).

These four interrelated domains of early development highlight the central accomplishments of early childhood and underscore the obligations of caregivers to provide relationships that are warm and nurturant, experiences that provoke the mind and brain, and protection from physical danger and biological hazards. In the final section, the accomplishments of infancy are reconsidered in light of the importance of the environment to early development, and the opportunities and vulnerabilities of the early years.

The Growth of the Body

Some of the most impressive developmental accomplishments of the early years are the most visible. The young child grows faster during the first 3 years than he or she ever will again (Behrman, 1992). Not only does the child grow physically larger but body proportions also change. The top-heavy newborn evolves into a 5-year-old with a body more closely resembling that of an adult. These changes in body proportions (together with the remarkable advances in brain development that integrate neural pathways governing behavior) help to account for the striking changes in motor coordination, balance, and dexterity that also characterize the early years. The physically uncoordinated newborn learns to sit up by 6 months of age, stand and walk shortly after the first birthday, and (impatiently, exuberantly, or anxiously) jump in place by the second birthday. The rudimentary grasping reflex of infants evolves into more sophisticated, deliberate eye-hand coordination that enables them to pick up small objects (such as a pea on a dinner plate) by the end of the first year. By age 2, toddlers are using their hands to build towers, and by age 3, to draw circles on paper.

These physical advances are also fostered by growth in sensory acuity. Because of changes in the eye, ear, and other sensory organs, and developments in brain organization, infants quickly learn to scan the visual field and to discriminate sounds in much more sophisticated ways. And there are other changes in the young child that derive from the growth of the body. Parents welcome the greater regularity of sleep-wake cycles, the diminishing of crying and unexplained fussiness, and the enhanced predictability in mood that derive from rapid growth in neurobehavioral organization.

There is a tendency in this culture to attribute these remarkable physical achievements to an inborn maturational timetable. Often overlooked is the extent to which these accomplishments rely on crucial catalysts from experience and the environment. But it is a truism of development that the periods of most rapid advance are often periods of greater vulnerability because of the many changes that occur in a short span of time. The rapid growth of the body is metabolically demanding, for example, which means that a nutritionally adequate diet is one of the most crucial requirements for healthy early physical growth. Deficiencies in iron and vitamins owing to chronic undernutrition in the early years can result in cognitive delays, listlessness, and diminished resistance to disease (Lozoff et al. 1998). Young children are also vulnerable to exposure to infectious diseases, drugs and other controlled substances, and environmental toxins (like lead-based paint). In children whose developing physical systems are still maturing, such exposure can result in more profound harm than if it occurs at a later age. Moreover, accidents are a leading cause of injury and death for the very young, owing to children's characteristically poor judgment about potentially dangerous circumstances.

Consequently, healthy physical development in the early years hinges critically on caregivers' determination to protect young children from the harms that might occur. This includes efforts to ensure a healthy, adequate diet; timely immunizations; early vision and hearing screening to detect and correct sensory deficits before they endure; regular health care; and efforts to monitor children's safety in a physical environment that is friendly to the needs and interests of young children.

The Growth of the Mind

How does the mind grow? Does it depend on crucial inputs from the environment? Or is it driven by its own innate information-processing abilities? What parent has not gazed at the casual play of a toddler and wondered if she or he is doing enough to stimulate intellectual growth? Developmental scientists respond to this parent's question in this way: the young mind is astonishingly active and self-organizing, creating new knowledge from everyday experiences. Sensitive parenting—not educational toys or Mozart CDs—provides the essential catalysts for early intellectual growth (see Flavell, Miller, & Miller, 2002; Gopnik, Meltzoff, & Kuhl, 2000).

Thinking and Learning

From birth, a newborn's mind is active even though behavior is disorganized. Consider all of the intellectual equipment that enables newborns to begin engaging the world with their minds (Bornstein & Lamb, 1992). From birth, newborns crave novelty and become bored with familiarity. Their eyes, ears, and other sensory organs are attuned to events that are new and from which they can learn. Their eyes are drawn to sharp contrasts and movement that help them discern the boundaries between objects and derive sophisticated inferences about object shape, size, rigidity, and wholeness. Newborns are capable of integrating knowledge gained from their different senses. They look toward the source of an interesting sound or gaze at an object that matches the texture of the pacifier in their mouths.

These early capabilities provide the foundation for astonishing growth in concepts, causation, memory, and even problem solving in the early years. Consider concept development. The mind of an infant naturally clusters objects together that are similar in shape, texture, density, and other properties; and a toddler's mind categorizes faces, animals, and birds according to their properties (like nose size or leg length). On this basis, 3- and 4-year-olds make remarkably logical inferences about new members of a category—appreciating that a dolphin breathes like the mammal it is rather than the fish it resembles (Wellman & Gelman, 1992)—and enjoy displaying their new knowledge, as any parent of a dinosaur-loving preschooler knows. Consider, also, causation and problem solving. Infants are fascinated with "making things happen" through their actions. For example, they rapidly learn how to pull on a tablecloth to reach the milk. By preschool, young children become adept at manipulating physical objects and people to obtain their goals. Memory development also proceeds at a rapid pace. A baby's fragile memory for the past develops into a young child's flexible memory for routine events. And with an adult's help, preschoolers can remember unique and personally meaningful experiences, such as a trip to Disney World (Hammond & Fivush, 1991), long afterward. Even numerical reasoning begins to emerge as an early awareness of the difference between small quantities grows into a young child's dawning ability to use number concepts (such as one-to-one correspondence) even before learning to count. Each of these accomplishments reveal an active mind that promotes its own growth by continuously revising its understanding based on how the world responds to its initiatives and observations.

Language

A young infant's innate readiness to learn from experience is apparent in other ways as well. Newborns have a natural capacity for discriminating speech sounds that are used in all the world's languages, even those they have never heard and which their parents cannot discriminate. Newborns are, in a sense, "citizens of the world," innately prepared to learn any language. It is only later in the first year that their speech perception becomes specific to the sounds of the language they overhear at home. Newborns also prefer the appearance of human faces to other sights and the sound of human voices to other sounds. Indeed, one experimental study (DeCasper & Spence, 1986) showed that newborns prefer, above all, the sound of their mother's voice reading a story that she had repeatedly recited late in her pregnancy.

In early childhood, even more significant advances occur in language development. A 3-year-old is already putting words together into simple sentences, mastering grammatical rules, and experiencing a "vocabulary explosion" that will result, by age 6, in a lexicon of more than 10,000 words. New words are acquired at an amazing rate (five to six new words daily) as children employ intuitive rules for understanding the meanings of words on their first exposure to them (Woodward & Markman, 1998). Young children thus quickly grasp the meanings of the words they overhear (even words they are not intended to hear). Language enables children to put their developing ideas and concepts into words they can share with others, and language revolutionizes thought by giving children access to the concepts, ideas, and values of other people. Although many important achievements in language development remain for the years that follow, early childhood establishes the basis for complex human reasoning and communication.

Learning and Relationships

All of this learning occurs in a social context, of course. Even newborns respond in special ways to social stimuli, orienting to the people who provide their care and who offer the most interesting and stimulating experiences from which they can learn.

Babies' interest in social sights, sounds, and speech focuses their active minds on interpreting and understanding human words, facial expressions, vocal intonations, and social behavior during even the most casually playful encounters.

The achievements of the mind draw upon, and contribute to, a young child's emotional and social development. A baby's delighted laughter, while kicking her legs to make the crib mobile shake, reveals the powerful emotional incentives that drive her to understand experience and master the world. Early word learning is built upon a toddler's interest in the intentions of an adult speaker. As young children begin to understand the hidden properties of animate and inanimate objects, they also discover the hidden psychological dimensions of other people and begin to explore how beliefs, desires, and emotions influence the human actions they observe. This is why promoting school readiness is not simply a matter of encouraging literacy and number skills. It must also incorporate concern for enhancing the social and emotional qualities that underlie curiosity, self-confidence, eagerness to learn, cooperation, and self-control.

Young children thus do not learn about the world by themselves. A young mind's innate capabilities and its incessant activity each provide powerful avenues for understanding when aided by everyday experience and the behavior of other people. Safe, secure environments and playthings within easy reach permit a young child to explore things that can be examined, combined, and taken apart. Additional catalysts for intellectual growth arise from the natural, spontaneous behavior of sensitive adults. Caregivers do many things to stimulate mental growth. They create daily routines that enable young children to anticipate, represent, and remember routine daily events, such as preparing breakfast together, going to day care, or taking a bath before bed. Caregivers structure shared activities that are manageable for the children and that promote new skills and pride in achievement, such as working on a jigsaw puzzle or sharing a story (Rogoff, 1990). Caregivers promote language growth, from their sing-song "parentese" (which is optimally suited to enable babies to learn the sounds of the native language) to the continuing verbal patter they share with barely conversational young children (which enables children to begin to understand the significance of their everyday experiences). Parents and other caregivers do many things intentionally to promote learning and cognitive growth, but the most important intellectual catalysts they provide are uncoached and arise naturally from their unhurried, untroubled, sensitive encounters with the children they love.

The Growth of the Person

Individuality flourishes during the early years. This is because the temperamental qualities that make each newborn unique become elaborated in the development of close attachments, the unfolding of emotional life, and the growth of self-regulation, self-awareness, and social understanding. Studies of early personality development show that the relationships a young child shares with caregivers are crucial to these accomplishments. For this reason, this is a period of great opportunity or vulnerability for psychosocial health, depending on the quality and stability of these relationships (Thompson, 1998).

Attachments: Secure and Insecure

The first attachments of a baby to its caregivers are as biologically basic as learning to crawl and walk (see Cassidy & Shaver, 1999). Throughout human evolution, close attachments have ensured species' survival by keeping infants protected and nurtured. The development of emotional attachments by age 1 is preceded by months of animated social interaction during which infants and their caregivers exchange playful smiles, gazes, touch, and laughter together. In the life of an infant, secure attachments provide a sense of security that enables confident exploration and offers reassurance in the face of stress.

A secure attachment reflects the warmth and trust of early caregiver-child relationships. It provides a foundation for positive relationships with peers and teachers, healthy self-concept, and emotional and moral understanding. However, although virtually all infants become attached to their caregivers—including fathers, regular child care providers, close relatives, and others, as well as mothers—not all infants develop the secure attachments that arise from sensitive, responsive care. The effects of insecure attachments can be observed in the distrust or uncertainty that young children feel with their caregivers, as well as negative self-image and difficulties in coping adaptively with stress.

A secure attachment early in life does not guarantee healthy psychosocial outcomes, however, any more than an insecure early attachment ensures later difficulty. Attachment security and its outcomes can change in childhood in response to changes affecting family interaction, such as marital stress, parental job change, or a sibling's birth. Sensitive, responsive care thus remains a continuing need of young children throughout the early years at home and in child care (Thompson, 2000).

Self-Regulation and Social Understanding

The early years provide lessons in relationships, including lessons in conflict management and cooperation. As they mature, toddlers become increasingly active, assertive, and goal-oriented, and their caregivers increasingly set limits and expect compliance. Throughout early childhood, adults "up the ante" in their expectations for the child's cooperation and consideration for others. Adults increasingly guide a young child's behavior by using indirect strategies like explanation and bargaining that rely on the child's developing capacities for self-control. At the same time, young children become much more competent at exercising self-regulation, especially when this skill is enlisted for achieving personally meaningful goals (like getting dessert; Kochanska & Thompson, 1997). Although young children do, in fact, become increasingly compliant with adult expectations as they mature, they also show a growing tendency to refuse before they comply, and to negotiate, compromise, and assert their own preferences in other ways. At the same time that attachment security is taking shape, therefore, caregiver-child relationships are also influenced by the behavioral expectations of adults and the willingness of young children to comply. This means that conflict—as well as warmth and security—becomes part of the parent-child relationship.

Beneath the surface of these difficulties of the "Terrible Twos," however, milestones in social understanding are emerging. Nothing focuses a young child's attention on what other people are thinking or feeling more than the realization that a conflict must be resolved. And because toddlers are acquiring a more sophisticated awareness that others' feelings and desires can be different from their own, the caregiver-child interaction becomes a laboratory for exploring these differences and their consequences (Dunn, 1988; see also Gopnik et al., 2000; Thompson, 1998). For instance, a 2-year-old whose hand inches closer to the forbidden VCR while carefully watching her parent's face is testing her best guess about the adult's expected reaction.

Other features of psychological understanding also curb the young child's misbehavior, including a growing capacity for empathy with another's feelings and a developing understanding of how adult expectations for behavior apply to specific situations. Caregivers contribute to this understanding when they firmly, but warmly, focus a toddler's attention on the consequences of misbehavior or the child's responsibility for causing harm to another (Zahn-Waxler & Radke-Yarrow, 1990). A 3-year-old, whose indoor roughhousing has resulted in a crying younger sibling, can learn from an adult about the connections between exuberant running and inadvertent collisions with a smaller person. Equally important, these encounters between a young child and an adult strengthen the child's understanding and concern for others' feelings and needs, which is one of the most important developing curbs on impulsivity and violence.

Self-Awareness

One of the most charming features of personality growth is how young children learn to answer the question "Who am I?" in ever more insightful ways. Developing psychological understanding provides avenues toward greater self-awareness. Infants gradually learn that there is a difference between "self" and "other." During the second year, children develop visual self-recognition (in a mirror) and verbal self-reference ("Andy big!"). This is followed by the period when an assertive 3-year-old refuses assistance and insists on "doing it myself" to assert competence and autonomy. During the preschool years, the child's self-correction in drawing, tying shoelaces, and performing other everyday activities reflects developing capacities for self-monitoring and the motivation to succeed (Cicchetti & Beeghly, 1990). Beginning at age 3, moreover, preschoolers begin to remember events with reference to their personal significance, constructing an autobiographical memory that helps to establish a continuous identity throughout life's events (K. Nelson, 1993). Self-awareness and self-understanding are highly dependent on the evaluations of others, of course, especially those to whom the child is emotionally attached. Consequently, the 2- to 3-year-old's emotional repertoire broadens beyond the basic emotions of infancy to include emotions like pride, shame, guilt, and embarrassment that are elicited in social situations in response to the evaluations of others (Tangney &

Fischer, 1995). A young child's relationships with others thus establish the cornerstone of self-concept through the image reflected in the eyes of another.

Temperament and Emotional Growth

Young children vary, of course, in their temperamental qualities. Inborn characteristics like mood, soothability, and adaptability affect young children's behavioral tendencies (for example, to approach or withdraw from unfamiliar peers), their emotional qualities, and their capacities to tolerate stress. As infants mature into young children, they begin to learn strategies for managing their emotions because doing so contributes to social competence, self-confidence, and feelings of well-being (Denham, 1998; Lieberman, 1993). Their strategies may be simple—such as looking away from a scary TV show or saying, "Mommy will come soon," during a lonely first day at preschool; or retreating to an adult when threatened by a peer—but they begin the lifelong process of learning to regulate emotions consistently with one's temperamental qualities.

Unfortunately, the close relationships with caregivers that ordinarily support and constructively guide emotional growth in the early years can also put young children at risk when these relationships are disturbed or dysfunctional. Sadly, some children are so buffeted by conflicted family environments, chaotic child care settings, or unpredictable challenges in daily experience that their capacities for managing their emotions quickly become taxed, and healthy personality development is imperiled. Emerging research in the field of developmental psychopathology reveals the surprisingly early origins of emotion-related disorders like depression, conduct problems, anxiety disorders, and social withdrawal. These studies also show how relationships with caregivers who are emotionally neglectful, physically abusive, or psychologically inconsistent can (especially when combined with risk factors like temperamental vulnerability) predispose certain young children to the emergence of psychopathology (Sameroff & Emde, 1989; Shaw, Keenan, & Vondra, 1994; Zeanah, 2000). Thus, the conclusion that relationships are central to healthy psychosocial growth in the early years is a double-edged sword. It highlights how sensitive caregiving provides many opportunities for enlivening early social and emotional capacities, but also how markedly inadequate care renders young children vulnerable to psychosocial harm.

The Growth of the Brain

In view of recent public excitement over early brain growth, it might have been appropriate to begin this summary of the early years with a discussion of brain development. Instead, this summary began with the growth of the mind and the person because developmental scientists know considerably more about cognitive, socioemotional, and personality growth than they know about brain development. Indeed, developmental neuroscience is a recent addition to the study of the child. Furthermore, processes of brain development are best understood when considered in relation to the pace and timing of concurrent mental, emotional, and social advances of early childhood because these behavioral achievements provide clues about what is likely to be happening within the brain.

Unfortunately, considerable misunderstanding of early brain development occurs when neurons and synapses are considered independently of the development of thinking, feeling, and relating to others (Thompson & Nelson, 2001). Time-limited windows of opportunity—during which critical stimuli from the environment are necessary for healthy brain development—are exceptional rather than typical, consistent with the gradual course of most features of early development. Brain development is lifelong, not limited to the early years, consistent with the enduring capacities for growth in thinking, feeling, and adapting throughout life. And although the talking, singing, and playing of caregivers are valuable stimulants of early brain development, so also are the caregiver's efforts to provide adequate nutrition; to protect young children from the hazards of drugs, environmental toxins (like lead), and uncontrollable stress; and to obtain early vision and hearing screening. Each of these elements is an important requirement of healthy brain growth.

Blooming and Pruning of Brain Connections

Developmental scientists' observations of early development provide other important clues for what to expect in the developing brain (Dawson & Fischer, 1994; Gibson & Peterson, 1991; Johnson, 1997). For example, the powerful innate capabilities that underlie the newborn's readiness to learn suggest that brain growth begins early and advances quickly during the prenatal months. And indeed it does. Brain development begins within the first month after conception, when the brain and spinal cord begin to take shape within the embryo. By the sixth prenatal month, nearly all of the billions of neurons (nerve cells) that populate the mature brain have been created, with new neurons generated at an average rate of more than 250,000 per minute. Once neurons are formed, they quickly migrate to the brain region where they will function. Neurons become differentiated to assume specialized roles, and they form connections (synapses) with other neurons that enable them to communicate and store information. Neurons continue to form synapses with other neurons throughout childhood. By the moment of birth, the large majority of neurons are appropriately located within an immature brain that has begun to appear and function like its mature counterpart.

Furthermore, given the newborn's hunger for novelty, attention to sensory experience, and preference for social stimulation, significant changes in the brain's neuronal architecture would be expected after birth. This is precisely what occurs, although the manner in which the brain becomes organized (or wired) in the early years is intriguing. Both before and after birth, an initial "blooming" of brain connections occurs; neurons create far more synapses with other neurons than will ever be retained in the mature brain. This proliferation of synapses creates great potential for the developing brain, but it also makes the young brain inefficient and noisy with redundant and unnecessary neural connections. Consequently, this proliferation is soon followed by a stage of "pruning" when little-used synapses are gradually eliminated to reach the number required for the brain to operate efficiently.

How are synapses selected for retention or elimination? Early experience plays an important role. Stimulating experiences activate certain neural synapses, and this triggers growth processes that consolidate those connections. Synapses that are not activated progressively wither over time. Through this "use it or lose it" principle, therefore, the architecture of the developing brain becomes adapted to the needs of everyday stimulation and experience. The effects of this principle can be observed behaviorally in the early years. Vision, for instance, is an example of this principle. During the early months of life, visual acuity increases because the neural pathways connecting eye to brain become consolidated while infants gaze at the world around them. But if infants experience prolonged visual deprivation (which can result, for example, from congenital cataracts), those pathways will remain unorganized. If the cataracts are removed in childhood, there may still be irreversible deficits in vision because the neural connections were never consolidated. In this respect, therefore, early vision develops according to a sensitive period that begins abruptly (at birth) but very gradually tapers off.

Other features of early behavioral development may also reflect the brain's early blooming and pruning of connections. Consider language learning. Newborns can discriminate universal speech sounds, but over time, their speech perception becomes limited to the sounds of their native language. This change in perception may reflect the initial proliferation of connections in brain regions governing language and their later refinement (Kuhl, 1993). Neuroscientists offer similar accounts to explain the early development of memory ability (C. A. Nelson, 1995), the growth of early categorization and thinking skills (Diamond, Werker, & Lalonde, 1994), and early emotional development and emotion management (Dawson, 1994). However, the blooming and pruning of brain connections for these capacities takes place on an extended timetable compared to the narrower window of opportunity that exists for vision.

The timetable for brain development thus varies by region, and it continues throughout life. Sensory regions, which govern sight, touch, hearing, and other sensations, undergo their most rapid growth early in life, while the brain areas guiding higher forms of thinking and reasoning experience blooming and pruning of brain connections into early adolescence. Indeed, the recent discovery that the mature adult brain generates new neurons (Eriksson et al., 1998) raises the possibility that brain development continues into maturity in yet unknown ways.

Brain Growth and Experience

At least two forms of brain development occur throughout life (Greenough & Black, 1992). The first, called "experience-expectant," describes how common early experiences provide essential catalysts for normal brain development. Without these essential experiences, brain growth goes awry. The dependence of vision on early visual stimulation is one example. Scientists believe that typical experiences of hearing, exposure to language, coordination of vision and movement, and other common early experiences likewise contribute to the young brain's developing organization. The developing brain "expects" and requires these typical human experiences and relies on them as a component of its growth.

The second form of brain development occurs throughout life. It is called "experience-dependent" and describes how individual experience fosters new brain growth and refines existing brain structures. These experiences can be unique to an individual. For instance, the brain of a musician who plays a stringed instrument differs from the brain of a poet who works with words and abstract ideas because they have exercised different brain regions throughout life (Elbert, Pantev, Weinbruch, Rockstroh, & Taub, 1995). In this respect, the experiences that refine brain functioning throughout life are individualized rather than typical. These experiences influence neural connections uniquely in different individuals, as they account for new learning and skills.

Vulnerability of the Developing Brain

The foundation for these achievements is established in the early years, however, and the rapid pace and broad scope of early brain growth means that the immature brain is a vulnerable organ. Beginning at conception and continuing after birth, healthy brain development is imperiled by exposure to hazardous drugs such as alcohol, cocaine, and heroin; viruses like HIV and rubella; and environmental toxins like lead and mercury. The brain is also vulnerable prenatally and postnatally to poor diets that lack essential nutrients such as iron and folic acid. Chronic maternal stress during pregnancy and after birth can also threaten healthy brain development because of stress hormones that have a toxic effect on developing brain structures (Gunnar, 2000). Stressful experiences of chronic abuse or neglect, as well as head injuries resulting from accidents, also pose significant risks. The greatest dangers to the developing brain arise, of course, from the combined and cumulative effects of these hazards such as when children in poverty are malnourished, exposed to hazardous drugs or environmental toxins, or experience head injuries. Enduring harm also arises when early problems are undetected and are allowed to endure uncorrected.

Parents and other caregivers contribute to healthy brain development by talking, singing, playing, and reading to a child. These activities are valuable, especially if they are developmentally appropriate and are attuned to a young child's interests. But more significant contributions occur when parents obtain prenatal and postnatal health care; protect children from environmental hazards, dangerous drugs, and viruses; secure appropriate immunizations, and early vision and auditory screenings; and prevent accidents. The continuing efforts of parents to keep stresses manageable and environments safe for secure exploration offer significant protections to the development of healthy brains and minds.

The Importance of the Environment

When scientists seriously consider the remarkable achievements of the first years of life, it is unmistakable that early experiences matter. The early childhood years are crucial to the quality of the life course. But parents are concerned about their young children not just as an investment in the future but also because children are themselves valuable. Parents seek to create every opportunity for healthy, optimal growth because of the excitement of contributing to enhancing the unique qualities that each child possesses. Likewise, practitioners and policymakers should also strive to strengthen the opportunities, and reduce the vulnerabilities, of early development because children merit society's commitment to them.

This is why the environment of a child matters: Because early experiences can enhance or diminish inborn potential, the environment of early experience shapes the opportunities and risks that young children encounter. The environment that influences early growth is multifaceted. The physical environment, for example, provides opportunities for toddlers to safely explore and learn, poses hazards for accidental injury, and enlivens young children's emotions by the barriers it sets to achieving goals. The biological environment (which begins to influence development prenatally) affects the developing brain and body through the quality of early nutrition, health care, immunizations, sensory screening, and protection from dangerous drugs, viruses, and environmental toxins.

The irreducible core of the environment during early development is people. Relationships matter. They provide the nurturance that strengthens children's security and well-being, offer the cognitive challenges to exercise young minds, impart many essential catalysts to healthy brain growth, and help young children discover who they are and what they can do. Remarkably, most of the significant ways that caregivers promote healthy development occur quite naturally during the course of sensitive adult-child interaction. For instance, the "parentese" that facilitates early language, the caregiving routines that promote predictability and memory skills, the patient structuring of an activity to make it manageable for a child, and the protective nurturance that manages a baby's emotions show that when sensitive adults do what comes naturally, their behavior is optimally suited to promoting early cognitive, socioemotional, and neurobiological growth. In a sense, just as children's developing brains intrinsically expect that eyes will see light and ears will hear sound because of their developmental self-organization, so also do children's developing minds and hearts expect that adults will talk in special ways to them and that caregivers will nurture them as they mature. Normal human development draws upon these natural and unrehearsed features of everyday early experience far more than it requires special educational toys, Mozart CDs, or flashcards.

Unfortunately, "doing what comes naturally" does not always support healthy early development when caregivers are depressed, stressed, absent, or otherwise have neither time nor energy to devote to caring for young children. In these circumstances, attachment relationships become insecure, conflict negotiation results in coercion, self-concept is shaped by denigrating evaluations of the child, and young children do not develop the sense of secure self-confidence that is their birthright. Society's commitment to ensuring the healthy development of every child requires far more, therefore, than standing on the sidelines and wishing parents the best in their efforts to benefit their offspring. It requires enabling parents to integrate work and child responsibilities constructively through family-friendly job conditions, welfare reform that does not endanger stable parent-child relationships, affordable and desirable child care arrangements, and wage policies that ensure adequate family incomes. It requires helping parents to obtain the prenatal and postnatal health care that screens children for developmental difficulties before they become severe, guarantees adequate nutrition, and can protect young children from debilitating diseases and hazardous exposures. Society's commitment to ensuring the healthy development of every child begins with the parent-child relationship and requires that the broader institutions affecting the family stand alongside parents in their efforts to ensure the well-being of young children.

The relationships that matter do not end with the immediate family. They also include the relationships that young children develop and depend upon in child care. Society's commitment to ensuring the healthy development of every child requires far more, therefore, than hoping that market forces make available high-quality, affordable care for young children. It requires equipping care providers with the knowledge and resources required to provide young children the kind of focused, sensitive care that offers essential catalysts to healthy psychological growth. It requires esteeming the relationships between children and caregivers sufficiently that there are incentives (in wages and benefits, the structure of child care work, and public support) for these relationships to provide stable, reliable support for young children. Society's commitment to ensuring the healthy development of each child requires that all the relationships that young children rely upon are valued and supported.

Recognizing that the early years are a period of unique opportunity and vulnerability means that the environments of early childhood should be designed so they facilitate, rather than blunt, the remarkable intrinsic push toward growth that is characteristic of every child. Doing so not only enhances the well-being of young children, but makes a long-term investment in the well-being of all individuals. A society that is concerned with problems of violence and self-control, school readiness, and social civility wisely takes note of the fact that the origins of these social, emotional, and intellectual qualities take shape early in the life course. In committing itself to the well-being of the youngest citizens, society can promote the well-being of all.

Conclusion

Although the processes of early development remain something of a mystery, enough is known to enable twenty-first-century parents, practitioners, and policymakers to foster the healthy growth of the body, mind, person, and brain. Because the early years are important, young children merit a high priority, even though they cannot speak for themselves. Because early relationships matter, society is wise to value those who relate to young children daily. Because children are active participants in their own development, the most sensitive care is that which is aligned with the child's interests, needs, and goals. Because experience can elucidate or diminish inborn potential, early environments must be designed to ensure young children's health, safety, and well-being. And because the early years are a period of considerable opportunity for growth and vulnerability to harm, society wisely does not take for granted the well-being of young children. Instead, we share responsibility as adults to guarantee for each child the opportunity to thrive in the early years of life.

References

Behrman, R. E. (1992). *Nelson textbook of pediatrics*. Philadelphia: W. B. Saunders.

Bornstein, M. H., & Lamb, M. E. (1992). *Development in infancy: An introduction* (3rd ed.). New York: McGraw-Hill.

Cassidy, J., & Shaver, P. R. (1999). *Handbook of attachment: Theory, research, and clinical applications*. New York: Guilford.

Cicchetti, D., & Beeghly, M. (Eds.). (1990). *The self in transition: Infancy to childhood*. Chicago: University of Chicago Press.

Dawson, G. (1994). Development of emotional expression and emotion regulation in infancy. In G. Dawson & K. W. Fischer (Eds.), *Human behavior and the developing brain* (pp. 346–379). New York: Guilford.

Dawson, G., & Fischer, K. W. (Eds.). (1994). *Human behavior and the developing brain*. New York: Guilford.

DeCasper, S. J., & Spence, M. J. (1986). Prenatal maternal speech influences newborn's perception of speech sounds. *Infant Behavior and Development, 9,* 133–150.

Denham, S. A. (1998). *Emotional development in young children*. New York: Guilford.

Diamond, S., Werker, J. F., & Lalonde, C. (1994). Toward understanding commonalities in the development of object search, detour navigation, categorization, and speech perception. In G. Dawson & K. W. Fischer (Eds.), *Human behavior and the developing brain* (pp. 380–426). New York: Guilford.

Dunn, J. (1988). *The beginnings of social understanding*. Cambridge, MA: Harvard University Press.

Elbert, T., Pantev, C., Weinbruch, C., Rockstroh, B., & Taub, E. (1995). Increased cortical representation of the fingers of the left hand in string players. *Science, 270,* 305–307.

Eriksson, P. S., Perfilieva, E., Bjork-Eriksson, T., Alborn, A. M., Nordorg, C., Peterson, D. A., & Gage, F. H. (1998). Neurogenesis in the adult human hippocampus. *Nature Medicine, 4,* 1313–1317.

Flavell, J. H., Miller, P. H., & Miller, S. A. (2002). *Cognitive development* (4th ed.). Englewood Cliffs, NJ: Prentice Hall.

Gibson, K. R., & Peterson, A. C. (Eds.) (1991). *Brain maturation and cognitive development.* New York: Aldine de Gruyter.

Gopnik, A., Meltzoff, A. N., & Kuhl, P. K. (2000). *The scientist in the crib: Minds, brains, and how children learn.* New York: Morrow.

Greenough, W. T., & Black, J. R. (1992). Induction of brain structure by experience: Substrates for cognitive development. In M. R. Gunnar & C. A. Nelson (Eds.), *Minnesota symposia on child psychology: Vol. 24. Developmental behavioral neuroscience* (pp.155–200). Hillsdale, NJ: Erlbaum.

Gunnar, M. R. (2000). Early adversity and the development of stress reactivity and regulation. In C. A. Nelson (Ed.), *The effects of adversity on neurobehavioral development: Minnesota symposium on child psychology, Vol. 31* (pp. 163–200). Mahwah, NJ: Erlbaum.

Hammond, N. R., & Fivush, R. (1991). Memories of Mickey Mouse: Young children recount their trip to Disneyworld. *Cognitive Development, 6,* 433–448.

Johnson, M. H. (1997). *Developmental cognitive neuroscience: An introduction.* Cambridge, England: Blackwell.

Kochanska, G., & Thompson, R. A. (1997). The emergence and development of conscience in toddlerhood and early childhood. In J. E. Grusec & L. Kuczynski (Eds.), *Parenting and children's internalization of values* (pp. 53–77). New York: Wiley.

Kuhl, P. K. (1993). Early linguistic experience and phonetic perception: Implications for theories of developmental speech perception. *Journal of Phonetics, 21,* 125–139.

Lieberman, A. F. (1993). *The emotional life of the toddler.* New York: Free Press.

Lozoff, B., Klein, N. K., Nelson, E. C., McClish, D. K., Manuel, M., & Chacon, M. E. (1998). Behavior of infants with iron-deficiency anemia. *Child Development, 69,* 24–36.

Nelson, C. A. (1995). The ontogeny of human memory: A cognitive neuroscience perspective. *Developmental Psychology, 31,* 723–738.

Nelson, K. (1993). The psychological and social origins of autobiographical memory. *Psychological Science, 4,* 7–14.

Rogoff, B. (1990). *Apprenticeship in thinking: Cognitive development in social context.* New York: Oxford University Press.

Sameroff, A. J., & Emde, R. N. (Eds.). (1989). *Relationship disturbances in early childhood.* New York: Basic Books.

Shaw, D. S., Keenan, K., & Vondra, J. I. (1994). Developmental precursors of externalizing behavior: Ages 1 to 3. *Developmental Psychology, 30,* 355–364.

Shonkoff, J. P., & Phillips, D. A. (Eds.). (2000). *From neurons to neighborhoods: The science of early childhood development.* Washington, DC: National Academy Press.

Tangney, J. P., & Fischer, K. W. (Eds.). (1995). *Self-conscious emotions.* New York: Guilford.

Thompson, R. A. (1998). Early sociopersonality development. In W. Damon & N. Eisenberg (Eds.), *Handbook of child psychology: Vol. 3. Social, emotional, and personality development* (5th ed., pp. 24–104) New York: Wiley.

Thompson, R. A. (2000). The legacy of early attachments. *Child Development, 71,* 145–152.

Thompson, R. A., & Nelson, C. A. (2001). Developmental science and the media: Early brain development. *American Psychologist, 56,* 5–15.

Wellman, H. M., & Gelman, S. A. (1992). Cognitive development: Foundational theories of core domains. *Annual Review of Psychology, 43,* 337–375.

Woodward, A. L., & Markman, E. M. (1998). Early word learning. In W. Damon, D. Kuhn, & R. S. Sigler (Eds.), *Handbook of child psychology: Vol. 3. Cognition, perception, and language* (5th ed., pp. 371–420). New York: Wiley.

Zahn-Waxler, C., & Radke-Yarrow, R. (1990). The origins of empathic concern. *Motivation and Emotion, 14,* 107–130.

Zeanah, C. H., Jr. (Ed.). (2000). *Handbook of infant mental health* (Rev. ed.). New York: Guilford.

Note: Minor changes have been made to this chapter as it was originally published in order to conform with the volume's editorial style. These changes have not altered the meaning of the chapter's content in any way.

3

THE ROOTS AND FRUITS OF PRETENDING

Marilyn Segal

T he blocks are being removed from the kindergarten classrooms and so are the dress-up areas. Despite extensive research that affirms the benefits of play, early childhood teachers have been informed that they must get children ready for school by preparing them to read and write. In response to this pressure, many early childhood teachers have shortened the time allotted to free play and have increased the time spent in didactic teaching. Educational materials take the place of play props, and teachers stand in front of the class holding up flashcards. "*A* is for apple," the teacher declares as she shows them the letter *A*.

Although getting children academically prepared for school is a commendable goal, it is also important to realize that naming letters and the sounds they make is a very minor part of what children need in order to do well in school. The children who thrive enter school with strong communication skills. They are confident and self-assured, adept at making friends, persistent, creative, and excited about learning. These are the qualities that children acquire through play.

In the spirit of playfulness, join me as I play with a metaphor. I have envisioned play, in all its wondrous complexity, as an imaginary tree. My play tree has strong roots, a sturdy trunk, and an array of branches with bright green leaves and colorful blossoms, which will become golden fruits. The roots of the play tree ground it in the soil, providing it with the nutrients that sustain its life. Its trunk is the essence of play and can be seen from different perspectives. Its branches sprout its leaves, its blossoms, its fruits, and its seeds. Play, like a tree on a summer day, provides shade from the sun, blossoms to admire, fruits to enjoy, and seeds that generate new trees.

The Roots of the Play Tree

Now, in a more serious vein, let us look at the roots of play that give and sustain its life. The roots of the play tree represent (a) secure attachment; (b) a developmentally appropriate environment; and (c) nurturing, interactive adults.

Secure Attachment

Secure attachment is a strong emotional bond between a baby or young child and a caring adult who is part of the child's everyday life—the child's attachment figure. This attachment develops over time as children experience the comfort of being held, spoken to, sung to, fed, carried around, and played with by a loving parent or substitute parent who is always there to read the child's cues and recognize and respond to his or her needs. Babies who are securely attached learn to self-regulate, which means that they can find ways, without the help of their attachment figure, to comfort themselves when they are tired or upset, for example, by sucking their thumb or by clinging to their "blankie." They learn to use their attachment figure as a secure base for exploration from which they wander further and further away and stay away for progressively longer periods of time without feeling insecure.

The grounding of learning in relationships begins very early. The more we learn about babies, the more we come to appreciate the power of early relationships. Babies come into the world wired for making connections. They are utterly dependent on their caregivers and, therefore, are programmed to elicit and respond to love and care. Secure relationships ready a child to interact with other children and adults and motivate the child to play.

A Developmentally Appropriate Environment

A developmentally appropriate environment encourages a child to play—to practice emerging skills, try out new ideas, and make new discoveries. We tend to think of a play environment in terms of furnishings and available toys, but it is much more than that. The size of the group, the lighting and the noise level, the room arrangement, the attention to safety, and the ambience of the room are all part of the environment. At each developmental age, different considerations must be taken into account in setting up and maintaining a classroom. In planning a classroom environment, teachers need to take into account the characteristics of the children who will be spending time there. The classroom environment should invite children to explore and discover and should not be overwhelming. Of course, what is likely to be interesting and what is likely to be overwhelming changes as the child grows, so the environment will always need changing. The following sections describe some basic considerations.

The environment for infants. In setting up an environment for babies, we need to recognize that babies react differently to stimulation. For some babies, the more stimulating the environment, the more alert and happy they are. For other babies, an overstimulating environment is stressful. Rather than play, stressed babies are likely to cry or fret or simply shut down and "zone out" or fall asleep. In setting up the environment, be sure to take into account the temperament of each baby. Other features of the environment that teachers should keep in mind include the following:

- *Lighting*—Most babies do best in a room that is neither too bright nor too dim. Young babies fall asleep when they are tired regardless of whether the room is light or dark. Making a room dark makes it difficult for the caregiver to monitor the babies while they are sleeping. A room that is too bright, particularly one that uses florescent lighting, may be too stimulating for some babies, and they may react by tuning out.

- *The size of the group*—Even when the ratio of caregiver to child meets licensing standards, a desirable practice is to limit the number of babies in a room. A room with too many babies is overwhelming for infants and distracting for caregivers.

- *Noise level*—Many caregivers believe that a baby's room should be kept quiet. In actuality, most babies are accustomed to hearing background noise and are not disturbed by it. Babies benefit from hearing language spoken and enjoy listening to music.

- *Room arrangement*—The room layout should include a contained play area where babies can interact with one another and safe places for mobile infants who are ready to explore.

- *Ambiance*—A baby room should be attractive, cheerful, and free of clutter. Interesting and age-appropriate toys should be within the infants' reach. Photos and pictures on the wall should be hung where babies can see them.

The environment for toddlers. The environment for toddlers needs to be home-like and attractive. It should accommodate both active toddlers who enjoy fast-paced play and timid toddlers who prefer quieter or less vigorous play. Other features of the environment that teachers should keep in mind include the following:

- *Room arrangement*—The room should be arranged so toys and books are within the children's reach at all times. Ideally, plenty of uncluttered floor space will allow toddlers to engage in physical play, and small, intimate spaces with soft materials will allow toddlers to escape if they need down time.

- *Easy clean up*—Shelves should be labeled with pictures so toddlers know exactly where each toy belongs. Cleaning up can be as much fun as taking toys off the shelves.

- *Décor*—Pictures and children's art work should be hung low enough for the toddlers to see but high enough so toddlers cannot take them off the wall. Nothing in the room should be within their reach if they are not allowed to touch it.

- *Toy selection*—Selected toys that are put out for play should include not only one-of-a-kind toys but also some toys that are identical so toddlers can play together without having to share. In addition, toy options should include toys like wagons, rocking boats, and riding toys built for two that encourage children to play cooperatively. Select toys and materials that enhance different facets of development, including materials for sensorimotor activities, musical toys, construction toys, manipulatives, dress-up clothes, cars and trucks, housekeeping toys, and other pretend play props that encourage imaginative play.

The environment for children from 3 to 5 years. The environment for children from 3 to 5 years should support the children's interest in playing with friends, making new discoveries, and learning about new things. It should also reflect their interest in reading, writing, and learning about numbers. Other features of the environment that teachers should keep in mind include the following:

- **Room arrangement**—The most effective way to arrange a preschool classroom is in interest centers. Most early childhood specialists suggest a construction center, an art and sensory play center, a math and manipulative play center, an imaginative play center, a discovery center with plants, animals, and a variety of science materials, a writing center, a listening center, and a special book nook where children can read together. These centers should further academic goals while simultaneously supporting play.

- **Décor**—The walls of a preschool room should be eye-catching and print-rich, full of boldly lettered signs, labels, captioned posters, messages, charts, and children's dictated words. Scrapbooks, albums, and child-created products should be displayed around the room. The name of an interest center should be posted in bold letters at the entrance to that center.

- **Toys and materials**—Each interest center should be well stocked with books, toys, and other items that engage the children's interest as well as invite exploration and problem solving. The math and manipulative play area should include counting books; shape, color, and number puzzles; matching and sequencing materials; and problem-solving toys. The imaginative play area, in particular, should include reading and writing materials such as menus, signs, notepads, diplomas, and an assortment of sturdy books. Children are most likely to learn their letters and words if these elements are a part of their play.

Nurturing, Interactive Adults

Parents and other caregivers support a child's play in many significant ways. Nurturing caregivers encourage children to play with other children, to explore their environment, and to engage in creative play activities. They help children build on and extend their play, providing just the right materials at just the right time. If, for instance, a group of children pretending to be firefighters are quarreling about who gets to hold the hose, the teacher can arrive with a play telephone for answering emergency calls, a gong for sending the firefighters to the scene of the fire, or a first aid kit to treat an injured victim. The following sections describe specific ways in which parents and other caregivers can foster play.

Organizing activities. The teacher or parent can organize activities that encourage children to play together. One teacher was worried because the boys in the class tended to play "monster chase" on the playground and the girls were afraid to go out, so she decided to introduce a more cooperative game. She told the children that someone had left the gate to the zoo open and 25 wild animals had escaped on the playground. She asked the children if they could go out on the playground and find the missing animals (earlier in the day the teacher had hidden the animals from the bag of miniature zoo animals in different corners of the playground). The whole class responded by running out to the playground to join the animal hunt.

Joining in the play. Another way in which teachers or parents can extend and enrich children's play is to become players. With infants, the parent or other caregiver not only initiates the play but also joins in when the baby signals playtime. In a childcare setting, routines like feeding and diapering provide the caregiver with special opportunities to play with the baby. Games such as "Peeka-Boo," "See-Saw," "Row, Row, Row Your Boat," "How Big Is the Baby," and "This Little Piggy" are perennial favorites. During the toddler period, circle games in which parents or teachers participate are always fun. "Ring Around the Rosy" is the all-time favorite. During the preschool period, the parent or teacher can assume a role in a pretend play scenario. A father may play the role of patient when his son is playing doctor or the role of being the horse when his daughter decides to be a cowgirl. A teacher may agree to be the customer when a child is pretending to be the server in a restaurant or when a group of enterprising preschoolers pretend to own a clothing store.

Being an appreciative audience. Another way that teachers or parents can enrich a child's play is by being an appreciative audience. Children love to have an audience when they climb to the top of a jungle gym, dog-paddle across a swimming pool, or put on a puppet show. No matter how busy a parent or teacher is, he or she always has time to share comments such as "Good job. I can't believe that you built such a great castle all by yourself" or "I am so proud of all of you. That was the best puppet show I have ever watched."

However, although joining the play of children can be fun for a teacher or parent, adults need to know when to step out and let the children take over. Among the most important benefits of play are the opportunities it provides for children to develop their own creativity, settle their own conflicts, and pursue their own ideas. Sometimes, the best thing that a parent or teacher can do for children is simply to let them play.

The Trunk of the Play Tree

With the sturdy roots of the play tree in place, let us move on to the trunk of the tree. The trunk of the tree represents the essence of play. As we walk around the tree together, we will examine the construct of play from different perspectives.

The Characteristics of Play

From one perspective, we focus on the characteristics of play. Several writers (Chance, 1979; Johnson, Christie, & Yawkey, 1987; Leiberman, 1977; Rogers & Sawyers, 1988) have agreed on its salient characteristics:

- Play is pleasurable and enjoyable; even if the player looks serious rather than mirthful when she is playing, she values the time she can devote to play.

- Play has no extrinsic goals; its motivations are intrinsic and serve no other objectives.

- Play is spontaneous and voluntary; it is not obligatory but is freely chosen by the player.

- Play involves active engagement on the part of the player; a passive on-looker who simply observes the play cannot be considered as a player.

- Play is all engrossing; when a young child is immersed in play, a parent or caregiver may have difficulty pulling him or her away from the play, even though the child is cold or hungry or has to relieve him- or herself.

- Play is a child's private reality; although a child may be able to tell you what is real and what is pretend, whatever is happening in his or her play represents his or her reality at that moment.

- Play is nonliteral, "allowing children to escape the constraints of the here and now and experiment with new possibilities" (Johnson et al., 1987, p.12).

The Stages of Play

As we walk around the play tree, our perspective on play changes. Rather than focus on the salient characteristic of play, we now seek to identify the sequence or stages in which play emerges. In describing the stages of play, theorists describe stages of social play, stages of cognitive play, and stages of symbolic play.

Stages of social play. In many early childhood textbooks, the stages of play are described as ways of relating to other children:

- *Solitary play* in which the infant might watch the mobile over his or her crib or the toddler plays alone, perhaps zooming his or her miniature trucks along the floor.

- *Parallel play* in which two children play side-by-side, occasionally glancing at each other.

- *Associative play* in which the children again are playing side by side but, at this stage, imitate each other and incorporate components of their counterpart's play.

- *Cooperative play* in which the children join together to create a happening or produce a product.

Although these four types of play are traditionally described as sequential, the same child or adult is likely to engage in more than one type of social play. An infant may engage in solitary play when he or she bats a mobile and in parallel play when he or she climbs on a mat alongside another baby. Preschool children may engage in solitary play when they put together puzzles individually, in associative play when they try on clothes in the dress-up area, and in cooperative play when they sit together and build a castle out of blocks. School children engage in all four types of social play. They engage in solitary play when they each manipulate a hand-held video game; in parallel play when they go Rollerblading™ with a friend; in associative play when they ride bikes with their chums, occasionally imitating one another's stunts; and in cooperative play when they build a fort together or put on a performance.

Stages of cognitive play. Focusing on cognitive rather than social stages, Jean Piaget (1962) describes a four-leveled sequence of mental representations:

■ *Functional play* in which the child associates an object with an action (e.g., a boy picks up a toy broom and tries to sweep or puts a play telephone to his ear).

■ *Constructive play* in which the child uses materials to build a structure (e.g., a girl places two rectangular blocks about 2 or 3 inches apart, sets a third block on top, and announces that she built a bridge).

■ *Dramatic play* in which one or more children play out a real or imagined event (e.g., two children pretend that they are going on a shopping trip).

■ *Games with rules* in which children play a game together, following a mental representation of the rules (e.g., two children play a board game or play a ball game according to their own agreed-on rules).

Stages of symbolic play. A related way of sequencing play skills is by symbolic stages. Lorraine McCune (1986) describes five levels of pretend play between 10 and 24 months, based on Piagetian theory:

■ *Presymbolic scheme, Level 1,* refers to the stage when an infant shows his or her understanding of object use or meaning through a brief action (e.g., the infant brings a brush to his or her hair, indicating that he or she knows what the object is, but there is no element of pretend).

■ *Self-pretend, Level 2,* refers to play in which a baby shows an awareness of the pretend nature of a self-directed activity (e.g., the baby pretends he or she is drinking from an empty bottle by making sipping noises, smiling broadly, and closing his or her eyes tightly while pretending to sleep).

■ *Decentered pretend, Level 3,* refers to two forms of pretending; either the child's play includes another person or object or the child engages in an activity that is usually performed by someone else (e.g., a child pretends that he or she is feeding a teddy bear or a child pretends to read a book to his or her mother).

■ *Pretend play combinations, Level 4,* refers to situations in which two or more different schemes are described in sequence (e.g., a child plays that he or she is baking a cake by mixing pretend batter, pouring it into a pan, and then placing the pan in the oven).

■ *Planned pretend, Level 5,* refers to pretend play situations in which a child reenacts an event and announces what he or she is going to do (e.g., "I'm going to pretend that me and my dolls are going on a picnic."). It also refers to symbolic play in which a child uses a prop to substitute for a real object (e.g., a child makes a sand birthday cake, using sticks to represent the candles).

The Perspective of the Teacher

As we complete the walk around our tree, we view play through the eyes of the teacher. Teachers, like children, are players. They enjoy playing and laughing with children and engaging in their imaginative play. They become familiar with the play style of the children in their class and recognize that child play is not simply a way of having a good time. Just about every early childhood teacher recognizes and believes Maria Montessori's maxim: "Play is the child's work."

Teachers recognize also that play is a window into the child's reality. When a child plays that she is the queen of the castle, the teacher recognizes that the child is expressing her wish to be powerful. When a child who has been in a car accident continues to crash the toy cars, the teacher recognizes that he was traumatized by the accident and that crashing the cars over and over again is his way of coping. When children whose mothers are pregnant make a game of putting the baby dolls in the oven, the teacher recognizes not only their ambivalent feelings but also the possibility that they may have heard the phrase "bun in the oven." In any case, the teacher knows that it is time to introduce stories about big brothers and sisters and to set up a classroom nursery.

When children get fascinated with the textures of wet sand or with the different sounds they can make with a pot and a spoon, observant teachers supply opportunities to extend their explorations. They can give the children other materials that extend their explorations or give them language that allows them to describe their discoveries. When children write "real words" instead of scribbles on their menus, puppet show tickets, or homemade books, it is time to escalate reading instruction.

The Branches of the Play Tree

Let us return to our play tree metaphor. Just as the branches of a real tree are the source of leaves, blossoms, fruits, and seeds, the branches of the play tree represent the many benefits of play. Play that involves motion and interaction helps children develop their physical skills. Play that involves sounds and words helps a child develop language skills. Play that involves rules helps children learn their own capabilities and the nature of social rules. Pretend or imaginative play—the kind of play that is being shortchanged in the attempt to prepare children for school—is critical because it benefits every facet of a young child's development and promotes school readiness. As we talk about the branches of our play tree, we will recognize how each of the critical attributes that enables a child to be successful at school is fostered by imaginative play.

Pretend Play as a Way of Making Friends

Vygotsky (Berk, & Winsler, 1995; Vygotsky, L. 1967) describes imaginative play as a social activity in the sense that it is a form of communication. As children pretend, their collective wishes are communicated to the group. At the same time, they learn to communicate through the use of language, gestures, and symbolic objects. Consider the following scene[1]:

> A mother and her 3-year-old son, Danny, were sitting at the breakfast table when Danny's father walked over to the table. He was about to sit at his usual place when Danny stopped him short. "No Daddy, don't sit there!" Danny shouted out. "Dandelion is sitting in that chair and you'll squash him." Dad responded, "I'm terribly sorry. I'll sit in another chair." Danny's father was used to his son's imaginary friend usurping his chair and good-naturedly moved to the other side of the table.

Like Danny, young children who have an imaginary friend are not unusual. Imaginary friends serve many purposes. They are companions, confidantes, agreeable playmates, protectors, and on occasion, scapegoats. Danny never snitched a piece of chocolate from the candy dish, but Dandelion, who happened to have a sweet tooth, frequently yielded to temptation. Although young children who create an imaginary friend may know, on at least some level, that their imaginary friend does not really exist, they have difficulty parting with a delightful delusion.

Children who do not have an imaginary friend may become attached to an object, a blanket, or a special doll or stuffed animal. They animate these inanimate objects and imbue them with human characteristics. Babies are quite likely to become attached to their blanket and use it as a security object. Toddlers may animate a doll, stuffed animal, or even an object like a key ring or a miniature car and turn it into a faithful companion. Geoffrey was attached to a screwdriver that he named Screw Ball. Screw Ball liked to do tricks during the day, but at night, he slept in Geoffrey's bed and scared away the monsters.

Even though children, as they grow older, might recognize that their "Lovie" is not really alive, they continue to believe that dolls and stuffed animals have feelings and should not be neglected. In fact, children who are attached to an imaginary or inanimate friend are developing a basic notion of what friendship is. A friend is someone who is always there, who does what you want without protests, and who is very much like oneself. As children get older, they replace inanimate or imaginary friends with real friends who are not as compliant as their Lovie but who are a lot more fun to play with.

Children who are good pretenders are likely to be good at making friends. Children like to play with a child who has good play ideas such as "Let's play house," "Let's pretend we're spacemen," or "Pretend that you and me are having a birthday party and all

---

[1] Several of the anecdotes and theoretical descriptions in the current chapter were derived from field research described in Segal and Adcock (1981).

the dolls bring us presents." Few children can resist these kinds of invitations. Even when children disagree over who gets to be the driver or who has to be the baby, they are honing their social skills. They are learning how to communicate and support their own position, how to make compromises, how to resolve conflicts, and how to mend fences after an altercation. Knowing how to initiate and maintain a friendship is an important skill that will help children make and keep new friends when they enter grade school.

Pretend Play as a Way of Developing Thinking Skills

Pretending is a form of thinking and learning as well as a form of play. Although pretending may seem effortless, it is an intellectually demanding activity. Creating a pretend reality is not easy; both concentration and inspiration are needed to keep the activity alive. Pretending represents a critical step in passing from the sensory-motor intelligence of infancy to the symbolic thinking of adulthood. As children pretend, they transpose their knowledge into symbolic form, and in the process, they begin to make the distinction between what is real and what is pretend. As we observe the imaginative play of infants, toddlers, and preschool children, we discover how intellectually challenging pretend play can be. The following sections describe the various forms of imaginative play.

Imitation and exploration. Imaginative play is a way of thinking that does not arise in a vacuum. It is built on the intellectual activity of infants and toddlers. During the early years, children experience the world as a medley of sensory impressions. To make sense out of their impressions, children try out different actions and watch what happens (e.g., they bat the rings on the cradle gym and listen to the noise those rings make). As babies carry out their experiments, they imitate the actions of other people and explore new ways of making things happen. Imitation and exploration are the twin sources of early knowledge, and by the time these babies become toddlers, they are masters of both. Consider the following scene:

> Jimmy,18 months, was sitting in the middle of a pile of toys. He picked up his teddy bear, cuddled it for a minute, then picked up a block and brought it to his teddy bear's mouth. His mother, who was watching him play, called to her husband. "Look!" she said to him, "Jimmy is pretending that he's feeding his bear."

Jimmy's mother had a right to be excited about her son's accomplishment. He was imitating an action he had experienced many times. After his mother fed him his pabulum, he would often attempt to give her a taste. This teddy bear episode was different. Jimmy was using a block to represent a spoonful of pabulum. He was making the leap from imitation to representative, or symbolic, thinking.

Greenspan and Lieberman (1994) describe the importance of this emerging representational capacity: "Children are no longer limited to somatic behavioral responses to environmental occurrences; they can now form mental representations, an ability with an enormous adaptive value" (p. 6). When Jimmy fed his teddy bear a block, he had a mental image of feeding his mother the pabulum.

Role play. An early form of imaginative play, which we see in the play of many 2-year-olds, is that of taking on a role. One of the first and most persistent roles that young children assume is the role of parent. By the age of 2, children have formed a notion of the key actions of the parent. They have abstracted the idea that parents, above all else, take care of children and babies. This caretaking may entail a host of tasks such as cooking, feeding, cleaning, washing, giving baths, or putting children to bed. It also includes emotional behaviors like hugging, kissing, and comforting. Each child abstracts his own blend of these parental behaviors.

When children first assume the role of their parent, they are likely to identify the role they are playing by selecting a particular item that represents the role. For the role of mother, children are likely to put on beads or an apron or toss a purse over their shoulder. For the role of father, they are more likely to select a tie, a belt, a lunchbox, or a briefcase. As children get older, their assumption of the parent role is elaborated. Their play reveals the characteristics they associate with the person whose role they are assuming. The following scenes provide examples:

> When visitors came to Jennifer's house one day, she invited them to dinner in her room. She served her guests pretend roast beef and potatoes but cautioned them not to eat quite yet because it was too hot. She sat at a little table with her guests and busied herself pouring drinks and urging them to have second helpings. Then she brought out brownies hot from the oven for dessert. When she finished this pretend eating, Jennifer cleared the dishes to wash them at the oven, which also doubled as sink and refrigerator. When the guests asked Jennifer why she did not eat some dinner herself, she looked a bit puzzled. For Jennifer, the parent role involved cooking and serving the food, not eating it.
>
> Jamie placed special emphasis on the parent as the runner of errands. His play routine was always the same. He put on a pair of old sunglasses and jumped into his red car. He pretended to shut the door and turn on the ignition. Making appropriate "vroom, vroom" sounds, he drove down the hall. At the far end of the hall, Jamie parked the car, hung up his keys underneath his invisible hook, and took off his sunglasses. The needed items such as a newspaper for daddy were always conveniently located in a particular spot on the wall. Then, donning his sunglasses and starting up his engine, Jamie drove home and delivered each of his purchases.

Each of these children played out the role of a nurturing parent, but in each case, a different characteristic had been abstracted as being the most salient.

Thematic play. Thematic play is an elaboration of role play where the focus is playing out a familiar or imaginary theme. Unlike role play, thematic play often involves two or more children, and the assignment of roles is only one facet of the play. Thematic play becomes increasingly more sophisticated as children grow older and have more real-world experience.

Two-year-olds at play, whether they are driving their trucks in the sandbox, feeding their dolls, or preparing dinner for the family, are hard at work replaying fragments of everyday experience. These bits and pieces of a familiar routine are repeated over and over again with little effort to integrate them into a longer sequence. When Bella served a tea party to her friends, the entire routine consisted of pouring tea, burping the baby, and pouring the tea again. Eric's teddy bear play consisted of putting the bear in the cradle, saying "goodnight teddy," lifting him out of the cradle, and starting all over again.

By the age of 3 years, children's play becomes less repetitive and is more likely to be sustained by language. We also see the beginning of peer play, which introduces the intellectual challenge of listening and responding to another player. In the following scenario, Mandy is playing with Derek, who is a little older than she is and who likes to direct the play:

Derek: Mandy, let's take the doll to the beauty shop and color her hair purple.

Mandy: Purple?

Derek: Purple is my favorite color.

Mandy: My doll has soap in her eyes! (*Mandy tries to wash the soap out, but Derek pulls the doll away.*)

Derek: We're losing the purple, Mandy.

Mandy: No—soap in her eyes!

Derek: There is no soap in her eyes.

Mandy: Yes—soap in dolly's eyes—soap in dolly's eyes.

Derek: Okay, I'll wash it.

Mandy: I'm making soup.

Children who are 4 and 5 years old are less likely than younger children to play out everyday themes. Their play, particularly if they are boys, is often fast-paced, exciting, and packed with danger, and the themes they act out are based on fantasy. Although children may borrow characters from a television show or a movie, the plots are usually their own invention, and the dialogue is spontaneous. The group in the following scenario models this type of play:

Harmon: 6, 4, 2, 1, blast off. Hold on gang. We're going to out the space!

Alfred: Hey, watch out, there's a spacecraft coming at us.

Daren: Bang, Bang. I blew it up with my space gun.

Harmon: Gimme the space gun. There's another one coming from behind.

Daren: (*banging on the floor*) Man, we just hit a planet.

Alfred: Yah, we just hit Mars. Get ready to fight. The martas are about to attack us!

The pretend play of 4- and 5-year-old girls is likely to be quite different than the danger-packed play of boys. When a group of girls decide to play out a theme such as going on a trip or throwing a birthday party, they are apt to spend much of their time deciding what to play, planning the action, assigning roles, and gathering props. In a preschool, it is not uncommon for a group of children to spend so much time talking about what they are going to do that, before they actually carry out any plan, it is time to change activities.

As children engage in pretend play, they are learning ways to communicate with one another, including sharing ideas; planning ahead; negotiating conflicts; and creating fun, exciting, creative, and novel ways to play out favorite themes. Children who have mastered these skills are socially adept as well as self-confident and enter school ready and eager to learn.

Pretend Play as a Way of Feeling Good About Oneself

In his early writings, Piaget (1962) described the relationship between imaginative play and preoperational thinking. According to his theory, the framework that preschool children use to interpret experience is unstable. Because the children have not learned to distinguish between feelings and concepts, they cannot adequately separate themselves as thinkers from their thoughts about the world. The reason imaginative play is so appealing to preschool children is that their feelings and ideas can coexist in harmonious confusion. Fears or unfulfilled wishes can be projected into a familiar reality and, at the same time, new ideas about reality can be explored within a context of emotional security. Pretend play is used to replay events, replay bad experiences, cope with anger and jealousy, and gain real power.

Replaying events. A favorite kind of pretend play for most children is replaying events. Favorite themes include birthdays, holidays, and outings. Although most of the events that children replay are happy events that they want to savor repeatedly, they may also reenact an event that was not completely happy, saving the happy parts and changing parts that were scary or unpleasant. In the following scene, Mandy replays and modifies an event that was important to her:

> Mandy had gone on a trip to Disney World with her family. On the way there, they ran out of gas and had to wait several hours for assistance. She had a wonderful time at Disney World except for a visit to the haunted mansion, which she thought was much too scary.
>
> Mandy replayed the Disney World excursion. She tipped over the kitchen chair, climbed on top, and positioned three dolls behind her, using the rungs of the chair as her steering wheel. "We go to Disney World! Vroom, Vroom, Vroom. Here we go! Gotta stop at the gas station. We don't wanna run out of gas. Vroom, Vroom, Vroom. We're almost there! Better stop at a gas station. Okay here we go . . . We're at the Small World. We're not going to Haunted Mansion. It's too scary!!! Let's go see Donald Duck and Mickey Mouse."

Another favorite form of pretend play for toddlers and preschoolers alike is assuming a power role "I'm the King of the castle! You're the dirty rascal." Frequently selected identities are prestigious power figures like mothers and fathers, super-heroes, monsters, teachers, doctors, firefighters, or astronauts. Sometimes, the power figures the children assume are benevolent or heroic. At other times, they are authoritarian or threatening, as Juan models in the following scene:

> When Juan was getting ready to enter kindergarten, most of his pretend play revolved around school. Juan always took the part of teacher. "Okay class. Everybody sit down at your seats. Listen to me and don't wiggle. We're gonna learn our numbers. Angelo, stop squirming! You need to be punished. I'm gonna hit you!" (Juan hits his dinosaur with a ruler.) "Now go home and tell your mother how bad you were."

Juan's play allows him to express his fears while maintaining control of the action.

Replaying bad experiences. In addition to using play as a way to express their fears and anxieties, children are also likely to use play as a coping strategy, as Alicia shows in the following scene:

> After a visit to the doctor during which she was given a shot, Alicia decided that her stuffed camel, Camilla, was not feeling very well. She laid a kitchen towel on the table and put her camel on top of the towel. "Got a look in her throat" Alicia announced sticking a spoon from the kitchen into her open mouth. "Oops, looks bad Camilla. Gotta give you a shot." For several days Alicia kept busy bringing each of her stuffed animals to her makeshift examination table, poking at various parts of their anatomy, and always deciding that what they really needed was a shot.

By repeatedly playing out scary or unpleasant events, children are able to master their fears and regain their composure.

Coping with anger and jealousy. Imaginative play helps children deal with feelings of anger, frustration, and jealousy. The most common source of jealousy is the birth of a new baby. The birth destroys the established pattern in a family, and the baby is likely to become the center of attention. In the next scene, Kori expresses her anger and jealousy through pretending:

> Kori reacted to the news of her mother's pregnancy by growing 10 babies in her tummy. When her brother was born, so were her 10 babies, but the babies were sent away to live in another house "near the drugstore on Huron Street." The real brother could not be dismissed as easily as the 10 imagined babies. Kori approached the problem by drawing a scribble on a piece of paper. "This is a picture of a crab for my baby brother. The crab has teeth. It can bite." That night, as she put Kori to bed, Kori's mother helped her daughter to express her angry feelings toward her brother. Talking about these feelings obviously helped. The next day, Kori drew another scribble. "I made a baby crab. It has no teeth. It won't bite my baby brother!"

Expressing negative feelings in words is not easy for children to do. No matter how accepting their parents are, children are aware that they are not supposed to be jealous, angry, or scared. Kori communicated her jealousy to her mother through her imaginative scribble. Cued into Kori's feelings, her mother was able to talk with her daughter about her feelings. Once Kori felt that she did not have to be ashamed of feeling jealous, she felt better about herself and could cope with her own feelings of jealousy directed at her brother.

Gaining real power. Although children enjoy the feeling of power they get from assuming the role of a power figure, imaginative play also gives children the opportunity to exert real power. By reversing roles with their parents, children can boss their parents around. Similarly, children who have imaginary friends have a silent scapegoat when they wet their pants or break a piece of bric-a-brac. Furthermore, imaginative play provides children with a quick rationalization for avoiding a parent's directive, as shown in the following two examples:

> Zachary did not want to wear the pair of pajamas his mother had selected. "But I can't wear those pajamas to bed," he explained to his mother. "The mouse and the kitty on the pajamas run all over me and tickle me all night long."
>
> Brittany's mother told her it was dinnertime and she had to put her toys away. "But Mother," Brittany responded, "I can't come to dinner yet. I have to give Princess and Wobbly Neck their dinner. It's not nice to eat dinner before you feed your children."

Whether a child uses imaginative play to boss around his or her parents, get him- or herself out of trouble, or ignore a parent's request, the strategy usually works. Parents have difficulty scolding a child, whatever the infraction, when his or her imaginative excuse makes them laugh.

Imaginative play enables children to make friends, think on an abstract level, feel good about themselves, and express and cope with bad feelings. Through play, children learn ways to initiate and maintain friendships, to engage in symbolic and abstract thinking, and to explore new ideas. Play boosts children's self-confidence and self-respect as well as enables children to face new challenges with enthusiasm and self-assurance.

A Final Thought

The metaphor of the play tree with its roots and fruits of play highlights the importance of play in preparing a child for grade school. The qualities that teachers look for when children first enter school—the ability to make friends, strong communication skills, a good self-image, self-assurance, persistence, creativity, and an eagerness to learn—are the qualities that children gain through play. Play is a vehicle for learning the things a child wants to know and for learning things the teacher wants to teach. Teachers and parents in today's world are often concerned that children who play too much will not be prepared for success in school. Six-year-old James Snyder (1981) gives us an answer to consider:

> The wind was bringing me to school
> And that is the fast way to get to school
> So why don't you let the wind bring you to school just like me?
> And you will be to school on time, just like I was. (p. 4)

References

Berk, L. E., & Winsler, A. (1995). *Scaffolding children's learning: Vygotsky and early childhood education.* Washington, DC: National Association for the Education of Young Children (NAEYC).

Chance, P. (1979). *Learning through play.* New York: Gardner Press.

Greenspan, S. I., & Lieberman, A. F. (1994). Representational elaboration and differentiation: A clinical-qualitative approach to the clinical assessment of 2- to 4-year-olds. In A. Slade & D. Wold (Eds.) *Children at play: Clinical and developmental approaches to meaning representation.* New York: Oxford University Press.

Johnson, J. E., Christie, J. F., & Yawkey, T. D. (1987). *Play and early childhood development.* Glenview, IL: Scott, Foresman and Company.

Lieberman, J. N. (1977). *Playfulness: Its relationship to imagination and creativity.* New York: Academic Press.

McCune, L. (1986). Symbolic development in normal and atypical infants. *The Young Child at Play: Reviews of Research, 4,* 45–61.

Rogers, C. S. & Sawyers, J. K. (1988). *Play in the lives of children.* Washington, DC: National Association for the Education of Young Children (NAEYC).

Piaget, J. (1962). *Play, dreams, and imitation.* New York: Norton.

Segal, M., & Adcock, D. (1981). *Just pretending: Ways to help children grow through imaginative play.* Englewood Cliffs, NJ: Prentice-Hall.

Snyder, J. (1981). [Untitled poem.] In R. Lewis (Ed.), *Miracles: Poems by children of the English-speaking world* (p. 4). New York: Simon and Schuster.

Vygotsky, L. (1967). Play and its role in the mental development of the child. *Soviet Psychology, 5,* 6-18.

REAL AND NOT REAL: A VITAL DEVELOPMENTAL DICHOTOMY[1]

Brian Vandenberg

Why do children play? From an evolutionary perspective, play is a puzzle. Play serves no obvious biological need; it is an activity that is divorced from immediate adaptive concerns, and it is done for the fun of it. Furthermore, it is children who most actively engage in play, which can involve considerable risk and a suspension of concerns about reality. There must be adaptive benefits to such a high-risk activity that children seem compelled to perform, yet none are obvious. One explanation that has been offered is that the adaptive functions of play are indirect, that, through play, important cognitive and social skills are stimulated (Rubin, Fein, & Vandenberg, 1983).

Another answer to why children play has been offered by Freud (1960) and Piaget (1962), who argue that play serves important functions in childhood, but the growth of reason results in the disappearance of play as an important factor in thought. In Piaget's terms, the play of young children reflects the distorting influence of the dominance of assimilation over accommodation. With development, assimilation and accommodation become more differentiated and integrated, creating a more stable cognitive structure. Under these conditions, assimilatively dominated activity is less distorted, and play is more adapted to realistic goals and activities. Or, as Freud indicates, "play is brought to an end by the strengthening of a factor that deserves to be described as the critical faculty or reasonableness" (Freud, 1960,

[1] Reprinted with permission from *Multiple Perspectives on Play in Early Childhood Education*, edited by Olivia N. Saracho and Bernard Spodek, 1998, Albany, NY: The State University of New York Press. Copyright 1998 by The State University of New York.

p. 128). These theories are compatible with the way that adults usually view children's play. Children outgrow their tendency to engage in playing house, school, and other fantasy themes, and their belief in fairy tales and myths such as Santa Claus erodes as the children come to see their logical shortcomings (e.g., "How can Santa fly around the world in one night?"). Childhood fantasy play and children's myths are developmentally idiosyncratic phenomena that disappear once individuals begin to develop these critical faculties.

Play and Myth

Fantasy, Belief, Reality

These approaches, which have dominated contemporary thinking about children's play, assume that play is secondary to other, more salient developmental functions. Play is an epiphenomenon that stimulates more important cognitive or social skills, or it is a childish activity that is usurped by reason. But what if we began our investigation by asking, "What are the features of a being that is capable of creating theories of play and interpreting their experience from these various vantage points?" This turns the process of investigation on end. Theories of play, instead of providing the assumptive framework for gathering data, become important data themselves. The answer to this question is that humans are myth-making beings who create reality through belief in stories they have constructed about reality. By myth, I don't mean mistake, as the word is sometimes used, but myth as a lived-in belief system that orders and gives meaning to life.

Thus, humans are myth-believing beings for whom reality is a trusted fantasy. To be human and to live in a meaningful way within a culture requires that we live in and through a sophisticated, abstract system that is largely imaginary. To be incapable of fantasy is to be barred from human culture. Children's fantasy play is an expression of this human capacity to create imaginary worlds that structure, energize, and give meaning to experience. Play is a manifestation of the fundamental properties of myth-making, and cognitive, social, and symbolic abilities are concomitant aspects of this process. The myths and fantasies of childhood are not eroded by the onset of reason; rather, they are replaced by more sophisticated adults myths about the importance of reason. Ironically, the mythical belief in reason by adults has led to the myth that adults have no myths.

Our reality is grounded in the myths, assumptions, beliefs, and ways of saying that compose intersubjective mutuality. Culturally sanctioned myths about what constitutes reality, if they are believed, create the reality. In Bateson's words, "propositions . . . about the world . . . are not true or false in a simple objective sense; they are more true if we believe and act upon them, and more false if we disbelieve them. Their validity is a function of our belief" (Ruesch & Bateson, 1968, p. 127). Or as William James asserts, "truths cannot become true till our faith has made them so" (James, 1956, p. 96). So, for example, egos, motives, crime, interest rates, GNP, money, God, or, for that matter, cognitive processes, social roles, play, and human development are abstractions that carry considerable ontological weight that is derived from the way they are embedded in the web of cultural assumptions about the nature of reality and from the beliefs about their status as real entities (Miller, 1973). When these concepts are evoked, they serve to order, orient, and organize us in a particular way to ourselves, to others, and to our world.

This does not mean that reality is a solipsistic fantasy or that the world simply can be wished away. The world has a tangible presence that is ignored at our peril. However, myths and beliefs about the world can vary greatly, and they influence the nature of our understanding and relation to it. For instance, the belief that "trees are for wood" engenders a much different experience and stance toward the world than "trees are for worship"; through our belief, we create the reality of our experience of trees. Cross-cultural comparisons reveal that there are a wide variety of myths and beliefs. Unfortunately, this insight is often overlooked, as we are prone to relegate the beliefs of others to the realm of fantasy and to reify our own as reality. As Sutton-Smith (1980) points out, "the cosmic constructions of ideology and religion are seen as ultimate meanings without which none of the rest makes sense. Other people's religions or ideologies are, of course, often designated as mere 'fairy tales,' mere 'child's play' " (p. 12).

The Real and the Not Real

While various cultures will use different myths and beliefs to organize experience, it is essential that individuals within a culture share a common ground of understanding and be able to discern what is real from what is not (within the shared framework). Failure to accurately and consistently distinguish the real from the not real has serious consequences. In Vygotsky's (1978) words, "to behave in a real situation as in an illusory one is the first sign of delirium" (p. 102). Thus, it is not enough to have the capacity for imaginative involvements; individuals must be grounded in the myths, beliefs, and ways of communication that form the basis of intersubjectivity that enable appropriate distinctions between real and not real.

But what is real and what is illusory? Bateson's (1972) analysis of play suggests that what distinguished the playful from the serious, the "real" from the "not real," is the metacommunication, "This is play." Metacommunication lifts thought out of the immediate welter of signals, creating a new level of communication. The reality of an exchange is not simply what a signal communicates but is determined by the metacommunication about how a signal is to be interpreted. The message, "This is play," is not expressed by a particular signal but, rather, is a "way of saying," whereby actions are exaggerated, repeated, jumbled, or transformed in some unusual or unique way (Miller, 1973; Schwartzman, 1978); the "saying is the playing" (Garvey, 1977). Play can be *anything*, said playfully. Playful saying is integral to the ongoing stream of communication that slides from the serious to the playful and back. The playful and the serious, the "real" and the "not real" are distinguished by the ways that communication is punctuated. The dynamic tension between "real" and "not real" is a necessary consequence of metacommunication, which assigns onto-logical values to signals. Metacommunication and increasingly complex linguistic and metalinguistic communications evoke an imaginary world where what is real, what is play, and what is madness is determined by how messages are framed and un-derstood. Reality is an imperative act.

Development is not simply the acquisition of information about a given world. Rather, it involves becoming grounded in an uncertain world that is beyond under-standing (Vandenberg, 1991). This is achieved through enculturation into the mean-ings, myths, rituals, social practices, and assumptions that order, orient, and organize individuals in common ways and provide a sense of reality that allows for confident action in the world. What is real and what is illusory is not an obvious, directly per-ceived dichotomy but is based upon discerning conventional markers of communica-tion. The challenge for children is to learn the appropriate ways of interpreting and punctuating communication so as to properly share the appropriate communicative ground of intersubjective meanings and to dwell within the sociocultural reality that is constituted from this common ground. It is crucial that children know what is serious and what is not and that they understand and trust the regularities and particularities of communication that are essential for appropriate participation in intersubjective mutuality.

However, this is not easily achieved. The complexity of adult communications, with the layers of metacommunication, linguistic signification, and the levels of ab-straction is stupefying to the uninitiated. Children, who are the uninitiated, gradually enter the assumptive world that is embodied in reflexive gestures, meanings, and ways of saying that provide a sense of grounded reality. Children are capable of distinguish-ing play from not play, but their appreciation of what is "real" and what is "not real" is labile and lacks the sophistication found in adult members of the culture.

Becoming Grounded

There is a close association between the development of capabilities to become in-volved in increasingly complex communicative exchanges and becoming grounded in increasingly sophisticated beliefs, myths, and intersubjective mutuality. The devel-opmental path of play is particularly revealing of the increasing capacity for sophis-ticated imaginative involvements and for complexly nuanced distinctions between the real and the not real. The following discussion will provide a brief overview of this developmental path of play and communication. There are, of course, wide indi-vidual difference and variations across contexts, so what is offered is meant simply as a general guide, not a universal proscription.

The first period, infancy, is marked by participation in intersubjective mutuality that requires coordinating actions with others using trusted signals that enable coop-eration and understanding. During this time, the basic coordinates of intersubjectivity are established, as are the essential skills for communicative exchanges; recognizing that a signal is a signal; learning to coordinate and sequence signals with another; adjusting communications based on feedback; establishing common referents; and repairing, clarifying, and correcting messages. Objects begin to be understood within the context of intersubjectivity, as the "environment" becomes imbued with sociocultural significance (Vandenberg, 1995). Adults are essential for the being of infants, and infants are exquisitely attuned to "being with" adults. Adults serve as an executive function, regulating and orienting infants' experiences and promoting and shaping their expression. Infants' communication and memory are limited to the behavioral plane, but mastery of this level is essential to the development of later, more complex and abstract communications. Communication is expressed through bodily movements, gestures, and vocalizations. Thus does the common ground of intersubjectivity become part of infants' neuromusculature (Vandenberg, 1995). During this developmental period reality is limited to the behavioral plane, is largely organized and structured by adults, and therefore is quite labile. But infants' communicative achievements also root them, in a primordial way, within the web of sociocultural intersubjectivity. These developments are reflected in the play of infants. Infants are capable of complex communications on the behavioral plane; they are capable of play, saying "This is play" about certain actions and objects (Rubin et al., 1983). This metacommunicative ability suggests that infants are capable of lifting themselves out of the stream of ongoing activity; they are not stimulus bound but are free from the welter of necessity.

Infancy gives way to early childhood, which is marked by the emergence of language, and the communicative tasks accomplished in infancy on the behavioral plane must now be learned on the more abstract, linguistic plane. Words are instruments of great power, allowing for significance within a vast horizon of sociocultural intersubjectivity. Language serves important intermental functions, as it is used as a tool for social influence and cooperation. It also affects transformation of intramental functions, which become abstract, conceptual, logical, measured, and selective. Thought has been freed from the immediate properties of the perceptual field, and children have gained access to the complex intersubjectivity of adult communication (Vygotsky, 1978). However, they are not stabilized in this world, or, rather, their stability is externally influenced and grounded. Children have not yet internalized their own voice, their attention is two-dimensional and fluid, and they are unable to assume executive control of their own thought—they must rely on authoritative voice of others (Wertsch, 1991).

The growing complexity and lability of children's reality is reflected in their play. Children during this age engage in a great deal of fantasy play, and it has been called the age of play. A central question is whether they really believe their imaginative involvements are real (e.g., Harris, Brown, Marriott, Whittal, & Harmer, 1991; Singer & Singer, 1990; Woolley & Wellman, 1993). While the research is not definitive, the fact that the question is even asked, and it is asked repeatedly, reflects uncertainty about how children view the ontological status of their believed in imaginings and whether they have yet learned to secure the boundaries between reality and illusion. Regardless of the research results, it is clear that, in actual practice, adults allow younger children considerable leeway in their assumptions about what is real and what is illusory; few adults would be concerned that 5-year-old children may be taking their stuffed animals or imaginary playmates too seriously.

Children's transition to middle childhood is characterized by greater communicative sophistication and stability of thought. During this time, inner speech becomes fully internalized and provides a means of self-organization and influence. But inner speech serves more than simply a cognitive-organizational function. Children appropriate the voices of authority for themselves, acquiring the valuings and ways of saying that confer power and a sense of grounding. Their self-organizing valuings embody the authority derived from the appropriated voices. It is also during this time that children become intensively involved in a context that shapes thought and behavior in ways that are highly valued by the culture: school. In school, children learn to decontextualize experience, acquire skills of literacy, and think rationally, all of which are critically important for participating in the realities of the culture (Wertsch, 1991).

This is also a time when childhood and adulthood are straddled. Children become capable of self-direction, are beginning to acquire a sense of authority about their own voice, are becoming capable of abstract thought, and are beginning to confront expectations about a cultural reality that is objectified and rational. It is an age where the playful can include imaginary playmates—or chess—and children are still allowed leeway in their imaginings; an age where the boundaries between the real and the illusory are not completely secured.

Adolescence marks a time of great change, as children enter puberty and must confront growing expectations and demands to become a more integral member of the culture. Childhood fantasies and imaginative involvements receive less leeway, and play becomes more realistic, rule-bound, and rational (Rubin et al., 1983). There is a change in adult evaluations of the reality of imaginative involvements, and there are increased expectations to be anchored in the realities of adulthood. When children between 4 and 8 years old have imaginary playmates, adults are usually not concerned, but after 12 years of age, imaginary playmates are likely a source of deep consternation for adults. Indeed, it may be a sign of mental illness, a sign that the adolescents have failed to properly assign ontological status to the appropriate communications. It is noteworthy that the diagnosis of schizophrenia is difficult and rare before the age of 8, one reason being that some of the most telltale clues of a "thought disorder," which is part of the diagnosis of schizophrenia and involves an inability to distinguish reality from fantasy, are ever present aspects of the thoughts of young children (Russell, Bott, & Sammons, 1989). There are greater expectations and far greater consequences for adolescents (and adults) to properly distinguish reality from illusion. Considerable emphasis is placed on reason, rationality, and detached objectification, and there is suspicion and fear associated with fantasy, irrationality, and imaginative involvement.

Development, then, can be said to be a process of "hardening of the categories."[2] The distinction between the real and the illusory becomes of utmost im-

---

[2] I am grateful to William Conroy for suggesting this phrase.

portance. There are increasing expectations that these boundaries will be understood and honored, and there are considerable sanctions for the failure to do so. Boundaries and demarcations between the real and the illusory are essential, as they allow for shared assumptions and values that are necessary for cooperative action, and it is crucial that individuals come to share this intersubjective grounding. Children acquire this grounding gradually, and the expectations for them to navigate the subtle and complex layers of messages of varying ontological status increases with development. Play offers insight into the complexity of the paths of becoming grounded in the myths, beliefs, assumptions, and ways of saying that define reality.

The preceding discussion suggests that reality is composed of trusted myths invested with belief, that the demarcation of the real from the not real is of critical importance in becoming grounded, and that the developmental path of play reveals an ever increasing complexity and significance of distinguishing real from not real, which requires investing belief and becoming grounded. The period of early childhood is a particularly salient time when play involvements flourish. The following discussion will explore several implications of this view of play for young children.

Play in Early Childhood

An essential feature of young children's play is their ability to communicate their intent to play and to enter appropriately playful exchanges with peers that require a mutual understanding of what is real and what is not. For example, a child who wishes to play with others must learn how to communicate, "This is play," "I would like to play," and "May I join you in you play?" These are supercharged overtures, for they require the signaling of understanding of what is to constitute the real and the not real, the manner in which the play is to proceed in relation to others, and one's role in the playful exchange. The watching child trying to negotiate entry into an ongoing play round is a paradigmatic event that reveals important features of human life. For such a child, an invitation into the playing group is more than just an opportunity to play; it is an issue of existence. To be outside the group is to be a nonentity; to join the play is to be accorded an officially sanctioned identity and status within a group of trusting and trusted players. This is at the heart of the process of coming to be grounded: to share a common myth framework and to trust that others will also. In doing so, one derives meaning through play and a sense of belonging and rootedness by sharing the trust of others. The play of preschoolers is one of the early steps in learning to negotiate one's place with others in joint, cooperative involvements.

Play in the preschool years can be about anything, said playfully. The act of transforming something from real to play is an act of lifting experiences out of the ongoing context of everyday involvement, highlighting them, and making them the object of investigation. Play affords children the opportunity to make visible, inspect, and understand experience that is otherwise hidden. The act of play is different from that which the playful act enacts. This is evidenced in an example, cited by Vygotsky (1978), of two young girls, who are sisters, who are playing at being sisters.

> They are playing at reality. The vital difference . . . is that the child in playing tries to be what she thinks a sister should be. In life, the child behaves without thinking that she is her sister's sister. . . . [A]s a result of playing, the child comes to understand that sisters possess a different relationship to each other than to other people. What passes unnoticed by the child in real life becomes a rule of behavior in play. (Vygotsky, 1978, pp. 94–95)

Signaling "This is play" is a transformational act. Real experiences are rendered "not real," the serious made playful, thus allowing it to be seriously reconsidered.

Many contemporary perspectives on play consider it a means for acquiring information, exercising cognitive functions, or elaborating social skills. But such explanations do not fully explain why play is so passionate, so thrilling, and so riveting for children. The emotional demeanor of play is in dramatic contrast with that usually associated with acquiring information, exercising functions, or practicing skills. Play is exciting because it flirts with an existential dichotomy of being and not being, real and not real. This vitality of "playing at the real", without consequences, allows children to dwell within possibilities, to try them out without suffering the penalties that would otherwise accompany such actions.

Dwelling within possibilities is contrary to the Freudian notion of play as mastery of past traumatic events. This is not to argue that children don't play out and play over past events. But the salience of these past events, the reason why they emerge in the present, is because of the way they influence, constrain, and structure children's anticipations of their future. Past, present, and future are not separate, self-contained features of time that exist independently. Rather, they are intimately linked to an organic temporality whereby children's playful involvements reflect their present, indwelling projections about their future that is based on their experience. Thus, the passion of play is a result of playing with the vital dichotomy of real and not real that has significance for how children anticipate their future.

But this is not all. The excitement of play results from the sheer exercise of freedom over necessity. For example, dramatic play such as playing house is a common form of play among preschoolers. In such play, children enact common meanings associated with family membership, and there is undoubtedly a component of hopeful projection of future possibilities. However, the children play with the script, new twists and alternatives are introduced, and the script is bent to the desires of the children; perhaps more favorable child-oriented behaviors are assumed by the mommy and daddy players, or the children in the family are more angry, demanding, and powerful. The children are uncovering the power and limits of public meanings and, at the same time, exercising their sense of freedom over them. It is thrilling to transform the real to the not real, to journey into forbidden areas of darkness behind the public mask of conventionality, and to become aware of one's freedom to do so in the process. The ease with which the real can be rendered not real by the simple signal "This is play" reveals the contingency and fluidity of the social construction of reality. Young children's play is a frolicking in this fluid contingency.

Children play with the social "facts" of their lives, but their play is also shaped by cultural factors, and there have been important changes that have altered the context of their play. During the first two thirds of the twentieth century, children's first encounter with schooling was kindergarten, which frequently was only half-day and not aimed at developing academic skills. However, during the past several decades, there has been a dramatic increase in the number of mothers who have entered the workplace, and children are now being placed in day care and preschools. Children's institutional life is beginning much earlier. Furthermore, there has been an increase in concern that children acquire the requisite cognitive and social skills needed in an increasingly complex, technological world (Garbarino, 1989). This has created a dilemma for how to approach this new class of institutionalized children. They are too young, by traditional wisdom, to be subjected to rigorous tutoring, but they should begin to acquire some of the necessary skills for academic survival.

Play is a particularly attractive solution to these dilemmas, for it preserves the mythic, playful aspects of childhood, yet at the same time, it offers the possibility of enhancing valued cognitive and social skills. What results is a "play curriculum." Toys are selected, play activities planned, adult tutoring and guidance offered that are aimed at very specific payoffs and goals. Adults, of course, have the responsibility to organize and guide children's activities in ways they think is most appropriate. The danger of play curriculum, however, is that the focus on adult intentions renders the activity no longer playful, that the concern for imparting educational lessons in play destroys the child's freedom, joy, and passion realized at the boundary of real and not real.

The changing historical conditions, which are forcing a redefinition of the meaning of early childhood, pose questions to early childhood educators. Are we to value play, joy, and frivolity for their own sake, even if they never lead to desired developmental outcomes? How much do we want our children to learn, and how early? At what expense? What is the role of institutions in the lives of young children? Confronting these issues brings a sharper appreciation of our values about play in the lives of our children—and in our own.

References

Bateson, G. (1972). *Steps to an ecology of mind.* New York: Ballantine.

Freud, S. (1960). *Jokes and their relation to the unconscious.* In J. Strachey (Ed.), *The standard edition of the complete psychological works of Sigmund Freud, Vol. VIII.* London: Hogarth.

Garbarino, J. (1989). An ecological perspective on the role of play in child development. In M. N. Block & A. D. Pellegrini (Eds.), *The ecological context of children's play* (pp. 16–34). Norwood, NJ: Ablex.

Garvey, C. (1977). *Play*. Cambridge, MA: Harvard University Press.

Harris, P. L., Brown, E., Marriott, C., Whittal, S., & Harmer, S. (1991). Monsters, ghosts and witches: Testing the limits of the fantasy—reality distinction in young children. *British Journal of Developmental Psychology, 9,* 105–123.

James, W. (1956). *The will to believe*. New York: Dover.

Miller, S. N. (1973). Ends, means and galumphing: Some leitmotifs of play. *American Anthropologist, 75,* 87–98.

Piaget, J. (1962). *Play, dreams and imitation in childhood*. New York: Norton.

Rubin, K. H., Fein, G. G., & Vandenberg, B. (1983). Play. In E. M. Hetherington (Ed.), *Handbook of child psychology: Vol. 4. Socialization, personality and social development* (pp. 693–774). New York: Wiley.

Ruesch, J. & Bateson, G. (1968). *Communication: The social matrix of psychiatry*. New York: Norton.

Russell, A. T., Bott, L., & Sammons, C. (1989). The phenomenology of schizophrenia occurring in childhood. *Journal of the American Academy of Child and Adolescent Psychiatry, 28,* 399–407.

Schwartzman, H. B. (1978). *Transformations: The anthropology of children's play*. New York: Plenum.

Singer, D. G., & Singer, J. L. (1990). *The house of make-believe*. Cambridge, MA: Harvard University Press.

Sutton-Smith, B. (1980). Children's play: Some sources of play theorizing. In K. H. Rubin (Ed.), *New directions for child development: Children's play* (pp. 1–16). San Francisco: Jossey-Bass.

Vandenberg, B. (1991). Is epistemology enough? *American Psychology, 46,* 1278–1286.

Vandenberg, B. (1995). Infant communication and the moral matrix of human life. *Family Process, 29,* 21–31.

Vygotsky, L. S. (1978). *Mind in society*. Cambridge, MA: Harvard University Press.

Wertsch, J. V. (1991). *Voices of the mind*. Cambridge, MA: Harvard University Press.

Woolley, J. D., & Wellman, H. M. (1993). Origin and truth: Young children's understanding of imaginary mental representations. *Child Development, 64,* 1–17.

Note: Minor changes have been made to this chapter as it was originally published in order to conform with the volume's editorial style. These changes have not altered the meaning of the chapter's content in any way.

SCHOOL READINESS AND CHILDREN'S PLAY: CONTEMPORARY OXYMORON OR COMPATIBLE OPTION?

Sharon Lynn Kagan and Amy E. Lowenstein

A scan of current literature might easily lead one to believe that the achievement of school readiness through children's play is an oxymoron, that readiness and play are so incompatible that they should not, and perhaps even cannot, be linked. Advocates of play cite rich scholarship that affirms the importance of play and child-initiated learning to children's development. Skeptics of play honestly query whether play can contribute to children's readiness for school and, if so, through what mechanisms and to what degree. These two approaches vie for prominence in practice, placing nothing less than the heart of the profession in question.

The purpose of this chapter is to confront this debate head-on and to examine the relationship between children's play and children's readiness for school. To do so, we discuss the history and development of the school readiness debate, explicating the work of the National Education Goals Panel (NEGP) as well as the history of children's play and issues surrounding it. We then examine the relationship between play and each of the five dimensions of school readiness identified by the NEGP, using research to solidify these linkages. Our findings are clear: play, though not the sole effective pedagogical strategy, is absolutely essential to advancing children's development and their readiness for school. Consequently, the challenge ahead is not to blithely romanticize or to falsely criticize play; it is to discern the purposes for and the conditions under which play is an optimally useful pedagogical strategy, fully realizing the heterogeneous effects on children's development and their school readiness. In short, we contend that play and its relationship to school readiness remain misunderstood, have become the subject of false debate, and are in need of explication.

Because we consider readiness and play to be separate constructs with distinct histories, we start by addressing each individually. The chapter begins with a discussion of readiness from both historical and contemporary perspectives. The next section addresses issues related to play, again from historical and contemporary perspectives. The chapter then presents the relationship between school readiness and play, citing research that demonstrates the role of play in achieving various dimensions of school readiness. The chapter concludes with a discussion of play as the exclusive or preferred strategy for early childhood pedagogy.

Understanding Readiness: Historical and Contemporary Perspectives

Concern about readiness is not new; parents, scholars, and practitioners have discussed the issue for more than a century. Although not using the term itself, Johan Pestalozzi discussed the concept of readiness as early as 1898 (Pestalozzi, 1915). Charles May and Rose-Marie Campbell (1981) noted that, although the concept of readiness was understood in the 19th century, the term did not appear in print until the 1920s. Moreover, the idea was not given serious attention until the end of that decade when the International Kindergarten Union named a "reading readiness" committee to promote better understanding of the concept (Holmes, 1927). Since that time, the educational and psychological literature on readiness has burgeoned with theoretical and empirical work, most of it contradictory. Much attention has been devoted to the following issues: distinguishing between readiness for learning and readiness for school, discerning differences between chronological and maturational conceptions of readiness, and determining correlates of school readiness.

Readiness for Learning and Readiness for School

Historically, two broad constructs—readiness for learning and readiness for school—have vied for attention, although they have often been intertwined and sometimes are not clearly defined themselves (Kagan, 1990b). The first construct, readiness for learning, has two different interpretations. Genetically driven, the first perspective focuses on very young children. It suggests that humans not only are born ready to learn but also are learners in utero. This perspective is based on scientific research that demonstrates that children are "programmed" or "wired" by endogenous forces to learn. From this perspective, children are always ready to learn; learning is regarded as innate and natural (National Research Council and Institute of Medicine, 2000). Another perspective on readiness for learning, and one that does not necessarily refute the first, emerges from learning theory and focuses on humans of all ages. From this perspective, leading theorists consider readiness for learning to be the level of development at which an individual has the capacity to undertake the learning of specific material—usually, the age at which the average group of individuals has the specified capacity (Good, 1973).

Learning theorists, however, debate precisely which forces affect readiness to learn. For example, Robert Gagne (1970) suggests that readiness for learning involves three factors: attentional set, motivation, and developmental status. Piagetians suggest that readiness for learning involves the integration of new stimuli with previously acquired information (Piaget, 1970). While Piagetians tend to focus on the importance of forces internal to the learner, Jerome Bruner and his associates attribute greater significance to environmental forces (Bruner, 1960). Thus, a range of opinion surrounds the construct of readiness for learning alone.

In contrast to readiness for learning, readiness for school is typically a more finite construct, embracing specific cognitive and linguistic skills (e.g., identifying four colors by name, copying a square, distinguishing a triangle from a circle, repeating a series of four or five numbers without practice). This emphasis is not surprising given that, historically, readiness for school has been equated with reading readiness (Gray, 1927). Over time, the press for school readiness also has been manifest in curricular domains such as arithmetic readiness (Ben-Yochanan & Katz, 1989) and handwriting readiness (Lesniak & Legien, 1983). In fact, in the literature, school readiness has been correlated with children's printing (Simner, 1989), drawing (Dunleavy, Hansen, Szasz, & Baade, 1981), self-concept (Morisset, 1994), perceptual skills (Solan, Mozlin, & Rumpf, 1985), fine and gross motor skills (Buttram, Covert, & Hayes, 1976; Oja & Juerimaee, 2002), social skills (Knoll & Patti, 2003), socioeconomic status (Coley, 2002), family size (Scott & Kobes, 1974; Scott & Seifert, 1974), father involvement (Fagan & Iglesias, 1999)—even the desirability of children's names (Busse & Seraydarian, 1978) and bioplasmic forces (Ogletree, 1985). Irrespective of academic domain, the construct of readiness for school typically involves a fixed standard of physical, intellectual, and social development sufficient to enable children to fulfill school requirements and to assimilate the curriculum content (Okon & Wilgocka-Okon, 1973).

Not surprisingly, readiness to learn and readiness for school—each representing different conceptual constructs and having different definitions—have yielded very different orientations. The former applies to students of all ages; the latter, primarily to young children at the prekindergarten or kindergarten level. Readiness for learning views the content of early education as fluid and evolving; readiness for school views it as more static and fixed. The former has been considered a "gate opener"; the latter, a gatekeeper. Though somewhat hyperbolic, these contradictions reflect a tension that has been problematic and has given rise to a third construct: maturational readiness.

Maturational Readiness

Maturational readiness accepts the basic tenet of school readiness: that it is correct to expect children to achieve a specified standard before entering school. But it also acknowledges the existence of children's individual time clocks. It suggests that, because all children do not develop at the same pace, they will not all attain the school readiness standard at the same time. Rather than place children in school environments that are too advanced for them or attempt to reform schools to accommodate children's individual differences, many maturationists advocate keeping children out of formal schooling until they are (maturationally or developmentally) ready. This type of readiness is not determined by chronological age but is assessed through the use of tests, whose creators suggest are quite effective in predicting success or failure in kindergarten.

This approach, advanced by Arnold Gesell and his adherents, provides children with the "gift of time" and offers an alternative to the conventional and somewhat arbitrary chronological standards of school readiness (Ilg & Ames, 1965). Its apparent sensitivity to individual children and its endorsement of the biological stages of development made it quite comprehensible and appealing. Gaining widespread acclaim, the construct of maturational readiness was fostered by many school districts throughout the nation and by many parents, who often elected to keep their children out of school for an additional year. Indeed, anecdotal accounts supported practices associated with this approach. Recently, however, in light of empirical data, the maturational view has been criticized for its influence in preventing scores of needy children (largely males) from enrolling in kindergartens that others contend might foster, rather than deter, their development (Shepard & Smith, 1988; Zigler & Child, 1969).

Theoretical Issues Surrounding Readiness

During the 1980s, theoretical formulations of the relationship between learning and development were reassessed. For years, advocates of maturational readiness had posited that development preceded learning; in fact, development was considered a prerequisite for learning. Premature instruction was frowned on until the child was developmentally ready to learn.

Another theory, suggesting that learning precedes development, surfaced. Advanced years ago by Lev Vygotsky (1978), it contends that children exhibit at least two developmental levels. The first, their actual developmental level, is the result of completed developmental cycles; the second represents their potential level of development. Between the two lies what Vygotsky terms the "zone of proximal development," the area between the actual developmental level, as determined by independent problem-solving, and the level of potential development, as determined through problem-solving under adult guidance or in collaboration with more capable peers (Vygotsky, 1978). Through adult "scaffolding" and in collaboration with peers, children working in their zone of proximal development reach new levels of development.

These different approaches to the relationship between learning and development have had tremendous implications for practice. From the maturationist perspective, which claims development precedes learning, the practice of keeping children out of school until they are developmentally ready is sanctioned, if not encouraged. Because readiness is viewed as an inherent condition of the child, children—not institutions—bear the burden of developmental proof (Willer & Brede-kamp, 1990). Abiding by this theory, schools and parents throughout America did what they felt was best and kept children out of school until the youngsters were pronounced "ready" to benefit from formal instruction.

In contrast, Vygotsky (1978) posits that children grow into the intellectual life around them, that their development is stimulated by learning. Offering the theoretical underpinnings for a fourth construct of readiness, this view suggests that children—ever-ready learners—need to be in environments where adults and peers will nurture their learning and, consequently, their development. Gaining acclaim, this fourth construct transfers the burden of proof of readiness from children to their external world (e.g., parents, schools, and other socializing institutions), making readiness a condition of the institution, not of the individual child. This construct is best summed up by the somewhat hackneyed admonishment that concern should focus not on whether children are ready for schools, but on whether schools are ready for children.

Contemporary Definitions of Readiness

Against this rather muddied backdrop, concern about readiness accelerated considerably with the establishment of six national education goals in 1989. The first goal, long debated, declared, "By the year 2000, all children in America will start school ready to learn" (U.S. Department of Education, 1995). Revolutionary in its intent and in the fact that it was declared an *education* goal, the readiness goal (as it came to be known) dramatically heightened attention to school readiness and legitimated mechanisms to address its accomplishment. Specifically, the NEGP, consisting of governors, congressmen, and policy leaders, was established to monitor the nation's progress in meeting the goals, and the Goal 1 Resource and Technical Planning Groups were created to carry out the NEGP's charges related to readiness.

But before the nation's progress on readiness could be measured, particularly in light of the history chronicled above, a clear definition of readiness needed to be developed. To that end, and after culling decades of research and the input of hundreds of scholars, the Technical Planning Group identified five dimensions of readiness in its 1995 report, *Reconsidering Children's Early Development and Learning: Toward Common Views and Vocabulary* (Kagan, Moore, & Bredekamp, 1995). The dimensions are: (1) physical well-being and motor development; (2) social and emotional development; (3) approaches toward learning; (4) language development; and (5) cognition and general knowledge (Kagan et al., 1995). Although the definition of readiness continues to be fine-tuned, the NEGP definition has amassed widespread support and provides a functional framework for our analysis of the contribution of play to the achievement of school readiness. Therefore, we accept that school readiness is composed of the five dimensions above; we will return to them later.

A noteworthy point is that, in addition to the five dimensions, the NEGP advanced important principles with respect to readiness. The group noted that the dimensions, though explicated separately, are inextricably linked. No single dimension can be considered a proxy for any other dimension; all five dimensions must be considered as a totality. The NEGP also noted that children vary on every measurable characteristic and that this variation can be explained, in large measure, by genetic, cultural, and contextual factors. Historically, however, conventional definitions of readiness have been more attentive to genetic and developmental variation than to cultural and contextual variation. For this reason, the NEGP stressed the importance of families, communities, and schools in developing children's readiness. Consistent with Vygotskian principles, the group emphasized that schools and communities must also be ready for children.

Questions persisted, however, with respect to what makes a ready school and a ready community. The NEGP established a national panel to define the elements of ready schools. The panel highlighted the importance of strong leadership, an orientation focused on results, effective transition efforts between preschool and elementary school, and meaningful parent engagement. Most important, ready schools are committed to the success of every child and every teacher. Ready schools are learning organizations where exciting curriculum and effective pedagogy merge to help children learn and make sense of their world (Shore, 1998).

Of critical importance, then, is to understand what constitutes *exciting curriculum* and *effective pedagogy*. To be exciting, the curriculum must be carried out with intentionality to address all five dimensions of learning. To be effective, the pedagogy must align with the changing needs of the children; it must incorporate multiple pedagogical strategies, with play among them. Although the NEGP made this clear, it did not define what was meant by play nor did it discuss how play should be manifest in the lives of young children to accomplish their readiness for school. To begin to address these critical issues, we turn first to a historical discussion of play and then to theories of play. Following that, we discuss the relationship between school readiness and play, particularly in light of contemporary and increasingly controversial debates about the viability of play as an effective pedagogical strategy in preparing young children for school.

Understanding Children's Play: Historical and Theoretical Perspectives

In terms of the history of the civilization, the fascination with children's play, which is documented more thoroughly elsewhere (Kagan, 1990a), is fairly recent. Although hints about children's play can be found in the Bible and in various writings from ancient civilizations to the European Renaissance, these descriptions were sketchy and of little importance, preventing empirical conclusions about the nature and quality of play (D. G. Singer & J. L. Singer, 1990; J. L. Singer, 1973). It is known that pre-Renaissance children tended to follow the patterns set by the adults in their presence; boys were involved in their fathers' trade and girls in housekeeping duties. In noble families, children were socialized to courtly routines and skills needed at the time. Although children's play was represented intermittently in various art forms (Shakespeare was sensitive to childhood fantasy in his writings; Brueghel's painting *Children's Play* depicts the vigorous play of village children), the nineteenth-century romantics were the ones who helped seed interest. In Germany, Goethe and Schiller explored the imaginative component of children's play. In England, Coleridge and Wordsworth were fascinated by children's imagination. Robert Louis Stevenson, in poetry, and Mark Twain, in fiction, sanctioned children's rights to imagine and fantasize. And, of course, educational pioneers Froebel and Pestalozzi advocated the use of play in child rearing and education.

Since that time, the issue of children's play has risen in prominence with scholars advancing various theories of play. The surplus energy theory (Spencer, 1896/1955) argues that children, not having to attend to daily survival activities, let out their excess energies in play behavior, rather than in work. Groos's (1901) instinctual theory explains children's play as a way of developing behaviors that are essential for later survival. In this view, play is seen as a necessary rehearsal—a preamble to adult life. G. S. Hall's (1906) recapitulation theory suggested that the individual's development cycle recapitulates the evolutionary history of the race: play, rooted in savage behavior, had to be worked through before one could go on to the realities of adult life. Psychoanalytic theory (Brill, 1938) offered a different interpretation: much of play is an attempt to satisfy drives; to resolve conflicts; and to cope, by repetition, with anxiety-provoking situations. For Piaget and cognitive theorists, play is viewed in a broader context. More than adaptive or conflict-resolving behavior, play is the mode through which children understand their experience and development. For Piaget, accommodation—the attempt to initiate, modify, and interact with the environment—is mastery play or, using Elkind's (1988) word, "work." Likewise, assimilation—the incorporation of the world to match our concepts—is associated with symbolic play or, using Elkind's word, "play."

Piagetian theory marked a turning point for early education. Sanctioning the adaptiveness of behavior, Piagetian theory fostered a role for adults as those who could enhance children's imaginative behavior. Piaget's theory could be translated into concrete classroom practice. Further, cognitive theory could be related to social learning and developmental theory. With Piagetian theory as a springboard, additional concepts of child's play emerged. Far too plentiful to recount here, the theories have explored play with respect to the affective domain, with Curry (1972) suggesting that play affords children a means of clarification and relief from emotional distress. The relationship of play to creativity and to convergent and divergent thinking has received much attention (Guilford, 1967), as has the relationship of play to personality structure (Berlyne, 1969). Clearly, the field does not lack theoretical or conceptual models of children's play.

The Relationship Between Play and School Readiness

As research demonstrated the importance of play in children's development, the commitment to encouraging the practice of play grew. Isaacs (1933) pointed out that early childhood educators had, even then, long cherished the belief that play can nourish children's intellectual and social development. In addition to theories that fortified the rationale for play, research documented the effect of play, and new curriculum and professional guidelines emphasized its importance. Volumes on the theory and practice of play have emerged, particularly to fend off the "back to basics" phenomenon that episodically swept preschool and early education programs. Buffering the importance of play, the National Association for the Education of Young Children (NAEYC) took a strong stand on what constitutes appropriate practice for young children. Through its work, *Developmentally Appropriate Practice in Early Childhood Programs* (Bredekamp & Copple, 1997), play emerged as a hallmark of appropriate early education environments, whether for infants, toddlers, preschoolers, or elementary-schoolers. Verifying the commitment to play, performance standards or program guidelines for many early education efforts (Head Start, Project Giant Step) encouraged providing opportunities for children to play, to initiate their own activities, and to participate in small group activities.

Although the term *play* has meant different things in each of these contexts, certain elements characterize children's play and frame our definition. These elements include the following: (a) children's freedom to select activities; (b) children's freedom to explore and invent, without a prescribed template for their work; (c) children's engagement in solitary or group activity that is purposeful to the child; and (d) children's engagement in fantasy-based, symbolic, or representational activity.

Despite general convergence on constructs associated with play and the preoccupation with the importance of play to children's development, research is actually quite limited with respect to the direct links between play and children's readiness for school. In part, this lack of research may be explained by the fact that, heretofore, readiness has lacked a functional and operational definition. The dearth of research may also be explained by a presumption that there are links between positive developmental outcomes and children's readiness for school. In an effort to make the links more explicit, we use the NEGP's definition of readiness and review the research on the relationship between play and each dimension of readiness.

Dimension 1: Physical Well-Being and Motor Development

Research shows that play is associated with children's physical well-being and motor development (Bredekamp & Copple, 1997; Fjortoft, 2001; Kagan et al., 1995). For example, indoor play equipment, including equipment with modifications made to provide access for children with disabilities, can promote gross-motor skills (Bredekamp & Copple, 1997). Examples of developmentally appropriate play equipment that can stimulate gross-motor skills include: cup stilts, small trampolines, steps, balance beams, hoops for jumping, jump ropes, a bean bag toss, scooter boards, a puppet show, a ring toss, a parachute, floor puzzles, hollow blocks, large Legos™, and strollers for dramatic play (Bredekamp & Copple, 1997).

Outdoor play has also been found to be associated with children's physical well-being and motor development. In Scandinavia, for example, where it has become popular for children to spend a significant amount of time outdoors in the natural environment, research shows that children's motor fitness is improved by play (Fjortoft, 2001). Fjortoft's work showed that children learn to cope with physical challenges and to move around in rugged terrain, which, in turn, improves their motor ability.

Children between the ages of 3 and 5 years who have not yet acquired sophisticated manual dexterity benefit from activities that develop their hand muscles and fine-motor skills, including drawing and painting, working with playdough, and constructing with Duplos™ or Legos™. These activities not only engage children but also prepare them for the demands of handwriting and other skills developed later (Bredekamp & Copple, 1997).

The development of sensorimotor skills is also enhanced through play. For example, coordinated movement such as that which occurs when a child kicks a ball that is rolling in his direction, requires the ability to use sensory information to guide motions. The child attempting to kick the ball rolling toward him must be able to distinguish the ball from other stimuli, focus attention on it, determine his distance from the ball, assess the speed at which the ball is moving, and then guide his own movement. One of the key aspects of sensorimotor development for classroom achievement is the development of eye-hand coordination, which is necessary for writing and drawing (Kagan et al., 1995).

Dimension 2: Social and Emotional Development

Considerable research validates the relationship between play and children's social and emotional development. The psychoanalytic view (Brill, 1938) suggests that play is the projection of the individual's inner or emotional life; hence, play, particularly sociodramatic play, has intrigued theorists and clinicians. Erikson (1950) supports the role of play in ego development. Play acts are "a function of the ego, an attempt to bring into synchronization the bodily and social processes of which one is a part even while one is a self" (p. 184). In symbolic role-taking (Fein, 1984), children demonstrate their perceptions of themselves and others. They struggle to come to terms with their senses of goodness and badness that are played out in fantasy play. They identify their own feelings and those of others (Hartley, Frank, & Goldenson, 1952). Through repeated contacts with playmates, children develop cooperative reciprocal relationships and gain mutual understanding and trust. Children can develop pro-social behaviors through play opportunities that foster self-confidence and the exploration of reality and make-believe.

Pretend or imaginary play is thought to provide a mental rehearsal for social development by offering a forum for experimentation with new roles and solutions (Burghardt, 1984). Pretend play has also been found to help children form their personalities and develop social skills (Sawyer, 2001). Children who develop imaginary playmates differ on a number of dimensions from those who do not (Taylor, 1999). Children with imaginary playmates generally have less sibling contact and have parents who believe fantasy to be valuable (Partington & Grant, 1984). They have a slight edge in verbal-literacy skills and, according to parents' reports, are better able to interact with adults and exhibit more "self-initiated" play (Manosevitz, Prentice, & Wilson, 1973).

Dimension 3: Approaches Toward Learning

The term *approaches toward learning* (which is closely related to, but less well-defined than physical, social, or emotional development) encompasses a range of attitudes, habits, and learning styles. Learning styles are malleable and are composed of aggregate variables that affect how children attitudinally address the learning process. These variables include: openness to and curiosity about new tasks and challenges; initiative, task persistence, and attentiveness; approaches to reflection and interpretation; capacity for invention and imagination; and cognitive approaches to tasks (Kagan et al., 1995).

Enmeshed within the approaches-toward-learning dimension is the array of efforts that enables children to approach formal learning tasks with confidence and zest. Many of these efforts are involved with representation through play and the arts. The idea has been suggested that representation evokes five major cognitive benefits (Eisner, 1990), among them, allowing the child to make permanent what could be fleeting or evanescent. Second, by altering the representation (as in an art activity or block play) a child "edits" or perfects his work, thereby preparing the way for an experimenting mindset. Representational activity is important to cognitive development because it enables children to make their ideas public, to set the stage for understanding the multiple forms that communication takes. It also, in Dewey's (1938) words, enables "flexible purposing," the ability to set a goal and to shift gears when necessary. Finally (and the observational experiences in Reggio Emilia support this benefit well), representational work allows children to become familiar with multiple genres through which to express unique aspects of the human experience.

Transcending representational work, the dimension involving approaches toward learning embraces constructs of reflection and interpretation that Wolf (1992) notes are referred to as the "socialization of thought"—the capacity to seek models, absorb information, and work through possibilities. These skills are precursors that enable children to form images of what is not present, to extend conventional thinking beyond the known, and to combine ideas and experiences in inventive and productive ways. Approaches toward learning also embraces the ability to complete tasks and to sustain attention to tasks over increasingly long periods of time. Children who are neither distractible nor distracting tend to fare better in school (Kagan et al., 1995).

Dimension 4: Language Development

Play has been found to accelerate communication in verbal and nonverbal youngsters. For young, nonverbal children, play is the means through which impulses, feelings, and fantasies are translated into actions; play offers a means of dealing with challenges. As a vehicle to stimulate language, play is ideal because it fosters the three basic functions of language: communication, expression, and reasoning. Bruner (1982) and others suggest that conversations are most likely to occur when children are in small groups, with or without an adult present. Clearly, language acquisition is enhanced when children are engaged in conversation rather than when they are simply passively exposed to language (Wells, 1983).

Research suggests that play, particularly symbolic behavior in play, is related to the understanding of written language (N. Hall, 1991; Pellegrini & Galda, 1993). Symbolic play, described by Isenberg and Jacob (1983) as "the process of transforming an object or oneself into another object, person, situation, or event through the use of motor and verbal actions in a make-believe activity" (p. 272), is an important source of literacy development because literacy consists of using words to represent objects, ideas, or actions (N. Hall, 1991). Three-year-olds' symbolic transformations in play have been found to predict their writing status at age 5, and their use of oral language in pretend play episodes has been found to predict their reading achievement (Roskos & Neuman, 1998).

Literacy objects and literacy-explicit play settings (e.g., a post office) have also been found to influence young children's literacy development. Well-crafted and print-enriched play centers that incorporate literacy roles, objects, and routines provide opportunities for children to explore and practice the functions and features of written language (Roskos & Neuman, 1998; Schroeder, 1997). Moreover, research shows that literacy-enriched sociodramatic play environments with primary, mixed-age learners make for a collaborative social context that fosters both literacy activity and helping behaviors. Children in these environments help one another with literacy learning; younger children seem to be the main beneficiaries (Stone & Christie, 1996). Supporting this finding, Smilansky (1990) offers a thorough review of the effect of sociodramatic play on children's reading comprehension, noting that "highly imaginative representation in kindergarten is one of the most relevant skills for school achievement" (p. 30).

Dimension 5: Cognition and General Knowledge

In terms of enhancing children's cognitive potential, play has been acknowledged as a primary vehicle for concept development and problem solving. Play brings children into contact with multiple stimuli that induce the development of categorization, generalization, and conceptual acquisition skills. For example, in the house corner, children categorize things to eat, things to cook with; at the water table, they learn which things sink and which float; they generalize from present object to objects not immediately available. In the science area, they learn concepts of time, for example, a seed planted today is a vine tomorrow. Natural play situations also provide countless opportunities for problem solving. Smith and Simon (1984) found in their review of 11 studies of play and problem solving that, compared with children in nonplay situations (e.g., direct instruction), youngsters in play situations are just as likely to solve problems successfully. They found that children in play conditions generate more responses than nonplay or control youngsters, suggesting that play enhances innovative and creative problem-solving behavior. Athey (1988), in summarizing the relationship between play and cognitive development, suggests that play contributes to a vast range of specific cognitive processes (association, hypothesis testing) and to generic functioning (information discrimination, generation, and abstraction).

Play: The Exclusive or Preferred Pedagogy?

The link connecting children's play, children's overall development, and school readiness is irrefutable. As has often been noted, children's play is children's work and vice versa (Elkind, 1986; Zigler, 1987). Moreover, the studies we have cited here empirically affirm the link between play and positive outcomes in all readiness dimensions.

The question at hand, then, is not whether play accelerates children's learning, but whether play is the exclusive or preferred pedagogy to do so. Consequently, it is important to look at studies that compare different pedagogical approaches. When comparing play-based and child-initiated pedagogy to teacher-directed pedagogy, for example, we see a reason for concern. Teacher-directed pedagogy is associated with children who are more distractible, less willing to follow directions, and less prosocial (Hart, Charlesworth, Burts, & DeWolf, 1993). Some teacher-directed instruction has demonstrated short-term academic gains, but concerns about the long-term effect of teacher-directed strategies on children's social development are prominent in the literature (DeVries, Reese-Learned, & Morgan, 1991). Indeed, Stipek, Feiler, Daniels, and Milburn (1995) have noted that, although children in more didactic programs had higher scores on reading achievement, their scores on achievement tests in math were not higher than those of children in less structured programs. Moreover, the work of Stipek and colleagues (1995) indicated that being enrolled in more didactic programs was associated with more negative outcomes on measures of motivation, in that children had lower expectations for their own academic accomplishment, were more dependent on adults, and evidenced less pride in their work. Notably, these findings did not differ between economically disadvantaged and middle-class children nor between preschoolers and kindergartners.

A noteworthy point is that preschool pedagogy varies greatly in the amount of play that is sanctioned, in the autonomy accorded children, and in the amount of structure imposed by the adults or the curriculum. Marcon (1999) has inventively and instructively categorized pedagogical strategies into three groups: child-initiated, academically directed, and middle of the road. Studying children over time, she has discerned that children whose preschool experience was more academically directed were retained less often in later grades, but by the end of fourth grade, they had earned significantly lower grades compared to children who had attended preschools with primarily child-initiated pedagogical approaches (Marcon, 2002). Research is coalescing to confirm that heavily didactic instruction with only modest amounts of play is not the most effective strategy to advance children's long-term development.

This finding, however, does not mean that some structure is injurious to children's development. Indeed, studies of the High/Scope program (formerly known as the cognitively oriented preschool program), which combines teacher- and child-directed efforts, demonstrate the benefits of a combined strategy. Widely used in Head Start and other early care and education programs, this combined strategy has been shown to advance children's early learning and development, particularly when compared with the use of highly structured and heavily didactic strategies (Schweinhart & Weikart, 1997). The High/Scope preschool curriculum is also associated with better outcomes later in life when compared with the Direct Instruction curriculum model, which teaches the academic skills and content assessed by intelligence and achievement tests (Schweinhart & Weikart, 1997). Specifically, the High/Scope curriculum was found to be associated with lower crime rates in young adulthood and fewer instances of emotional impairment or disturbance during schooling than the Direct Instruction model (Schweinhart & Weikart, 1997). These results are attributed to the emphasis on planning, social reasoning, and other social objectives in the High/Scope curriculum, which are absent from the Direct Instruction curriculum (Schweinhart & Weikart, 1997).

Slavin's Success for All program provides an example of a structured intervention nested within a child-oriented setting, thereby yielding a blended pedagogical approach (Slavin & Madden, 2001). The structured portion of the intervention provides research-based strategies in reading, writing, and language arts; one-to-one tutoring for children struggling in reading; and active family support activities. The program documents success, particularly with low-income children (Slavin & Madden, 2001). Specifically, Success for All has been found to improve children's reading achievement, reduce grade retention, and increase attendance among low-income populations (Madden, Slavin, Karweit, Dolan, & Wasik, 1992).

Our review of the literature—however brief—suggests that, although much more research is needed, evidence is pointing toward three findings. First, the benefits of highly didactic and very structured approaches to pedagogy seem to be limited, particularly over the long term. Second, significant social, emotional, and cognitive benefits are associated with balanced pedagogical approaches that embrace some structure, including teacher-directed activities, as well as opportunities for child-initiated and play-based activities. Finally, child-initiated strategies, long associated with play, provide a means to achieving positive outcomes for children and families. Indeed, we support the critical importance of self-directed learning and play as the essential pedagogical strategy for young children, the sine qua non of high-quality early childhood education. But this is not an indication that child-initiated strategies should be the exclusive approach; play can be effectively combined with teacher-directed efforts to yield positive outcomes for children.

The literature is clear: Diverse strategies that combine play and more structured efforts are effective accelerators of children's readiness for school and long-term development. Apparently, just as children need intentionality in their exposure to all dimensions of development, so too may they need exposure to play-based and child-initiated as well as teacher-directed pedagogical strategies. Clearly, no single strategy can be expected to work for all children, all the time. A variety of approaches can and should be sanctioned, including play, guided instruction, self-directed instruction, and group learning.

The challenge, however, in calling for multiple approaches is knowing which strategy to use for which children, for how long, and under what conditions. For example, when is it appropriate to rely more heavily on play-based approaches? What characteristics in children predispose them to various pedagogical preferences? Under what conditions (e.g., level of teacher competence, desired outcome) is it appropriate to use each strategy? Are certain dimensions of school readiness more amenable to one pedagogical approach than others?

These empirical questions beg not only for more research but also for more sophisticated research. Rather than advocate or investigate one pedagogical or curricular approach, we need to be ecumenical, experimental, and probing. We must be willing to posit different pedagogical scenarios; implement them; and when they are ready, evaluate them, taking particular note of variations in dosage of each type of pedagogy, of exogenous variables (e.g., culture, setting, and context), and of endogenous variables (e.g., level of individual child and teacher characteristics). Only then will we better understand effective ways to maximize instructional pedagogy for young children. Having made this assertion, let it be clear that play, rather than being eliminated, must be elevated to a central position in this inquiry. To do otherwise would be to invalidate not only the traditions of early care and education but also the lessons from a great deal of research.

References

Athey, I. (1988). The relationship of play to cognitive, language and moral development. In D. Bergen (Ed.), *Play as a medium for learning and development* (pp. 81–101). Portsmouth, NH: Heinemann.

Ben-Yochanan, A., & Katz, Y. J. (1989). Validation of a school readiness battery for a referred sample of Israeli elementary school students. *Perceptual and Motor Skills, 68*(2), 651–654.

Berlyne, D. E. (1969). Laughter, humor and play. In G. Lindzey & E. Aronson (Eds.), *The handbook of social psychology* (Vol. 3, 2nd ed., pp. 795–852). Reading, MA: Addison-Wesley.

Bredekamp, S., & Copple, C. (Eds.). (1997). *Developmentally appropriate practice in early childhood programs* (Rev. ed.). Washington, DC: National Association for the Education of Young Children.

Brill, A. A. (Ed.). (1938). *The basic writings of Sigmund Freud*. New York: Modern Library.

Bruner, J. (1960). *The process of education*. New York: Random House.

Bruner, J. (1982). *Under five in Britain* (Vol. II). Oxford Preschool Research Project. Ypsilanti, MI: High/Scope Foundation.

Burghardt, G. M. (1984). On the origins of play. In P. K. Smith (Ed.), *Play in animals and humans* (pp. 5–41). New York: Basil Blackwell.

Busse, T. V., & Seraydarian, L. (1978). The relationships between first name desirability and school readiness, IQ, and school achievement. *Psychology in the Schools, 15*(2), 297–302.

Buttram, J., Covert, R. W., & Hayes, M. (1976). Prediction of school readiness and early grade achievement by classroom teachers. *Educational & Psychological Measurement, 36*(2), 543–546.

Coley, R. J. (2002). *An uneven start: Indicators of inequality in school readiness* (Policy Information Report). Princeton, NJ: Educational Testing Service. (ERIC Document Reproduction Service No. ED466473)

Curry, N. E. (1972). *Current issues in play: Theoretical and practical considerations for its use as a curricular tool in the preschool*. Unpublished thesis, University of Pittsburgh.

Dewey, J. (1938). *Experience and education*. New York: Macmillan.

DeVries, R., Reese-Learned, H., & Morgan, P. (1991). Sociomoral development in direct-instruction, eclectic and constructivist kindergartens: A study of children's enacted interpersonal understanding. *Early Childhood Research Quarterly, 6*(4), 473–517.

Dunleavy, R. A., Hansen, J. L., Szasz, C. W., & Baade, L. E. (1981). Early kindergarten identification of academically not-ready children by use of Human Figure Drawing developmental score. *Psychology in the Schools, 18*(1), 35–38.

Eisner, E. (1990). The role of art and play in children's cognitive development. In E. Klugman & S. Smilansky (Eds.), *Children's play and learning: Perspectives and policy implications* (pp. 43–56). New York: Teachers College Press.

Elkind, D. (1986). Formal education and early childhood education: An essential difference. *Phi Delta Kappan, 67*(9), 631–636.

Elkind, D. (1988). Play. *Young Children, 43*(5), 2.

Erikson, E. H. (1950). *Childhood and society* (2nd ed.). New York: Norton.

Fagan, J., & Iglesias, A. (1999). Father involvement program effects on fathers, father figures, and their Head Start children: A quasi-experimental study. *Early Childhood Research Quarterly, 14*(2), 243–269.

Fein, G. G. (1984). *Play and behavioral flexibility*. In P. K. Smith (Ed.), *Play in animals and humans* (pp. 159–173). New York: Basil Blackwell.

Fjortoft, I. (2001). The natural environment as a playground for children: The impact of outdoor play activities in pre-primary school children. *Early Childhood Education Journal, 29*(2), 111–117.

Gagne, R. M. (1970). *The conditions of learning*. New York: Holt, Rinehart & Winston.

Good, C. V. (Ed.). (1973). *Dictionary of education* (3rd ed.). New York: McGraw-Hill.

Gray, W. S. (1927, January). Training and experience that prepare for reading. *Childhood Education*, 210–214.

Groos, K. (1901). *The play of man*. New York: Appleton.

Guilford, J. P. (1967). *The nature of human intelligence*. New York: McGraw-Hill.

Hall, G. S. (1906). *Youth*. New York: Appleton.

Hall, N. (1991). Play and the emergence of literacy. In J. F. Christie (Ed.), *Play and early literacy development* (pp. 1–25). Albany: State University of New York Press.

Hart, C., Charlesworth, R., Burts, D., & DeWolf, M. (1993, March). *The relationship of attendance in developmentally appropriate or inappropriate kindergarten classrooms to first and second grade behavior.* Poster session presented at the biennial meeting of the Society for Research in Child Development, New Orleans, LA.

Hartley, R. E., Frank, L., & Goldenson, R. (1952). *Understanding children's play*. New York: Columbia University Press.

Holmes, M. C. (1927, January). Investigations of reading readiness of first grade entrants. *Childhood Education*, 215–221.

Ilg, F. L., & Ames, L. (1965). *School readiness: Behavior tests used at the Gesell Institute*. New York: Harper & Row.

Isaacs, S. (1933). *Social development in young children*. New York: Schocken.

Isenberg, J., & Jacob, E. (1983). Literacy and symbolic play: A review of the literature. *Childhood Education, 59*(4), 272–276.

Kagan, S. L. (1990a). Children's play: The journey from theory to practice. In E. Klugman & S. Smilansky (Eds.), *Children's play and learning: Perspectives and policy implications* (pp. 173–187). New York: Teachers College Press.

Kagan, S. L. (1990b). Readiness 2000: Rethinking rhetoric and responsibility. *Phi Delta Kappan,* (December), 272–279.

Kagan, S. L., Moore, E., & Bredekamp, S. (Eds.). (1995, June). *Reconsidering children's early development and learning: Toward common views and vocabulary* (Goal 1 Technical Planning Group Report 95-03). Washington, DC: National Education Goals Panel.

Knoll, M., & Patti, J. (2003). Social-emotional learning and academic achievement. In M. J. Elias, H. Arnold, E. Budd, & C. S. Hussey (Eds.), *EQ + IQ = Best leadership practices for caring and successful schools* (pp. 36–49). Thousand Oaks, CA: Corwin Press.

Lesniak, T., & Legien, M. (1983, May). Application of a graphological method in assessment of children's reading and writing readiness. *Psychologia Wychowawcza, 26*(3), 293–302.

Madden, N. A., Slavin, R. E., Karweit, N. L., Dolan, L. J., & Wasik, B. A. (1992, March). *Success for All: Longitudinal effects of a restructuring program for inner-city elementary schools* (Report No. 28). Baltimore: Johns Hopkins University Center for Research on Effective Schooling for Disadvantaged Students.

Manosevitz, M., Prentice, N. M., & Wilson, F. (1973). Individual and family correlates of imaginary companions in preschool children. *Developmental Psychology, 8*(1), 72–79.

Marcon, R. A. (1999). Differential impact of preschool models on development and early learning of inner-city children: A three-cohort study. *Developmental Psychology, 35*(2), 358–375.

Marcon, R. A. (2002, Spring). Moving up the grades: Relationship between preschool model and later school success. *Early Childhood Research and Practice, 4*(1). Retrieved July 8, 2003, from http://ecrp.uiuc.edu/v4n1/marcon.html

May, C. R., & Campbell, R.-M. (1981). Readiness for learning: Assumptions and realities. *Theory into Practice, 20*, 130–134.

Morisset, C. E. (1994). *School readiness: Parents and professionals speak on social and emotional needs of young children* (Report No. 26). Baltimore: Center on Families, Communities, Schools, and Children's Learning, The Johns Hopkins University.

National Research Council and Institute of Medicine. (2000). *From neurons to neighborhoods: The science of early childhood development.* Committee on Integrating the Science of Early Childhood Development. J. P. Shonkoff and D. A. Phillips (Eds.). Board on Children, Youth, and Families, Commission on Behavioral and Social Sciences and Education. Washington, DC: National Academy Press.

Ogletree, E. J. (1985). *An interpretation of Rudolf Steiner's theory of child development and school readiness.* ERIC Document Reproduction Service No. ED259827.

Oja, L., & Juerimaee, T. (2002, October). Physical activity, motor ability, and school readiness of 6-year-old children. *Perceptual & Motor Skills, 95*(2), 407–415.

Okon, W., & Wilgocka-Okon, B. (1973). *The school readiness project.* Paris: UNESCO.

Partington, J. T., & Grant, C. (1984). Imaginary playmates and other useful fantasies. In P. K. Smith (Ed.), *Play in animals and humans* (pp. 217–240). New York: Basil Blackwell.

Pellegrini, A. D., & Galda, L. (1993). Ten years after: A reexamination of symbolic play and literacy research. *Reading Research Quarterly, 28,* 162–177.

Pestalozzi, J. H. (1915). *How Gertrude teaches her children* (L. Holland & F. C. Turner, Trans.). Syracuse, NY: C. W. Bardeen.

Piaget, J. (1970). *Science of education and the psychology of the child.* New York: Orion Press.

Roskos, K., & Neuman, S. B. (1998). Play as an opportunity for literacy. In O. N. Saracho & B. Spodek (Eds.), *Multiple perspectives on play in early childhood education* (pp. 100–115). Albany: State University of New York Press.

Sawyer, R. K. (2001). Play as improvisational rehearsal: Multiple levels of analysis in children's play. In A. Goencue & E. L. Klein (Eds.), *Children in play, story, and school* (pp. 19–38). New York: Guilford Press.

Schroeder, K. (1997). Literacy behaviors in the spontaneous play of a multi-national group of first graders in a small overseas school. In W. M. Linek & E. G. Sturtevant (Eds.), *Exploring literacy* (pp. 17–27). Platteville, WI: The College Reading Association.

Schweinhart, L. J., & Weikart, D. P. (1997). The High/Scope preschool curriculum comparison study through age 23. *Early Childhood Research Quarterly, 12,* 117–143.

Scott, R., & Kobes, D. A. (1974). *The influence of family size on learning readiness patterns of socioeconomically disadvantaged preschool blacks.* Washington, DC: Department of Health, Education, and Welfare. (ERIC Document Reproduction Service No. ED107385)

Scott, R., & Seifert, K. (1974). *Family size and learning readiness profiles of socioeconomically disadvantaged preschool whites.* Washington, DC: Department of Health, Education, and Welfare. (ERIC Document Reproduction Service No. ED107358)

Shepard, L., & Smith, M. (1988). Escalating academic demand in kindergarten: Counterproductive policies. *Elementary School Journal, 89*(2), 135–145.

Shore, R. (1998). *Ready schools: A report of the Goal 1 Ready Schools Resource Group.* Washington, DC: National Education Goals Panel.

Simner, M. L. (1989). Predictive validity of an abbreviated version of the Printing Performance School Readiness Test. *Journal of School Psychology, 27*(2), 189–195.

Singer, D. G., & Singer, J. L. (1990). *The house of make-believe: Children's play and the developing imagination.* Cambridge, MA: Harvard University Press.

Singer, J. L. (1973). *The child's world of make-believe: Experimental studies of imaginative play.* New York: Academic Press.

Slavin, R. E., & Madden, N. A. (2001). *One million children: Success for all.* Thousand Oaks, CA: Corwin Press.

Smilansky, S. (1990). Sociodramatic play: Its relevance to behavior and achievement in school. In E. Klugman & S. Smilansky (Eds.), *Children's play and learning: Perspectives and policy implications* (pp. 18-42). New York: Teachers College Press.

Smith, P. K., & Simon, T. (1984). Object play, problem-solving and creativity in children. In P. K. Smith (Ed.), *Play in animals and humans* (pp. 199–216). New York: Basil Blackwell.

Solan, H. A., Mozlin, R., & Rumpf, D. A. (1985). The relationship of perceptual-motor development to learning readiness in kindergarten: A multivariate analysis. *Journal of Learning Disabilities, 18*(6), 337–344.

Spencer, H. (1896/1955). *Principles of psychology.* New York: D. Appleton.

Stipek, D., Feiler, R., Daniels, D., & Milburn, S. (1995). Effects of different instructional approaches on young children's achievement and motivation. *Child Development, 66*(1), 209–233.

Stone, S. J., & Christie, J. F. (1996, Spring/Summer). Collaborative literacy learning during sociodramatic play in a multiage (K–2) primary classroom. *Journal of Research in Childhood Education, 10*, 123–133.

Taylor, M. (1999). *Imaginary companions and the children who create them.* New York: Oxford University Press.

U.S. Department of Education. (1995). *Goals 2000: A progress report.* Washington, DC: Author.

Vygotsky, L. S. (1978). *Mind in society: The development of higher psychological processes.* Cambridge, MA: Harvard University Press.

Wells, G. (1983). Talking with children: The complementary roles of parents and teachers. In M. Donaldson, R. Grieve, & C. Pratt (Eds.), *Early childhood development and education* (pp. 127–150). New York: Guilford Press.

Willer, B., & Bredekamp, S. (1990). Redefining readiness: An essential requisite for educational reform. *Young Children, 45*(5), 22–24.

Wolf, D. P. (1992). *Approaches to learning: A perspective on children coming to school ready to learn.* Manuscript prepared for the Goal 1 Resource Group on School Readiness for the National Education Goals Panel.

Zigler, E. (1987). Formal schooling for four-year-olds? No. *American Psychologist, 42*(3), 254–260.

Zigler, E., & Child, I. L. (1969). Socialization. In G. Lindzey & E. Aronson (Eds.), *Handbook of social psychology* (2nd ed., pp. 450–589). Reading, MA: Addison-Wesley.

6

FOSTERING SCHOOL ACHIEVEMENT AND CREATIVITY THROUGH SOCIODRAMATIC PLAY IN THE CLASSROOM[1]

Jerome L. Singer and Mawiyah A. Lythcott

P lay has often been derided as a trivial childhood activity that has little value in fundamental education. Yet there is evidence that various forms of pretend play can enhance school readiness, social skills, and creative accomplishment. We propose that play methods strengthen the child's use of private consciousness and organized mental structures while sustaining interest and excitement about remembering and learning. Following a review of early and more recent studies documenting the uses and consequences of forms of imaginative play guided by teachers with daycare or elementary school children, we suggest ways in which such play can be linked to cognitive theories of Bruner and Epstein and to Sternberg's conception of the tripartite dimensions of successful intelligence, especially the creative and practical components.

Our human capability for creating alternative mental models of our physical and social environments, a manipulatable virtual reality in thought and imagery, is a critical resource we need to draw on and to strengthen in the educational process. We have reason to believe that this feature of the human condition may emerge naturally in the child's second year of life with the beginnings of symbolic or make-believe play. Its flowering in the preschool years is dependent upon favorable environmental condi-

[1]Reprinted with permission of the Mid-South Educational Research Association Board of Directors. From "Fostering School Achievement and Creativity Through Sociodramatic Play in the Classroom" by J. L. Singer & M. A. Lythcott, 2002, *Research in the Schools, 9*(2), pp. 41–50. Copyright 2002 by Mid-South Educational Research Association Board of Directors.

tions, especially the encouragement by parents or other key adults (Lewin, 1935; Piaget, 1962; D. G. Singer & J. L. Singer, 1990; Vygotsky, 1978). Observational and experimental research with children aged 3 to 5 has indicated that pretend or imaginative play is linked not only to greater daily enjoyment but also to a series of generally adaptive and specific school readiness skills. Such skills include improved verbal fluency, imagery, delaying capacity or self-control, persistence, cooperation, less unwarranted aggression, and greater signs of early creativity (Russ, Robins, & Christiano, 1999; Shmukler, 1982–83; D. G. Singer & J. L. Singer, 1990; D. G. Singer, J. L. Singer, Plaskon, & Schweder, 2003; J. L. Singer & D. G. Singer, 1981).

In the period of middle childhood or the early school years, social constraints and enhanced brain capacities foster the internalization of public play into private interior monologues, daydreams, and other imagery sequences, as well as into short and longer-term playfulness (Piaget, 1962; J. L. Singer, 1973, 1975). The urge to engage in more play, which has seemingly "gone underground," does not fully disappear, however. It appears to resurface throughout the lifespan, and this tendency has important educational implications (Hellendoorn, van der Kooij, & Sutton-Smith, 1994; McCaslin, 1984; Rosenberg, 1987; D. G. Singer & J. L. Singer, 1990). Our intent in this paper is to examine how various forms of make-believe or sociodramatic play have in the past and can in the future be applied to the goals of "formal" education and the enhancement of "successful intelligence," the latter defined as combining the "abstract," "practical," and "creative" components drawn from the research of Sternberg (1999).

Before turning to a specific research review of how play has been used in the classroom, we want to clarify our broader theoretical perspective. Too often, groups of parents, policymakers, and educators have derided play as a trivial, if enjoyable, childhood activity, but one that has little value in fundamental "three Rs" education. A deeply thoughtful recent paper by cognitive psychologists John Anderson, Lynne Reder, and the Nobel Prize winner Herbert Simon (1998) has identified two supposedly antagonistic positions in education, the Behaviorist and the Radical Constructivist. The former position emphasizes repetition and drill as keys to learning in keeping with the association learning emphasis of Objective Behaviorism. The Radical Constructivist position proposes that true education establishes optimal conditions designed to bring out "from within" the child's inherent ability for exploration and problem solving. The Radical Constructivist might propose that fostering spontaneous play and curiosity in children may be enough to generate adaptive cognitive development and information-processing skills. Extreme examples of this position have surfaced periodically, as in the nursery schools that distorted John Dewey's "Progressive Education," or in elementary schools that have especially emphasized "social promotion."

Anderson, Reder, and Simon (1998), basing their approach on the research developments in cognitive psychology in the past quarter century, argue for a "hybrid" position. Without denying the associationist or "neural connectionist" position, they also propose that much cognition derives from symbol representations, knowledge based on organized mental structures such as schemas, scripts, and prototypes, some linguistic, some taking the forms of images or episodic memories and mental rules. Research indicates that while learning can occur through simple reading of associated material, even better results can be found when the children or adults actively seek to generate answers based on earlier acquired schemas.

Anderson et al. (1998) are careful to point to the importance of practice and repetition as critical features of learning, but they also call attention to data that indicate that "mindless recitation" can be fruitless educationally. As they conclude, the predicament that teachers face is "find[ing] tasks that provide practice while at the same time sustaining interest" (Anderson et al., 1998, p. 255).

We are proposing in this review that the use of various forms of teacher-directed sociodramatic play or other features of narrative thought (Bruner, 1986) or the cognitive-experiential self (Epstein, 1999) in the classroom can serve an important role in early education. Using play initiated by teachers but further practiced on their own by children can establish conditions for active rehearsal. Such conditions may promote in children the self-generated search for "successful intelligence" in its abstract, practical, and creative forms. A componential analysis of which features of the educational objective require individualized practice and which need group experience can yield more effective later generalization (Anderson et al., 1998). Our position here is that play methods can strengthen the child's utility of private consciousness and organized mental structures like schemas and scripts while sustaining interest and excitement about remembering and learning.

The Emergence of Play Approaches in School Settings

Earlier books have reviewed the first examples of how children's pretend play was identified as a formative basis for the adaptive role of the human imagination (D. G. Singer & J. L. Singer, 1990; J. L. Singer, 1973). One can trace the origins of thought about the role of play in the speculative but insightful writings of the German poet Schiller and the Dutch folklore specialist Groos; Freud's (1908/1962) astute linkage of adult literary creativity to childhood play; Piaget's (1962) observations on play, dreams, and imitation; and the work of Vygotsky, Luria, Leontiev, and Elkonin in Russia (Grigorenko, Ruzgis, & Sternberg, 1997). This connection of early childhood play to youthful fantasy and adult imagination was taken a step further in the 1920s and early 1930s by one of psychology's few geniuses, Kurt Lewin, the founder of experimental methods for child, social, and personality study. In an implicit criticism of some of the Montessori Group's tendencies to drastically restrict play in their nursery schools, Lewin called attention to the importance of encouraging the development of an imaginative "life-space." Education for reality, he proposed, calls for children to develop the capacity for playing mentally with pasts and futures, which then afford the youngsters a clearer sense of what their own needs are and what possibilities exist for moving toward their goals (Lewin, 1935). It is intriguing to read that, even in the former Soviet Union, psychologists like Elkonin came to recognize how important sociodramatic play can be for school readiness. Instead of formal teaching in the preschool, these researchers advocate allowing children the chance for complex "scenario role-play" such as playing with building blocks. Such games contribute to imaginative development, mental flexibility, self-control, and attentiveness (Burmenskaia, 1997).

Within the elementary school setting, we can trace the use of play methods to a series of teachers, some with backgrounds in theater but with interests less in dramatic career training than in enhancing all the development of imagination, motor skills, character, and judgment of children (Rosenberg, 1987). When and how did educators in the United States begin to introduce dramatic play into the elementary school curriculum? We must first make a distinction between formal dramas such as the annual school play in which children portray characters from ancient history or actually revive popular plays and musical comedies like *Grease*, *Oliver*, or *Annie* and the creative, improvised exercises first popularized in education by Winifred Ward (1960) in the 1930s. Winifred Ward, a wonderful classroom storyteller, is often considered the key figure in the past half-century in spreading the message that good teaching and imaginative or sociodramatic play go hand in hand. She wrote that "drama comes to the door of every school with the child" (Ward, 1960, p. 1). For Ward, listening to stories was a start, but the real opportunities for developing imagination, social skills, and approaches to problem solving came through improvised drama, writing, and acting in playlets and eventually trying out more formal roles. Nellie McCaslin (1984), the author of a major textbook on drama in the classroom, extends these benefits to include heightened social awareness, an opportunity for acceptable emotional expressiveness, and improved speech pronunciation and usage.

Programs that engage children's natural inclination to pretend usually begin with rhythm and movement, improvisation, and mime and gradually move to simple exercises that foster self-expression and the communication of emotions. Great sensitivity to group interaction is necessary in order to sustain a general sense of participation and to avoid isolating and scapegoating those children who are shy or who lack pretend play skills, perhaps because of inexperience. Today we recognize that the values of caring, sharing, concern for the weak and the disadvantaged, and responsibility are important features of a full curriculum. The creative educator seeks to foster the internalization of these values at two levels: through the content of the plays the children enact and through their actual participation in writing the play, assigning parts, rehearsing, preparing scenery, helping each other learn lines, and building simple sets or props. There is something for everybody in the process and since the central focus is story-telling, it draws on earlier make-believe experience (McCaslin, 1984).

Helane Rosenberg, working with her group at Rutgers University, has produced a delightful and practical volume on stimulating creativity and imagination in the schoolroom. The book includes dozens of simple, concrete procedures for engaging children's attention and generating imaginative activity in a playful but ultimately educational fashion (Rosenberg, 1987). She proposes that dramatic play can enhance, on one hand, imagery and related internal capacities, and, on the other, overt social and behavioral skills. Through the interactive process the child develops a new sense of an inner self, a heightened awareness of autonomous skills, and a sense of connectedness. Dramatic play, by enriching inner experience and also by fostering social interaction, can help the 7- to 12-year-old confront and resolve the inherent human tension between connection and autonomy.

The Rutgers Imagination method Rosenberg outlines involves three major aspects:

■ Participants plan, play, and evaluate using their ability to imagine, enact, and reflect

■ The tools include images, scripts, and modest props produced by the participants.

■ A sense of organization or at least some formal structure (circular, hierarchical, or linear) sustains the exercises, often with the limited but clear guidance of the instructor.

Extensive use is made of individually constructed props, of photographs that are easily available from family albums, and of paintings and drawings produced by the children themselves. Children not only act, they also write, design, direct, and criticize. Once again, children's natural inclination to pretend and their joy in storytelling are subtly and effectively enlisted for exercises that enhance their self-esteem and social adaptiveness.

The work of Ward, McCaslin, and Rosenberg, among others, has been evaluated chiefly through anecdotal report. Especially influential, however, has been the contribution of Sara Smilansky (1968), who conducted some of the earliest controlled studies designed to assess the effectiveness of classroom applications of sociodramatic or thematic-fantasy play. Smilansky and, later, Dina Feitelson, a reading specialist, carried out their work in Israel at a time when that nation was seeking to assimilate large numbers of Sephardic Jewish immigrants (chiefly from Arabic countries) into its then predominately Western Europeanized cultural tradition (J. L. Singer & D. G. Singer, 1981). The studies indicated that training in various forms of imaginative play not only enhanced the spontaneous tendency to engage in such play but also yielded evidence of better adjustment to school, better reading readiness skills in language usage, and in the case of the Feitelson group [J. L. Singer & D. Singer, 1981] more signs of divergent or creative thought.

In the United States, Joan T. Freyberg (1973) used a similar approach with a group of inner-city educationally disadvantaged kindergarten children. With just a little more than 2 hours of actual training time (eight 20-minute sessions of exposure to various play themes such as "boat and sailors in a storm," "family around the dinner table," and "magic genie performing tricks"), the scores for spontaneous schoolyard make-believe in the experimental group doubled while there was almost no change in the untrained control group. Along with these demonstrated increases in imaginative play, there was also evidence of greater positive emotionality and signs of better persistence in play and in more behavioral sequences. The children exposed to training showed more verbal communication when observed later in the school-yard, used longer and more complex sentences and more verbal labeling, and were more discriminating in their use of language.

Similar training approaches are now widely found in the literature (Freyberg, 1973; Saltz & Brodie, 1982; Smilansky, 1968). Some controversy remains over whether this kind of training has special advantages over other kinds of more direct and focused training in enhancing cognitive skills. While admitting that studies have shown fantasy play training to have resulted in significant improvements in verbal intelligence, mathematical readiness, perspective-taking, concentration, complexity of play, conservation or object-constancy on Piagetian tasks, Peter Smith raises the issue on whether such play training is better than instruction that focuses only on the specific ability in question. At the same time, he believes that such training is valuable in dealing with emotional problems and in reducing conflicts and that it may also foster more motivation and peer interaction, a finding we observed in our own studies (Smith, 1982).

Eli Saltz at Wayne State University in Detroit has conducted some of the most extensive studies on thematic play as a stimulant for cognitive and emotional development in poor, inner-city children and has also re-examined various findings, including his own, using play training. With Jane Brodie he has shown that attempts to attribute the positive effects of fantasy play training on verbal skills primarily to better "rapport" or "verbal encouragement" cannot explain the results (Saltz & Brodie, 1982). These studies involved 4 to 6 months of training with groups ranging from 30 to 150 participants. These represent some of the most extensive and careful training studies thus far available. Saltz's thematic play training yielded evidence comparable to Freyberg's in vocabulary usage. He and Brodie acknowledge that short-term training, which enhances performance on measures of originality, leaves open the question of how extensive such results may be. Will they generalize to creativity in other situations? Our data from specific studies are as yet too sparse to be certain, although we do have evidence that adults who are more creative report that they were more likely to play imaginatively, daydream, or have imaginary playmates as children (Saltz et al., 1977; Saltz & Brodie, 1982).

While some remain skeptical about the advantages of thematic or fantasy play training, especially in relation to specific cognitive objectives, most careful observers of children's play have recognized that for the promotion of social competencies or other constructive emotional and adaptive skills, techniques such as imaginative play may be more useful than formal drill training (Brainerd, 1982). The findings of Saltz and his group showed that thematic play training led to greater self-control and longer waiting ability in children, and Freyberg (1973) found more positive emotions and persistence.

In summary, there is a long tradition supported recently in the last 35 years by controlled research that has suggested the usefulness with preschoolers or early elementary school-aged children of some forms of imaginative play for both the cognitive and social skills needed for effective school performance. Let us turn next to examining recent research that points to the value of imaginative play for enhancing specific school readiness or school performance skills.

Recent Research on Specific School-Adaptive Skills

Language and Literacy

Pretend play has been consistently linked to cognitive and intellectual growth as well as the development of prosocial skills (Fein, 1981). Engaging in dramatic play can result in an increased number of mental constructs in very young children, allowing them to experience themselves in new ways, both as an individual and as a member of a group (Ghiaci & Richardson, 1980). In sociodramatic play, children are given the opportunity to test and revise their ideas about space, time, and cause-and-effect relations (Levy, Wolfgang, & Koorland, 1992). They are able to interact and use new language as they design, negotiate, and carry out the "script" of their play (Levy et al., 1992); find creative, divergent ways to solve problems (Swink & Buchanan, 1984); and practice verbal and narrative skills that are important to the development of reading comprehension (Pellegrini, 1980; Pellegrini & Galda, 1982).

Early language development is a primary feature of sociodramatic play. Smilansky (1968) delineated several different ways that words are used to take the place of reality during dramatic play: (a) changing personal identity, (b) changing the nature of objects, (c) substituting for action, and (d) describing situations. Jerome Singer and Dorothy Singer (1981) found that preschool children who are more frequently engaged in spontaneous pretend play also made use of more future and past tense verbs as well as more adjectives and probabilistic terms in their speech. Levy and her colleagues (1992) studied a group of 4-year-old children who frequently were engaged in adult-supervised dramatic play. This play took place in a spacious setting with available props related to themes (e.g., hospital, restaurant, grocery store) to which they had previously been introduced as a group through books, field trips, and videos. During their sociodramatic play, these children exhibited an increase in the total number of words in their conversation as well as an increase in the length and syntactical complexity of their utterances. They also used more targeted theme-specific vocabulary words as well as general concept words regarding color, shape, quantity, and time than a non-sociodramatic play control group (Levy et al., 1992).

Sociodramatic play is an arena for developing general representational skills that are eventually employed in other domains such as reading and writing. Yawkey (1986) highlights a specific element of sociodramatic play as particularly important, called *decentering*. This term refers to the child's abilty while playing to recognize and employ the fact that a toy action figure or a pretend setting may have multiple facets or uses. A prime example of decentering in sociodramatic play is the child's use of everyday objects in novel ways. For example, suppose that, among children playing together, a block becomes a phone. To these children, the block now has two identities, that of the real world and that of the pretend world, a conception that enhances their ability to think flexibly and inventively. Leslie (1987) has elaborated on this approach, integrating it with the burgeoning theory and research on "theory of the mind." Studies at Yale have shown that spontaneous imaginative play of children was indeed linked to theory of mind abilities and to the capacity of sustaining multiple identities of objects (Rosen, Schwebel, & J. Singer, 1997; Schwebel, Rosen, & J. Singer, 1999).

There are also a group of studies which identify the direct associations between play and literacy that occur when children incorporate book plots, themes, or characters into their play scripts. Saltz, Dixon, and Johnson (1977) differentiate between sociodramatic play and what they call *thematic-fantasy play*. Sociodramatic play entails acting out realistic events in everyday situations (e.g., going to the grocery store, the doctor's office, etc.) while thematic-fantasy play involves acting out themes that are more removed from day-to-day reality. Since a major benefit of imaginative play lies in its capacity to encourage children to disengage themselves from concrete stimuli in their environment and think about objects and events not immediately present, Saltz et al. (1977) hypothesized that children will profit the most from play that removes them the farthest from reality, that is, thematic-fantasy play. To test this theory, the researchers compared children who had been trained in enacting fairy tales (thematic-fantasy condition) to children who had been trained in enacting everyday events (sociodramatic condition) on receptive language skills, interpretation of causal relations, sequential memory, impulse control, and empathy (Saltz et al., 1977). Subjects in the thematic-fantasy condition performed better than those in the sociodramatic condition across all domains.

Thematic-fantasy play has been shown to benefit children's reading comprehension as well (Pellegrini & Galda, 1982). In a sample of children in Grades K–2, subjects were read the same book and placed in one of three experimental conditions: (a) thematic-fantasy play in which they acted out the story they had just heard, (b) discussion in which they talked about the story, and (c) drawing in which they drew pictures of the story (Pellegrini & Galda, 1982). These three groups were then compared on their performance on both a story comprehension and a story recall task. Results indicated that children in the thematic-fantasy condition fared better on both tasks than children in the discussion and drawing conditions (Pellegrini & Galda, 1982). Furthermore, in the thematic-fantasy condition, children who played roles calling for more active participation in the story re-enactment scored better on recall than children with less active roles, indicating that the more verbal exertion the child must put into a dramatic fantasy, the better he or she is able to retell the story (Pellegrini & Galda, 1982).

What particular aspects of thematic-fantasy play are important in reading comprehension? Marbach and Yawkey examined this matter in a 1980 study of aural language recall among 5-year-olds. The children were individually read a short, developmentally appropriate story and then asked to re-enact the story using either their body, puppets, or art supplies, depending on the experimental condition to which they were randomly assigned. After the re-enactment task, subjects listened to a tape-recorded playback of the story in which every 10th word was omitted. Subjects were then asked to say the missing word, a task that served as an assessment of language recall. Children in the self-action condition performed significantly better on the recall task than children in the puppet-action or artwork conditions. Marbach and

Yawkey (1980) propose that the play that solely involved manipulation of one's body was more direct, immediate, and meaningful than the other two types of play, due to greater cuing potential. Here we see a clear exemplification of the principle suggested in the analysis of Anderson et al. (1998) about the value of a more motivating, contextually rich form of teaching than simply drill and repetition.

While acting out a story simply using one's body is effective in remembering it, it is not merely the movement that contributes to improved story recall. There is some suggestion that the resolution of conflict among kids who are acting out a story together is the key element in story comprehension and recall. In a study done by Pellegrini (1984), children were read a story, then either acted it out in a group (thematic-fantasy play condition) or listened to each other's verbal reconstruction of the story followed by a discussion of how each version was different and/or similar to the others (accommodation questioning condition). In both experimental conditions, subjects were exposed to both a verbal rebuilding of the story and conflicting views of the story, but only subjects in the thematic-fantasy condition were exposed to physical play. After participation in one of these two conditions, the children were assessed on story recall, immediately after the experiment as well as 1 week later. While children in the thematic-fantasy play condition performed better than children in the accommodation questioning condition in immediate story recall, there was no significant difference between the two groups 1 week later, indicating that resolution of conflict is an important element of reading comprehension, independent of imaginative play (Pellegrini, 1984).

Several studies have examined the benefits of incorporating literacy material and activity into sociodramatic play (Neuman & Roskos, 1997; Stone & Christie, 1996). Literacy behavior refers to different types of reading and writing that can be integrated into children's play, such as reading labels on containers, reading aloud to another child or a stuffed animal, or writing to create props such as a sign in a store or a menu in a restaurant. Incorporating such behaviors into play not only helps the child develop his or her own reading and writing skills but may also help other children (Stone & Christie, 1996). During naturalistic observation of sociodramatic play among 3- and 4-year-olds, Neuman and Roskos (1997) noticed that children's demonstrations of reading and writing were varied according to the nature of the activity. For example, the same child who wrote slowly and carefully when addressing an envelope in the post office wrote quickly when taking orders in the restaurant (Neuman & Roskos, 1997). In classrooms, pretend play areas can be designed so that children have access to literary tools and related supplies such as magazines and an appointment book to use in a doctor's office or notepads and a calendar to use in a play office (Neuman & Roskos, 1997).

Play and School Readiness

Beyond vocabulary skills and literacy preparation, what other capacities do preschool children require to be effective upon their entry into elementary school? The important issue of school readiness was raised in the Carnegie Report (Boyer, 1991) and elaborated in relation to the potential role of early childhood television programming (J. L. Singer & D. G. Singer, 1993). Specific components of what children require have been outlined by D. G. Singer et al. (2003) and include, in addition to vocabulary, cognitive skills such as counting, knowledge of numbers, shapes, and the ability to form constructs or schemas. Great importance is also attached to emotional awareness, self-control, and prosocial behaviors such as civility, cooperation, and sharing.

Yawkey (1986) early on pointed to the importance of spontaneous and adult-directed imaginative play in children's development of skills outlined above. He not only conducted research to demonstrate this position but also, from a theoretical point of view, anticipated the key role of the creative features of such play for the more general concept of intelligence (Marbach & Yawkey, 1980; Yawkey, 1986). Pellegrini also pioneered in research demonstrating the implications of thematic-fantasy play in helping children acquire components of the cognitive structures that underlie school readiness and later effective school performance (Pellegrini, 1980, 1984; Pellegrini & Galda, 1982). Ghiaci and Richardson (1980) demonstrated through research with preschoolers how cognitive constructs were developed and strengthened through play exposure. A number of studies by other investigators have shown that both creative abilities and more formal cognitive skills emerging with imaginative play are also carried over and extended into the elementary school years (Russ, Robins, & Christiano, 1999; Shmukler, 1982–83).

Sociodramatic play allows children to test out a variety of different personae, thus developing the ability to see things from another's perspective. The benefits of role-playing for children include emotional awareness, increased sensitivity to others, and feelings of power over the environment, as shown in a study looking at the effects of sociodramatic play on children's locus of control (Swink & Buchanan, 1984). The construct of locus of control, embedded in Rotter's (1972) social learning theory, involves the extent to which an individual believes that he or she has control over situational events. An internal locus of control, the belief that events occur as a result of one's own behavior and/or permanent characteristics, has been associated with intellectual proficiency and higher school performance. Individuals who attribute situational events to fate, chance, or other people are thought to have an external locus of control, which has been correlated with high anxiety, abnormal behavior, and low motivation. Swink and Buchanan (1984) assessed children's locus of control both before and after engaging in either goal-oriented sociodramatic play or non-goal-oriented sociodramatic play. Non-goal-oriented play involved typical sociodramatic play techniques while goal-oriented play entailed enactment of scenes that explored specific themes such as one's being new at school, conflict, or loneliness as well as role-reversal and analyzation of behaviors and consequences. Children in the goal-oriented play condition displayed a significant increase in internal locus of control, as opposed to children in the non-goal-oriented condition, who showed no significant change. Swink and Buchanan (1984) felt that the significant change in locus of control among children in the goal-oriented condition was due to role-reversal and overt sharing of emotions, which they believe may have contributed to empathy development.

Implications for Education

─────────────────────────

We began this paper by citing the important cognitive analysis of the school learning process by Anderson et al., (1998), which sought to integrate repetitive rehearsal of new material with broader, contextually oriented approaches. The literature we reviewed on uses of play for motivating and for establishing social contexts in which new material can be enacted and re-enacted seems to represent an extension of this cognitive psychology position. We also hinted early on of two further theoretical approaches in which the value of play-based teaching can be understood. One of these is the conception currently best exemplified in the writing and research of Bruner (1986), Epstein (1990, 1999), and J. L. Singer (1973, 1975), which emphasize two major forms of human thought: (a) the logical-sequential and (b) the narrative, cognitive-experiential or imaginative orientations. The second line of research that we believe supports the importance of using forms of symbolic play in school settings derives from the redefinition of effective intelligence introduced by Sternberg and his collaborators (Sternberg, 1999; Sternberg & Grigorenko, 2000). In this "tripartite" view, intelligence involves abstract abilities, practical or daily life problem-solving skills, and, finally, creative abilities that are characterized by flexibility and transformative qualities. Let us examine how using play as one feature of school experience can contribute to the enhancement of preschool and elementary school children's capabilities in enhancing their narrative or cognitive-experiential thought processes and also their likelihood of using creative thought as a feature of their intelligent behavior.

Enhancing Narrative, Cognitive-Experiential, or Imaginative Thought

─────────────────────────

Bruner (1986) has proposed that human thought can be ordered along two dimensions: the "paradigmatic," which involves logical ordering of experience into abstract or even mathematical forms, and the "narrative," which involves constructing *possible* realities. Paradigmatic thought usually takes verbal forms and is also reflected regularly in direct communication to others. This mode seeks for truth and is, as all scientific hypotheses, ultimately falsifiable. In contrast, the narrative mode, while sequential only to the extent that it is communicated to others in a series of statements, may be thought of first in bursts of images, usually visual and auditory, but sometimes even olfactory, gustatory, tactile, or kinesthetic. It is expressed as a story and can also emerge as what cognitive psychologists call "episodic" or "event" memories or as fantasies and daydreams. As Bruner has proposed, the objective of narrative is not truth, but verisimilitude or "lifelikeness." One can identify gaps in logic in a story sequence, but those very surprising gappy features (as in much poetry, in the novels of Franz Kafka and Thomas Pynchon, or in Philip Roth's recent

Zuckerman novel series) are designed to communicate the sometimes comical or playful, but often sinister, irrationalities of the human condition. For Bruner (and the growing number of child psychologists and personality researchers who reflect his influence), the narrative mode involves a subjunctive orientation, the formulation through images and remembered dialogues of possible personal life stories or of more or less realistic potential futures. The imaginative facet of human experience largely reflects Bruner's narrative process. For the generation of a creative product, a fictional story, film script, or scientific theory or research study, both paradigmatic and narrative processes would have to be operative.

A similar formulation, supported by a series of research studies, has been proposed by Seymour Epstein (1990, 1999). His Cognitive-Experiential Self-Theory (CEST) also incorporates two modes by which people adapt to their physical and social milieus: a rational and experiential system. A major extension of Epstein's approach is his linkage of the experiential system to human emotionality. The rational system is characterized by deliberateness and greater effort; it works through abstraction, verbal thought, or language and even may be a very recent evolutionary development. The experiential system involves the accumulation of concrete experiences ("episodic memories") into tentative, emotionally nuanced, story-like generalizations or models of one's life situation or of the world. At its lower or moderately complex levels of operation, it proceeds rapidly, smoothly, seemingly without effort. Events are generally represented in images but can also be expressed in metaphors, prototypes, or stereotypes in stories. Epstein does point out that the more mature forms of the experiential mode (again a reflection presumably of imagination) when functioning along with the rational system may become the basis for intuitive wisdom or creativity.

As Epstein's research has demonstrated, the experiential system, while in the crudest form susceptible to misjudgments and the "childlike" thinking that often characterizes all of us when we gamble or buy lottery tickets, may also have important adaptive features. It allows us to experience and express the emotions that often guide us in altruistic directions through empathy with others and self-knowledge. It helps us to establish imagery-rich contexts for the situations we confront and to provide a fuller set of possibilities for ultimately more rational decision making. J. L. Singer's work extending William James's stream of consciousness has called attention to the adaptive role of fantasies, daydreams, and the imagery of memories or possible future events (J. L. Singer & Bonanno, 1990). The studies of early childhood imaginative play as a precursor of our later capability for internally miniaturizing and manipulating the complex physical social milieu in which we must "navigate" also suggest that playful activity in school may contribute to ultimate human competence (D. G. Singer & J. L. Singer, 1990).

An example of how the two systems may operate to yield a significant creative scientific product has been presented by Bruner (1986). He had occasion to interview the great pioneer of atomic physics, Niels Bohr. Bohr has recently attained a new burst of extra-scientific fame as the fictionalized protagonist in a powerful London and Broadway hit play, *Copenhagen*. Bohr actually described for Bruner a situation in which he learned that his son had stolen a pipe from a neighborhood store. As he tried to imagine the situation, Bohr realized how difficult it was to picture his son, on one hand, as a much-loved youth and, on the other hand, as a thief who deserved punishment. This led him to a further sequence of images featuring the classic perceptual illusion of the figure-ground shifts between a vase and a face that one finds in every psychology textbook. Only one image can be maintained at a time. From these cognitive-experiential imagery or narrative sequences Bohr, apparently cued by his current struggle with a scientific problem, realized that it was impossible to conceive simultaneously of the position and the velocity of an electron. Here he must have shifted more into the paradigmatic mode as he proceeded mathematically to outline his formal conception of complementarity in quantum physics.

The position that we are advocating for education is that the narrative, experiential, or imagery-daydream features of thought, while perhaps earlier in evolution and potentially more "primitive" than rationality, are capable of modification in more adaptive directions for children by some of the play methods described earlier. Through adult-guided or encouraged thematic play, children can learn to develop their acceptance, extension, control, and direction of their narrative or imaginative tendencies. These applications of basic experiential thinking can also lead to what Epstein (1990) has called "constructive thinking," a socially and physically useful capability, which his research distinguishes clearly from abstract intelligence. This adaptive emphasis links the narrative, imaginative, or experiential systems to the "Tripartite Theory of Intelligence" of Sternberg (1999), to which we shall turn to next.

Three Components of Successful Intelligence

Although Epstein (1990) has occasionally referred to constructive thinking as "Emotional Intelligence," he has not sought to formulate a more systematic theory of the nature of intelligence generally. This task has been undertaken chiefly in the past two decades by Sternberg, who has argued on theoretical and empirical grounds against the long-standing popular and professional psychological acceptance of the unitary or "g" factor theory of intelligence. Sternberg's series of factor analytic studies has shown that one can identify three major forms of intelligence that demonstrably predict different kinds of adaptive or "successful" performance in specific settings. Abstract intelligence, which is generally what is measured by the major "IQ" tests or by academic selection tests like the SATs or GREs, generally predicts school grades or competencies in analysis, discrimination, or criticism of quasi-mathematical or other forms of what Bruner would call paradigmatic thought. To predict effective achievement in other settings, with other tasks, or in creative accomplishment, one needs to measure practical or creative intelligence, which are statistically relatively independent of abstract ability.

Of particular relevance for the school applications of play approaches is the extensive and ongoing research by Sternberg and his collaborators on the training of teachers for incorporating distinctive features of the three intelligence systems into classroom curricula with children (Sternberg, 1999; Sternberg & Grigorenko, 2000).

For example, in the Creative Thinking curriculum, teachers are encouraged to present students with opportunities, strategies, and exercises that (a) redefine problems; (b) question oft-accepted assumptions; (c) find ways to "sell" creative ideas whether they represent new works of art, new technologies, or business techniques; (d) generate a range of new ideas; (e) consider that some strongly held views may actually be inverted or reversed; (f) try reasonably risky behaviors or conceptions; (g) tolerate ambiguity; (h) seek to identify one's own most cherished or "true" interests; and (i) try various exercises involving delay of gratification, etc. In implementing these approaches to foster the creative components of intelligence, one sees at once many opportunities to not only discuss the issues but also become engaged in story-telling or enacting quasi-dramatic scenes or playlets.

In striving to enhance Practical Intelligence, the curriculum emphasizes motivation, impulse control, perseverance, overcoming fears of failure, avoiding misattribution of blame, overcoming dependency, etc. Throughout the elaboration of this phase of the curriculum, there are numerous situations in which the type of thematic play outlined by Saltz, the sociodramatic play of Smilansky, and the classroom enactment exercises outlined by McCaslin or Rosenberg may all be employed.

In summary, we propose that well thought out uses of forms of story-telling, imaging, spontaneous and thematic role-play, and related forms of interaction have a key role in education for children from the preschool through the high school level. To pass off play as a time-wasting diversion even though children enjoy it is to ignore the growing body of evidence that supports its potential for enhancing school readiness, social skills, and creative accomplishment. From their earliest years, we have evidence that children who are encouraged in imaginative play show later indications of increased creativity and cognitive or emotional competence (Russ et al., 1999; Shmukler, 1982–83). The demonstrated effectiveness of the Sternberg approach necessarily involves introduction of forms of play even at older age levels. We need as a society to confront more squarely the critical role of this imaginative form of human endeavor in the socialization and adaptive education of our children.

References

Anderson, J. R., Reder, L. M., & Simon, H. A. (1998). Radical constructivism and cognitive psychology. In D. Ravitch (Ed.), *Brookings papers on educational policy* (pp. 227–255). Washington, DC: Brookings Institution Press.

Boyer, E. L. (1991). *Ready to learn: A mandate for the nation*. Princeton, NJ: The Carnegie Foundation for the Advancement of Teaching.

Brainerd, C. J. (1982). Effects of group and individualized dramatic play training on cognitive development. *Contributions to Human Development, 6,* 128.

Bruner, J. (1986). *Actual minds, possible worlds*. Cambridge, MA: Harvard University Press.

Burmenskaia, G. V. (1997). The psychology of development. In E. L. Grigorenko, P. Ruzgis, & R. J. Sternberg (Eds.), *Psychology of Russia: Past, present, future* (pp. 215–249). Commack, NY: Nova Science Publishers.

Epstein, S. (1990). Cognitive-experiential self-theory. In L. Pervin (Ed.), *Handbook of personality* (pp. 165–193). New York: Guilford Press.

Epstein, S. (1999). The interpretation of dreams from the perspective of cognitive-experiential self-theory. In J. A. Singer & P. Salovey (Eds.), *At play in the fields of consciousness* (pp. 51–82). Mahwah, NJ: Erlbaum.

Fein, G. G. (1981). Pretend play in childhood: An integrative review. *Child Development, 52,* 1095–1118.

Freud, S. (1962). Creative writers and daydreaming. In J. Strachey (Ed.), *The complete psychological works of Sigmund Freud* (Vol. 9, pp. 141–154). London: Hearth Press. (Original work published 1908)

Freyberg, J. T. (1973). Increasing the imaginative play of urban disadvantaged kindergarten children through systematic training. In J. L. Singer (Ed.), *The child's world of make-believe* (pp. 129–154). New York: Academic Press.

Ghiaci, G., & Richardson, J. T. E. (1980). The effects of dramatic play upon cognitive structure and development. *The Journal of Genetic Psychology, 136,* 77–83.

Grigorenko, E. L., Ruzgis, P., & Sternberg, R. J. (Eds.). (1997). *Russian psychology: Past, present, future.* Commack, NY: Nova Science Publishers.

Hellendoorn, J., van der Kooij, R., & Sutton-Smith, B. (Eds.). (1994). *Play and intervention.* Albany: State University of New York Press.

Leslie, A. M. (1987). Pretense and representation: The origins of "theory of mind." *Psychological Review, 94,* 412–422.

Levy, A. K., Wolfgang, C. H., & Koorland, M. A. (1992). Sociodramatic play as a method for enhancing the language performance of kindergarten age students. *Early Childhood Research Quarterly, 7,* 245–262.

Lewin, K. (1935). *A dynamic theory of personality.* New York: McGraw-Hill.

Marbach, E. S., & Yawkey, T. D. (1980). The effect of imaginative play actions on language development in five-year-old children. *Psychology in the Schools, 17,* 257–263.

McCaslin, N. (1984). *Creative drama in the classroom.* New York: Longman.

Neuman, S., & Roskos, K. (1997). Literacy knowledge in practice: Contexts of participation for young writers and readers. *Reading Research Quarterly, 32,* 10–32.

Pellegrini, A. D. (1980). The relationship between kindergartener's play and achievement in prereading, language, and writing. *Psychology in the Schools, 17,* 530–535.

Pellegrini, A. D. (1984). Identifying causal elements in the thematic-fantasy play paradigm. *American Educational Research Journal, 21,* 691–701.

Pellegrini, A. D., & Galda, L. (1982). The effects of thematic-fantasy play training on the development of children's story comprehension. *American Educational Research Journal, 19,* 443–452.

Piaget, J. (1962). *Play, dreams, and imitation in childhood.* New York: Norton.

Rosen, C. S., Schwebel, D. C., & Singer, J. L. (1997). Preschoolers' attributions of mental states in pretense. *Child Development, 66,* 1133–1142.

Rosenberg, H. S. (1987). *Creative drama and imagination.* New York: Holt, Rinehart & Winston.

Rotter, J. B. (1972). *Applications of a social learning theory of personality.* New York: Holt.

Russ, S. W., Robins, A. L., & Christiano, B. A. (1999). Pretend play: Longitudinal prediction of creativity and affect in fantasy in children. *Creativity Research Journal, 12,* 129–139.

Saltz, E., & Brodie, J. (1982). Pretend-play training in childhood: A review and critique. *Contributions to Human Development, 6,* 97–113.

Saltz, E., Dixon, D., & Johnson, J. (1977). Training disadvantaged preschoolers on various fantasy activities: Effects on cognitive functioning and impulse control. *Child Development, 48,* 367–380.

Schwebel, D., Rosen, C., & Singer, J. L. (1999). Preschoolers' pretend play and theory of mind: The role of jointly conducted pretense. *British Journal of Developmental Psychology, 17,* 333–348.

Shmukler, D. (1982–83). Preschool imaginative play and its relationship to subsequent third grade assessment. *Imagination, Cognition and Personality, 2,* 231–240.

Singer, D. G., & Singer, J. L. (1990). *The house of make-believe: Children's play and the developing imagination.* Cambridge, MA: Harvard University Press.

Singer, D. G., Singer, J. L., Plaskon, S. L., & Schweder, A. E. (2003). A role for play in the preschool curriculum. In S. Olfman (Ed.), *All work and no play: How educational reforms are harming our preschoolers* (pp 59–101). Westport, CT: Greenwood Publishing Group, Inc.

Singer, J. L. (1973). *The child's world of make-believe: Experimental studies of imaginative play.* New York: Academic Press.

Singer, J. L. (1975). *The inner world of daydreaming.* New York: Harper & Row.

Singer, J. L., & Bonanno, G. (1990). Personality and private experience: Individual variations in consciousness and in attention to subjective phenomena. In L. Pervin (Ed.), *Handbook of personality* (pp. 419–444). New York: Guilford Press.

Singer, J. L., & Singer, D. G. (1981). *Television, imagination, and aggression: A study of preschoolers.* Hillsdale, NJ: Erlbaum.

Singer, J. L., & Singer, D. G. (1993). *Public broadcasting: Ready to teach. A report to the 103rd Congress and the American people.* Report prepared for the Corporation of Public Broadcasting pursuant to Public Law, 102-356. Washington, DC: Corporation of Public Broadcasting.

Smilansky, S. (1968). *The effects of sociodramatic play on disadvantaged preschool children.* New York: Wiley.

Smith, P. K. (1982). Does play matter? Functional and evolutionary aspects of human and animal play. *Behavioral and Brain Sciences, 5,* 139–184.

Sternberg, R. J. (1999). The theory of successful intelligence. *Review of General Psychology, 3,* 292–316.

Sternberg, R. J., & Grigorenko, E. L. (2000). *Teaching for successful intelligence.* Arlington Heights, IL: Skylight Professional Development.

Stone, S. J., & Christie, J. F. (1996). Collaborative literacy learning during sociodramatic play in a multiage (K–2) primary classroom. *Journal of Research in Childhood Education, 10,* 123–133.

Swink, D. F., & Buchanan, R. (1984). The effects of sociodramatic goal-oriented play and non-goal-oriented role play on locus of control. *Journal of Clinical Psychology, 40,* 1178–1183.

Vygotsky, L. S. (1978). *Mind in society: The development of psychological processes.* Cambridge, MA: Harvard University Press.

Ward, W. (1960). *Drama with and for children* (Bulletin 30). Washington, DC: U.S. Department of Health, Education, and Welfare.

Yawkey, T. D. (1986). Creative dialogue through sociodramatic play and its uses. *Journal of Creative Behavior, 20,* 52–60.

Note: Minor changes have been made to this chapter as it was originally published in order to conform with the volume's editorial style. These changes have not altered the meaning of the chapter's content in any way.

7

EXAMINING THE PLAY-LITERACY INTERFACE: A CRITICAL REVIEW AND FUTURE DIRECTIONS[1]

Kathleen Roskos and James Christie

The idea that a seemingly frivolous activity such as play can promote children's literacy development is very intriguing and has prompted a large amount of research activity over the past several decades. In order to assess the status of this line of inquiry and provide guidance for future research, we undertook a critical analysis of 20 recent investigations of the play-literacy interface. We first attempted to understand the "story" that each study told—how the problem was framed, the solution path, the claims that were made, and the evidence that supported these claims. Then we engaged in critical analysis of the studies, challenging both what was said (i.e., the claims) and what was not said and not addressed. We agreed with the major claims of 12 of the 20 studies, judging the research to be sound and complete. These studies supplied strong evidence that play can serve literacy by (a) providing settings that promote literacy activity, skills, and strategies; (b) serving as a language experience that can build connections between oral and written modes of expression; and (c) providing opportunities to teach and learn literacy. However, our critical analysis of these studies also revealed a number of limitations and unresolved issues, including concerns about definitions, theories, methodology, lack of progress

[1] Reprinted with the permission of Sage Publications Ltd. From "Examining the Play-Literacy Interface: A Critical Review and Future Directions," by K. Roskos & J. Christie, 2001, *Journal of Early Childhood Literacy*, *1*(1), pp. 59–89. Copyright by Sage Publications Ltd.

in establishing causal connections with development, and dominance of the "play as progress" rhetoric.

Read not to contradict and confute, nor to believe and take for granted, nor
to find talk and discourse, but to weigh and consider.

—Sir Francis Bacon

That play and literacy share common boundaries in the developing mind of the young child is, to use a phrase of Kagan's, "a pleasing idea" (cited in Whitehurst & Lonigan, 1998, p. 848). The possibility that, by engaging in joyful play, children also build meanings and develop skills closely associated with reading and writing is intuitively appealing to researchers and educators alike. The idea is not new, framed theoretically by Piaget (1962) and Vygotsky (1978) and researched as early as 1974 by Wolfgang. What is new, however, is an emergent literacy perspective, which brings this pleasing idea more squarely into view. In sharp contrast to the readiness position, an emergent perspective stretches the process of literacy development to include budding literacy-like behaviors (e.g., pretend reading) as legitimate and contributory and treats social contexts (e.g., bedtime reading) as important venues for exposing children to literacy knowledge and practices. Through this lens, children's early "hands on" experiences with language and literacy in everyday social activities give rise to the internal mental processes that are needed to do the intellectual work of reading and writing activity. Play activity in particular affords these experiences, creating bold and subtle opportunities for children to use language in literate ways and to use literacy as they see it practiced. From an emergent perspective, therefore, the play-literacy interface grows more prominent and more significant, opening up new possibilities for investigating and understanding the interrelationships between these two very complex domains of activity.

In this paper, we review the recent empirical research that assumes an emergent literacy stance in examining relationships between play and literacy. At this point in the play-literacy line of inquiry, such a review is both timely and useful for several reasons. Although a relative newcomer to the field of early literacy research, the play-literacy connection has been one of the most heavily researched areas of early literacy in the last decade (Yaden, Rowe, & MacGillivray, 2000). And, although Pellegrini and Galda (1993) examined some of this early work just 7 years ago, discussing symbolic play-literacy links, research work has steadily grown and extended into additional areas since that time (Roskos & Christie, 2000). Moreover, interest in play as part and parcel of a developmentally appropriate early literacy curriculum has surged as the concept of emergent literacy has taken hold in the early childhood professional community. Regrettably, the benefits of play for literacy acquisition are not well-articulated and understood, which makes it increasingly difficult for educators to defend play as an opportunity for literacy experience and learning. Many early childhood teachers already feel pressure to alter play in ways that better serve discrete literacy goals or to abandon it as a curricular tool altogether (see, for example, Lubeck, 2000). Finally, the scientific pursuit of the play-literacy interface also involves paying attention to the various discourses that give meaning to play and literacy as objects of knowledge (Sutton-Smith, 1995). The study of the play-literacy interface is itself shaped and contoured by the historical and sociopolitical voices of the times. These social meanings speak through the research problems that are studied and the solution pathways that eventually wend their way into the everyday lives of children. To bolster and strengthen inquiry, it is important to remain alert to these persuasive discourses.

To conduct the review of research, we have chosen to use a critical analysis approach, which treats research reports as texts subject to critical reading (Jupp, 1996). In this respect, we depart from the more typical technical evaluation of studies and meta-analyses, which focus on the integrity of research design, the validity of statistical findings, and effect sizes. Our emphasis rather is on analyzing the definitions, explanations, and solutions put forth as conceptualizations and to challenge them, not only for what is said, but for what is not said. This cultivates understanding out of which critical points emerge that chart the way for further productive research work. We begin with a brief overview of the beginnings of the play-literacy line of inquiry, then turn to the critical analysis of studies conducted during the past decade, and conclude with our interpretation, which we hope assesses the research situation clearly and honestly and informs future research on this important topic.

Early Research on Play and Literacy

Research on play and literacy conducted in the late 1970s and 1980s was primarily grounded in theories of Piaget (1962) and Vygotsky (1976). Both theories placed heavy emphasis on the cognitive connections between play and literacy. As Pellegrini and Galda (1993) point out, "For both theorists symbolic play was an important venue in which children could practice (Piaget) or learn (Vygotsky) using representational media" (p. 165). This cognitive perspective led to a series of correlational studies that examined the relationship between children's participation in dramatic play (play involving make-believe transformations and role-playing) and general measures of early reading achievement such as the Metropolitan Readiness Test. Results did show positive correlations between play and these types of literacy measures (e.g., Pellegrini, 1980). As with all correlational studies, however, it was not possible to determine the causal direction between the two variables. The possibility also existed that a third variable such as underlying cognitive maturity may have been responsible for the relationship between symbolic play and scores on the literacy tests.

In the mid-1980s, a new perspective on early literacy development—emergent literacy—came into prominence and radically changed the way in which the connections between literacy and play were viewed (Hall, 1987; Teale & Sulzby, 1986). According to this perspective, children construct their own knowledge about written language as they interact with others in everyday activities that involve reading and writing. During this same period, ecological psychology also began to have an impact on play/literacy research. According to psychologists such as Barker (1978) and Gump (1989), children's behavior is greatly influenced by aspects of the physical environment. Combined with emergent literacy, this ecological perspective supplied a solid rationale for the literacy-enriched play settings that became a key feature of play/literacy research in the late 1980s and early 1990s. If one wants children to engage in literacy activity during play, then play settings should contain materials that create an environmental "press" for play-related reading and writing activities—books, signs, menus, calendars, pencils, markers, paper, note pads, bank checks, etc.

During the late 1980s and 1990s, researchers began to investigate the effects of adding literacy-related props to dramatic play settings in preschool and kindergarten classrooms. Results indicated that these print-enriched play settings result in large increases in emergent reading and writing activity during play (Christie & Enz, 1992; Hall, May, Moores, Shearer, &Williams,1987; Morrow, 1990; Neuman & Roskos, 1990; Vukelich, 1991). While attempts were also made to link children's play in print-enriched setting with gains in literacy development, the results were inconclusive. For example, Neuman and Roskos (1990) found that adding literacy materials to play centers resulted in a significant gain in preschoolers' scores on Clay's (1972) Concepts About Print test. However, Christie and Enz (1992) and Vukelich (1991) failed to find connections between literacy-enriched play settings and children's Concepts About Print scores.

Piaget and Vygotsky's theories continued to generate interest in cognitive connections between play and literacy, but to a lesser extent than during the preceding decade. Pellegrini, Galda, Dresden, and Cox (1991), for example, found that children's use of symbolic transformations in play at age 3½ predicted children's emergent writing, but not emergent reading, at age 5. Emergent reading, on the other hand, was predicted by children's use of metalinguistic verbs such as *talk, write,* and *read*. The children's ability to talk about language ("going meta," as Pellegrini puts it) predicted their reading acquisition.

In addition to pointing out cognitive connections between play and literacy, Vygotsky (1978) also emphasized the role of adult-child interactions in development. This social-interactionist view fit nicely with the tenets of emergent literacy. According to Vygotsky's construct of "the zone of proximal development," adults or more competent peers can help children to engage in activities that they cannot do on their own. Researchers used this construct as a rationale for investigating the effects of direct adult involvement (Christie & Enz, 1992; Morrow, 1990; Schrader, 1990; Vukelich, 1991) and peer interaction (Neuman & Roskos, 1991) in literacy-related play. Results indicated that certain types of adult involvement did increase the amount of literacy activity during play. In addition, Vukelich (1991) found that the combination of a literacy-enriched environment and adult mediation led to significant increases in children's knowledge about the functions of writing. Neuman and Roskos's (1991) ethnographic study revealed that children use strategies such as negotiating and coaching to help each other learn about literacy during play.

Considerable progress, therefore, was made during the first decade and a half of research on the play-literacy interface. There was a shift from correlational studies that looked for global, indirect connections between play and literacy to experimental and qualitative studies that sought direct links between the two phenomena. A very effective instructional strategy—the literacy-enriched play center—emerged from this research, and we learned a considerable amount about the effects of adult-child and peer interaction on the play/literacy relationship.

Method

As indicated earlier in our introduction, we took a less traveled approach to a review of current research, engaging in a critical analysis of research reports as texts. Critical analysis examines assumptions that undergird research reports and considers other possible accounts that may be concealed or ruled out. It tends toward the theoretical in that the emphasis is on how a set of abstract ideas and concepts is translated into an inquiry or problem-solution "story." The goal is to first understand the inquiry as the author meant it and then to evaluate it for "fit" with more general understanding and worth (Hodder, 2000; Jupp, 1996). The result is *a criticism* in the social science sense that identifies the major issues or "basic intellectual oppositions" in a field of inquiry on which further productive work might turn.

Data Collection

We focused our critical analysis on a set of 20 play-literacy studies published within the last decade (1992–2000) that represented a second wave of this research. Integrative reviews of play and literacy-related relationships have been conducted with some regularity over the past 20 years, providing benchmarks of progress in this line of inquiry (in chronological order: Fein, 1981; Christie & Johnsen, 1983; Pellegrini & Galda, 1993). Limiting our analysis to studies within the past decade, therefore, followed this trend and built on this work but also offered an alternative approach to more traditional research reviews conducted in the past.

We selected studies based on four criteria: (a) implicit or explicit assumption of play-literacy connections; (b) publication in a scholarly, refereed document (e.g., journal or book) between 1992 and 2000; (c) presentation as a research report (i.e., in the research genre); and (d) emphasis on the early childhood period (children ages birth–8). Studies were identified through three successive sweeps of the professional literature. Initially, we scanned the PsychINFO and ERIC online databases for articles from 1992–2000 that met the inclusion criteria of play (or pretend play or dramatic play) and literacy (or early reading or writing or emergent literacy). This initial search yielded a total of 189 records that included articles, studies, book chapters, and dissertations. From this collection, we culled those articles that met our four criteria, yielding a total of 17 studies. In our third sweep, we manually searched edited books (e.g., Roskos & Christie, 2000; Spodek & Saracho, 1998) and the full text of retrieved papers for studies that did not emerge from the computer search. This strategy yielded 7 studies, 4 of which duplicated those found in prior searches. This produced a collection of 20 studies that investigated the play-literacy interface in early childhood in a research report genre. The design features of these studies are summarized in Table 7.1.

Table 7.1 Design Features of Play-Literacy Studies

Study Play/Literacy Interface	Subjects	Setting	Duration	Methodology	Focus on
Bergen & Mauer (2000)*	14 children (age 4)	free play centers (Year 1) clinical play sessions (Year 2) parent phone interview about outdoor play (Year 3)	3 years	quantitative	symbolic play phonological awareness print awareness, reading achievement
Branscombe & Taylor (2000)*	5 children (age 5)	kindergarten classroom	8 months	qualitative	narrative development
Christie & Stone (1999)	22 children (age 5) 27 children (age 5–7)	literacy-enriched play centers in a kindergarten (Year 1) and a K–2 multi-age classroom (Year 2)	4 weeks	qualitative	peer collaboration
Dever & Wishon (1995)*	3 children (age 6)	literacy-enriched play center in a Grade 1 classroom	8 weeks	qualitative	adult mediation literacy/play behaviors
Dunn, Beach, & Kontos (1994)	30 teachers & 60 children (age 3–4)	30 child-care classrooms	1 day per site	quantitative	classroom literacy environment language and cognitive development
Einarsdottir (1996)*	20 children (age 5)	literacy-enriched play settings in 2 preschools (Iceland)	2 years	quantitative	interest in reading literacy development
Fein, Ardila-Rey, & Groth (2000)*	37 children (age 5)	2 kindergarten classrooms	12 weeks	quantitative	shared enactment & author's chair fantasy play literacy activity
Makin, Hayden, & Diaz (2000)*	158 child-care staff & an unspecified number of parents	79 early childhood classrooms (Australia)	7 months	quantitative	staff & parent perspectives on literacy literacy/play behaviors
Neuman (2000)	30 mothers (mean age = 19) and 6 of their children (ages 1.5–4)	literacy-enriched play center in a lab preschool connected with an adult basic education program	6 months	quantitative	adult mediation
Neuman & Gallagher (1994)	6 mothers (mean age = 20) and their 6 children (ages 3–4)	literacy-enriched prop boxes used in the home	12 weeks	quantitative	adult mediation child participation in literacy play vocabulary development

Study	Participants	Setting	Duration	Method	Focus
Neuman & Roskos (1992)	91 children (age 3–5)	literacy-enriched play centers in 2 day-care centers	6 months	quantitative & qualitative	play duration and complexity
Neuman & Roskos (1993)	177 children (age 3–5)	literacy-enriched play centers in 8 Head Start classrooms	5 months	quantitative & qualitative	adult meditation literacy/play behaviors environmental print reading functional print knowledge
Neuman & Roskos (1997)	30 children (age 3–4)	literacy-enriched play centers in an Even Head Start classroom	7 months	quantitative & qualitative	literacy/play behaviors literacy knowledge purposes for reading & writing
Pickett (1998)*	10 children (age 6–7)	literacy-enriched play center (blocks) in a Grade 1 classroom	3 weeks	qualitative	adult mediation literacy/play behaviors
Roskos & Neuman (1993)	6 teachers & 45 children (age 3–5)	literacy-enriched play centers in a day-care classroom	6 weeks	qualitative	adult mediation
Rowe (1998)	16 children (age 2–3)	preschool classroom & author's home	9 months	qualitative & case study	book-related dramatic play literary response
Sonnenschein, Baker, Serpell, & Schmidt (2000)	40 children (age 5) & their parents	home	3 years	quantitative	parent attitudes about literacy home literacy activities literacy development
Vedeler (1997)	6 children (age 6)	play room in a kindergarten (Norway)	11 weeks	quantitative	sociodramatic play & other play activity syntax (literate language)
Vukelich (1994)	56 children (age 5)	literacy-enriched play settings in 3 kindergarten classrooms	15 weeks	quantitative	adult mediation concepts about print environmental print reading
Walker (1999)*	17 children (age 4–5)	Head Start classroom	8 weeks	qualitative	narrative features of play process writing-like behaviors

Note. * studies in which we disagreed with the authors' claims.

Data Analysis

Unlike some other areas of qualitative analysis (e.g., Spradley's domain analysis [Spradley, 1979]), there are no well-formulated procedures for conducting critical analysis. Although the analytic aims seem clear, namely to understand what the text says and then to evaluate it for what it does and does not say, how to achieve such aims remains a murky endeavor. At best, Jupp and Norris (1993) suggest two relevant questions that may guide the critical reading of a research report as a document. One of these essentially asks, What is said? The goal is to find out what the problem is, how it is explained, and the solution path preferred. The second question asks, What is not said? And the aim is to identify what is "not seen" as problematic, what explanations are missing or rejected, and which solutions are not preferred.

Working to specify these questions more finely, we developed a coding matrix that allowed us to summarize what authors stated, explained, and systematically pursued as research problems and also the conclusions they drew as solutions to those problems and on what evidentiary basis (see Appendix A). The matrix consisted of eight key prompts and related probes derived from descriptions of analytic strategies (Miles & Huberman, 1994) and explanatory discourse (Brown & Armstrong, 1984). This matrix provided an analytic tool that aided the critical reading of each study in a consistent manner.

To test the coding matrix, we each applied it to a sample study, which led to a few minor modifications and clarifications. Then, after achieving an interrater reliability of nearly 100% on three studies from the collection, we divided up the remaining studies (making sure that we did not code our own studies) and summarized each using the matrix system. This provided us with a synopsis of the research information germane to our aims of understanding and criticism.

For the next phase of our critical analysis, we adapted a syntopical reading technique described by Adler and van Doren (1972). Syntopical reading is a form of interpretive reading that attempts to synthesize authors' concepts and claims on a topic around a common set of terms and propositions. It involves reading to understand what each author said, establishing a neutral set of main ideas, and considering authors' competing points in relation to it. The goal is to define the questions the authors attempt to answer and evaluate how successful they are in addressing these issues. For our purposes of criticism, the syntopical reading and analysis consisted of four steps, described below. The first two steps helped us to understand what the authors said, while the last two steps allowed us to evaluate their texts and infer issues.

In Step One, our goal was to build up a common set of terms across the collection. We identified the specific terms authors used to describe the play-literacy interface and how they explained the interface as a research problem. For example, Branscombe and Taylor (2000) refer to play as " through oral, written, and acted stories" and literacy as "story in the literate sense" and examine this interface based on a theoretical rationale or set of reasons why this seems plausible. This first step helped us to understand what the authors were attempting to explain with their research studies.

Step Two consisted of determining the authors' propositions (i.e., claims, assertions, and arguments) arrived at through the research process. In other words, what did the author conclude and based on what evidence? Grasping this, we then might understand more fully what the author meant to say and on what grounds. Dunn, Beach, and Kontos (1994), for example, claim that day-care environments do not afford much literacy activity and materials during playtime and support their claim with observational data (surveys, rating scales) gathered from 30 centers in the Midwest. Examining the authors' claims in this way allowed us to generate a general set of questions (or propositions) that the authors tried to answer.

Having built an understanding of the authors' texts, we next turned to the critical phase of the analysis. Our goal here was to judge the texts, examining specific concepts and claims against the common set of terms and propositions and determining the extent to which authors' evidence and reasoning shed light on the research problem. This allowed us to think within alternative systems of thought, recognizing and assessing assumptions, implications, and consequences that pointed to issues facing the field. Beginning with Step Three, we evaluated each research report by either agreeing or disagreeing with it or suspending judgment about it (see Appendix B.) The basis of agreement or disagreement rested on qualities of soundness and completeness in the report. To determine soundness, we probed the extent to which a report was informed (i.e., provided knowledge relevant to the problem and made assertions based on facts and evidence) and logical (i.e., combined ideas and concepts in clear, accurate, orderly, and mutually supporting ways). To assess completeness, we observed whether the report solved the stated research problem and led to implications of importance that followed from the evidence. Disagreements were documented by evidence of a lack of soundness or completeness in the text of the research report. If neither agreement nor disagreement seemed fully warranted based on our critical reading of the text and discussion, then we agreed to suspend judgment. The results of this analysis yielded points of agreement and points of criticism.

Finally, in Step Four, we worked inductively to define the issues revealed by our syntopical reading of the texts and to examine the different ways authors addressed (or overlooked) these issues, thus gaining insights into the character of the play-literacy interface as a domain of study. Further interpretive analyses of the "conflict in the opposing answers" around the issues also provided opportunity to examine the scientific discourses influencing the research work.

Results

Our critical analysis of the authors' research reports as written texts produced results in three main areas that constitute a critical review of the set of 20 studies. The first of these is a *description of the collection-as-a-whole,* which summarizes its key features and evaluates its qualities as scientific work. Another involves *the concepts of play and literacy* that authors use to examine what they see as problematic and the theories they employ to explain the shared boundaries between these two concepts. And a third is concerned with the *authors' claims and the evidence gathered to support them*. In each of these areas, we first summarize the gist of the texts and then step back to offer points of criticism.

Description of the Collection-as-a-Whole

The total set of 20 studies addressed a broad range of play-literacy topics that stretched across descriptions of environmental exposure (e.g., Dunn, Beach, & Kontos, 1994), observations of play-language relationships (e.g., syntax, Vedeler, 1997), analyses of play-narrative links (e.g., story sense, Branscombe & Taylor, 2000), documentation of literacy outcomes (e.g., reading environmental print, Vukelich, 1994), and examinations of play-literacy interactions (e.g., peer collaboration, Christie & Stone, 1999). The collection-as-whole was representative of established research problems in the field (e.g., play-narrative relationships) but also reflected newer areas of inquiry (e.g., peer and adult mediation of literacy in play activity).

Observations of children—their actions, language, knowledge, and thinking—dominated the set, a total of 15 reports, and occurred primarily in the indoor play environment within institutional settings such as day-care centers, Head Start classrooms, preschools, and elementary schools (85% of studies). As one might expect, 16 of the studies involved children between the ages of 3–5, the most popular age range for play research (Christie & Johnsen, 1987). It's noteworthy that 4 (20%) of these reports provide data on children in the 6–7 age range (primary graders). Research on school play is typically confined to the preschool and kindergarten levels. Rowe (1998), on the other, expanded the age range in the opposite direction, observing very young children (ages 2–3) who are entering the representational period of the preschool years.

Another popular topic was the adults' role in facilitating literacy in play connections. Three studies, for example, directly examined adult mediation of children's literacy in play. Neuman (2000) and Neuman and Gallagher (1994) evaluated the effects of family literacy programs that attempted to improve teenage mothers' play interactions with their children. Roskos and Neuman (1993) investigated how experienced preschool teachers interacted with children during literacy play. Two other studies considered the play environment but dealt only marginally with adults' direct involvement in designing the environment for play/literacy interactions (Dunn, Beach, & Kontos, 1994; Makin, Hayden, & Diaz, 2000).

The collection contained a good mix of methodology. Ten of the studies relied solely on quantitative methodology, while another seven used only qualitative procedures. In a promising development, three other studies used both quantitative and qualitative methods (Neuman & Roskos, 1992, 1993, 1997). The quantitative studies used a broad spectrum of methods to collect data, ranging from systematic observation to standardized tests. Some studies simply reported descriptive data, whereas others used inferential statistics. On the qualitative side, constant comparison was the preferred data analysis strategy, employed in virtually all of the studies.

However, looking beyond these descriptive features of the collection about which we might readily agree, points of disagreement emerge about the collection as a whole that challenge its scientific value. Our initial critical analysis led us to question the soundness (e.g., availability of information, the quantity and quality of evidence) and completeness (adequacy of research tasks) of eight studies and, ultimately, to disagree with their claims. As a result, these eight were excluded from further analyses. (See studies marked with an asterisk in Table 7.1.) Our points of disagreement with these studies were threefold: missing information, insufficient evidence, and inadequate solution paths. Two examples suffice to illustrate these points.

Consider, for example, Dever and Wishon (1995), who pose a formidable research question: What are play's benefits for literacy learning in first grade? This is a fundamental question and a significant one if we are to understand the role of play in early literacy development. The solution path they chose, however, is not well-matched to this problem, gathering evidence of literacy behaviors in play events instead of literacy performance (knowledge and skills) in relation to types of play activity engaged in by the children (e.g., exploratory play, dramatic play, rough and tumble play). As a result, information needed to inform the problem is unavailable and, consequently, the report is incomplete. The research work done, in other words, is not up to the research task, and thus opens the door to untenable conclusions.

The report of Bergen and Mauer (2000) provides another case in point. They take on an intriguing research problem—the relation of symbolic play to children's developing phonological awareness in the early years. Oral language is at the interface of this relationship (i.e., how children's language use in play might draw their attention to the sounds of language apart from its meaning). Children's playful use of words in the flow of play, for example, has not gone unnoticed (Weir, 1962). Illuminating this potential intersect would certainly benefit developmental research as well as early childhood literacy pedagogy. Yet, the report does not shed light on the theoretical ideas and research that might inform this question nor build a case for the argument; namely, that exploring sounds in play might benefit children's developing phonological awareness so necessary in learning to read. In addition, there were problems in how symbolic play was operationalized across the 3 years of this longitudinal study. During the first year (preschool), play consisted of free play in literacy-enriched centers. In the second year (kindergarten), play was assessed during structured clinical play sessions with games. During the final year of the study (Grade 1), telephone interviews were used to find out about children's home play behavior. This lack of consistency in how play was defined severely limits the conclusions that can be drawn about play's relationship with phonemic awareness.

Setting these eight studies and our judgments of them aside, we agreed with the major claims, assertions, and arguments of the remaining 12 studies in the collection, judging the research work as sound and complete and, thus, a solid evidentiary base for further analyses. All 12 authors identified and framed their research problems along well-delineated theoretical lines and channeled research tasks to find acceptable solutions in response to these problems. The real strength of these reports, though, resides in the consistent, systematic (and sometimes painstaking) data collection and analyses that characterize many of them. Rowe's (1998) analysis, for example, coupled constant comparison of videotaped events over a 9-month period in the preschool setting with a case study of her own son, lasting 13 months. She used extensive triangulating of multiple data sources and "expert" checks of her analyses and findings to confirm her conclusions.

Still, there are specific weak spots in this remaining set of 12 studies that warrant brief description. One of these results from too much scatter in the topics selected for investigation such that studies do not build on one another to establish a line of inquiry. Most studies were isolated efforts, providing information about some aspect of the play-literacy interface, but with no follow through. There are several notable exceptions (e.g., Neuman, 2000; Neuman & Roskos, 1992, 1993, 1997; Neuman & Gallagher, 1994). Neuman and Roskos, for example, focused their 1992 study on the effects of placing literacy objects in play settings. The 1993 study investigated adult mediation of play in literacy-enriched settings and its impact on children's environmental print recognition, and the 1997 investigation examined the impact of these settings on other aspects of children's literacy knowledge.

Another limitation concerns the very narrow range of research strategies used to analyze data. Like "Johnny-one-notes," these researchers preferred constant-comparison to all other qualitative analytic strategies, which limited the scope of vision and interpretation. Metaphor, for example, might provide a richer and more complete means for describing phenomena and moving to a more inferential level with data. Roskos and Neuman (1993) were the only investigators to employ this technique, developing a metaphor to represent each of the roles that teachers used to facilitate children's play.

A third weak spot, also related to diversity, is the dominance of Vygotskian and Piagetian theories as the "drivers" of research efforts to the near exclusion of other explanatory models. In addition, Vygotsky's explanatory influence appears limited to the symbolic connection between play and literacy and to social interaction. Minimal attention is paid to *play* as a "zone of proximal development" in and of itself or to the material culture as a mediator of literacy knowledge and practice in the play environment. In other words, while researchers have made heavy use of Vygotsky's theory, they have focused on narrow parts of his theory, ignoring some potentially important links between play and literacy.

Concepts of Literacy and Play

What is the interface of play and literacy as an object of study in the 12 remaining studies? To arrive at an answer to this question required identifying the researchers' terms for these constructs and discovering how they explained concepts so as to join them together. Understanding the researchers' terms, in turn, laid the groundwork for a critical analysis of the interface. We first describe the researchers' definitions of play and literacy and then bring them to terms, so to speak, by analyzing what is and is not explained by them.

What's striking from the outset is the authors' very liberal definitions of play. In fact, with the exception of two authors (Rowe, 1998; Vedeler, 1997), none provides an explicit definition of play to guide observations of children's behavior. For many ($n = 7$), play is loosely defined as any activity occurring in play centers or around play props. Vukelich (1994), for example, described play "as a social context" embedded in kindergarten classroom play centers; Christie and Stone (1999) referred to it as "collaboration" in a literacy-enriched play center at school; and Neuman and Roskos (1992, 1993) imply that play involves "transformations" in play settings. Others describe play as "entertainment" arising out of home experiences (Sonnenschein, Baker, Serpell, & Schmidt, 2000) or as global interactions that transpire in the play environments of early childhood settings, namely, day care (e.g., Dunn, Beach, & Kontos, 1994). Rowe (1998) is the sole author to include the generally held properties of play in the body of the report (see Christie, 1991), and only Vedeler (1997) specifies what constituted dramatic play, setting 40% or more role-play utterances in an episode as the criterion. For most of these researchers, therefore, play remains a fuzzy construct; it is what children do in play places or settings.

Literacy, however, is another matter, and here our authors tend to be more explicit, but also more conservative. Definitions range from a multi-modal semiotic view of literate behavior (e.g., response to books; see Rowe, 1998) to literacy practices (e.g., problem-solving strategies; see Neuman & Roskos, 1997) to the traditional sense of literacy as phonological awareness, word identification, and reading comprehension (Sonnenschein et al., 2000). All of the authors take pains to clarify what constitutes literacy in the context of their research and the behaviors that give evidence of children's literacy understandings and skills. Vukelich (1994), for instance, is quite clear that the ability to read environmental print is indicative of emergent reading. Similarly, others articulate the behaviors, performances, activities, and processes that define early literacy and allocate considerable text to clarifying their terms. Yet, unlike play where there is little activity that is not termed play, literacy is confined to a narrower strip of activity that involves primarily reading and writing. Children scribble and write, they pretend read, they respond to books that have been read to them, they use print. Vedeler (1997) is the single researcher who stretches the literacy concept to include the syntax of oral language as a forerunner in the learning to read process. In general, then, the majority of these authors keep a tight rein on what they mean by literacy, confining it primarily to print-based experiences.

How do these authors merge these two concepts to discover, describe, and examine their common boundaries? They use three thick theoretical ideas to pull play and literacy together. One is characteristically Piagetian, grafting play and literacy onto the development of recall, when children first imitate what they see (deferred imitation) and then say what they remember. The mental work of memory—conscious recollections of facts or past events—is at the root of pretend play schemes and also the manipulation of a second-order symbol system such as print. The interface, therefore, is at the level of representation, and the basic idea is that, in both play and literacy, children must recall facts and experiences held in memory to make new meanings in context, whether three dimensional as in play or two dimensional as in text.

Another is essentially Vygotskian, emphasizing the social interaction between individuals as the source of literacy knowledge. Play, like other social contexts, provides a social situation that (a) exposes children to literacy concepts and skills; (b) creates sociocognitive conflicts (different points of view) that generate adaptations in individual thinking; and (c) promotes elaboration of literate thinking through more complex social exchanges. In pretend play, the need to coordinate social actions with others gives rise to opportunities that may involve literate ways of thinking (e.g., narration) as well as use of literacy knowledge, tools, scripts, and skills. The interface, here, is at the level of appropriation, which is concerned with what children may take from their encounters with others in social situations, such as play in which literacy may be embedded.

A third idea is fundamentally ecological, embracing Bronfenbrenner's basic concept of the person-environment dynamic; namely, that individuals both shape and are shaped by their surroundings. Children are active, intentional entities of their environments; they help shape them. In turn, the situations they encounter cue them and also are embedded in larger environmental spheres with physical, social, and cultural properties that influence directly and indirectly the child-environment interaction. Play is a system of activity (an environment) that arises from individual intentions as well as setting influences both near (the immediate surroundings) and far (socially held views of play). As such, it affords an opportunity to exercise individual literacy ideas and skills, even as it presses for certain kinds of literacy knowledge and interactions. This dynamic, complex process contributes to developmental trajectories that may more or less favor literacy achievement at school. Thus, the interface in this case is at the level of activity, concerned with its social organization (e.g., groupings, roles, power relations) as well as its psychological content (e.g., tasks, tools, mental work).

How well do our authors do at conjoining play and literacy at these different interfaces? As might be expected, they are better at articulating some of these conceptually dense regions than others. Representation, for example, is clearly drawn in the work of Rowe (1998), where children remember and make sense of books in multimodal ways, and that of Vedeler (1997), where children practice their syntactic abilities in play. Several authors describe the power of social interaction in scaffolding children's appropriation of literacy knowledge, processes, and skills (e.g., Neuman, 2000). To various degrees, different authors also outline the activity settings of home, day care, and preschool that support or constrain children's opportunities to engage in literacy practices of meaning and challenge to them (e.g., Neuman & Roskos, 1997).

Yet, much remains uncharted along these common boundaries of play and literacy. We would argue, in fact, that most authors are centrists not veering far from classic interactionist explanations of the play-literacy relationship (i.e., locating its physical and social processes in interactions with the immediate world or among individuals). In the direction of sociocultural explanations, for example, macro-level or societal processes are overlooked as having any bearing on children's appropriation of literacy concepts in play or the nature of the play activity itself. How the shift to a global economy and results-oriented policies, such as the Head Start Reauthorization mandating that all children learn 10 letters of the alphabet, impact play and literacy in play-like activity remains unexplored.

And in direction of individual systems, the role of children's bio-psychological resources (e.g., affect and motivation) and their "developmentally instigative charac-teristics" (e.g., willingness to explore particular features of objects and symbols in the environment) are virtually ignored in examinations of activity and representation (Bronfenbrenner, 1995). Children contribute to their own development, and this may be especially relevant in the case of play "as a playground" for exploring cultural symbol systems and related tools. Yet the dispositional proclivities that propel some children over others to take advantage of the literacy opportunities in their play envi-ronment are not well-charted, being mostly confined to two personal characteristics: age and gender.

Nor do authors attend very well to a holistic, integrative view of literacy in play activity as a micro-system (or eco-cultural niche) that involves simultaneous interactions with three features of the immediate environment: persons, objects, and symbols. This is to say that, in joining play and literacy, authors fail to grapple with the dynamics of literacy-embedded play as experienced through patterns of co-occurring gestural and talk interactions that constitute activity. They remain fixed on the parts of activity and their attendant properties, whereas the play expe-rience itself occurs as a whole—a web of relationships that holds the meaning that the experience has for playing and for learning to read and write. There is also a need for a shift from the monocular focus on the shared "essential elements" be-tween literacy and play (Pellegrini & Galda, 2000, p. 68) to a binocular vision of play processes as patterns of interaction that are turned into experience by and for children (Johnson, 2000).

Claims and Evidence

As the final step in our analysis, we identified the authors' conclusions in order to develop an understanding of what they proposed as answers or solutions to their research questions. We sought more than a literal understanding of their points, how-ever, working to achieve a nuanced interpretation and analysis of the significance of the research findings. That is, we hoped to see subtle differences, levels, and ironies among the authors' claims so as to create a helpful interpretation. Our approach was two-tiered: to establish a set of neutral claims that shed light on the interface, and to which each author contributed, and to engage in a discussion of this set, "reading between the lines" so to speak, so as to reveal what the authors imply or do not imply in their claims.

Taking up the matter of the authors' conclusions first, we gleaned from this list a set of four claims. At the very core and integral to the others is the foundational as-sertion that play serves literacy. In some measure, some form, some process, play is mustered into the service of literacy and thus contributes to the literacy development of young children. Each author makes this basic claim either by showing how play can be pressed into service, as in supplying its environment with literacy information and tools (Neuman & Roskos, 1992; Vukelich, 1991), or how it may go untapped, as in limiting access to literacy resources or orientations in play (e.g., Dunn, Beach, & Kontos, 1994; Sonnenschein et al., 2000).

Three closely connected propositions embrace this core claim. One is that a literacy-enriched play environment (social and physical resources) promotes literacy activity, skills, or processes. Several authors assert, for example, that stocking the environment with literacy materials and tools stimulates literacy interactions in the course of play (Dunn, Beach, & Kontos, 1994; Neuman & Roskos, 1992, 1997). Others cite evidence that adult involvement and intervention infuse literacy ideas, processes, and skills into play activity (e.g., Neuman, 2000; Vukelich, 1994). Still others show the value of peers as provocateurs and informants in play settings (e.g., Christie & Stone, 1999). There is, in sum, a general consensus that the play environment can be engineered to enhance the literacy experiences of young children.

A related claim is made that play is a language experience for young children that builds connections between oral and written modes of expression. Sociodramatic play, for example, was found to recruit more advanced syntactic utterances and sentence expansions that are linked to reading success (Vedeler, 1997). Rowe's (1998) young players of 2 and 3 years of age mingled toy play, gesture, and talk to express their understandings of favorite books, thus building their "comprehension of the act" of reading books. Through guided participation during play, the teenage mothers in Neuman's study (2000) developed the distancing strategies of their young children so fundamental to meaning making in the decontextualized medium of print. The authors, therefore, find for and argue that the language of play can connect to the language of literacy, and thus contribute to the young child's literacy development.

The authors also claim that play is an opportunity to teach and learn literacy. Neuman and Gallagher (1994) show how young mothers can become better teachers of language and thinking when at play with their children. Vukelich (1994) describes how adults can demonstrate and express literacy to children while they play. And Christie and Stone (1999) illustrate how multi-age grouping in a play setting allows children to teach one another. Play provides chances to learn literacy, too. As they play, children learn to read words, such as environmental print (Neuman & Roskos, 1993; Vukelich, 1994); they learn to comprehend books (Rowe, 1998); and they develop phonological awareness and print motivation (Sonnenschein et al., 2000).

As these supporting claims attest, therefore, play serves literacy in various ways and that it does so is the most fundamental claim of all. Given the recency of play-literacy line of inquiry, that such claims can be made based on sound evidence is a testament to the strength, appeal, and fruitfulness of the play-literacy relationship. Still there are controversies that swirl around this set of claims and intellectual oppositions that confront them and expose their weaknesses. Consider, for example, the foundational claim that play serves literacy, from which we might infer that indeed literacy is "king" and play the "jester-clown." So positioned, play and literacy are in a power relation wherein play is subordinated to the loftier goal of learning to read and write—a power struggle not to be taken lightly, as Lubeck (2000) has observed. "The professional commitment to play," she writes, "has begun to be eroded in a political climate dominated by language of standards and outcomes" (p. 3). What is not asked wholeheartedly and with conviction is how literacy might also serve play, thus enhancing and deepening this significant life experience for young children. Do more advanced emergent readers and writers engage in more complex play that in turn boosts their intellectual power? How do early experiences with writing and reading impact different forms of play? And, while Fein, Ardila-Rey, and Groth (2000) accepted the challenge of this question, more potent research designs are needed to trace the spread effect of literacy curriculum experiences into play corners. Does an emphasis on emergent literacy in the early childhood curriculum limit play? What does a literacy emphasis portend for those "serious play" functions that give "push to variation," and thus develop children's combinatorial behaviors, their flexibility with materials and ideas, and fluency with rules and conventions (Bruner, 1972)? Questions like these expose what needs to be asked if play and literacy are to enter into a dialogic relationship—one that informs and instructs both domains to the improvement of each in the early childhood curriculum.

The claim of environmental enrichment for purposes of literacy enhancement also warrants closer scrutiny because the question must be asked: If more resources (both social and physical) are allocated to literacy in play, what areas are given short shrift? What is ignored because literacy receives more attention? Resources, as we all well know, are finite, and the degree to which teachers (as social resources) allot time and energy to reading and writing in play means they are not doing other things in play, such as building concepts about social relationships or helping children learn to manipulate and create with their material world. They may overlook broader aspects of environmental design and provisions (physical resources) that produce "an amiable environment rich with learning opportunities, media, and materials" (Gandini, 1998, p. 162). Preoccupation with literacy may, in fact, inhibit the growth of a hybrid environment in which a richly layered network of situations creates conditions for complex learning. It's important to ask, What might this literacy emphasis in play mean for the many developing languages of young children that equip them for an ever-changing and evolving world (Katz, 1998)? Thus, it is important to probe and investigate as to what occurs when the play environment is enriched (or overstuffed) with literacy and to document not only what is gained but also what may be lost and the consequences for children's play activity in early childhood.

Play as a language experience tied to literacy is challenged by two controversies. One is the degree to which all young children engage in or have access to the kinds of play (e.g., sociodramatic play) claimed to do the linguistic groundwork on which literacy depends. We simply do not have sufficient research data to fully address this issue of incidence. Who engages in pretend play, in what cultural ways, and how often are important questions, along with the degree to which such play is allowed and encouraged in educational settings. Early education programs, for example, vary widely as to the time allotted for play. Further, just as the nature of the play language experience can be linguistically strong, good, and true, it can be semantically and syntactically weak, mean-spirited, and headed in the wrong direction. Children can be exposed to language practices in play that give them an edge but just as easily exposed to those that limit growth and instill feelings of insecurity and resistance.

Finally, the proposition that play offers an educational opportunity in that literacy can be taught and learned within its boundaries must be cross-examined. Present evidence points to the potential of play for luring young children into literacy activity and kindred processes. Adults can show, and children will do. They can guide participation, and children will follow. But the danger, of course, is the spreading expectation in the minds of adults that a certain measure of play must be purposeful and such purpose must be bent to literacy outcomes. What this might mean for young children's indoor play in the early childhood curriculum is hard to say, but it is necessary to pose the possibility that play may become a site for literacy lessons and to seriously consider the consequences. Presently, there is little known as to how teachers view literacy-embedded play, how they plan for it, how it impacts children's play life, or to what extent it improves children's literacy achievements. For example, what do teachers need to know to plan for literacy in play effectively and well? What factors influence children's participation? And, fundamentally, does such play help children advance as readers and writers? If so, how? These are questions that invite further and deeper investigations about the role of play in literacy learning and development.

Critical Issues and Recommendations

The collection of 20 studies discussed in this critical review makes a substantial contribution to our understanding of the relationships between play and literacy. Most noteworthy, researchers have made considerable progress in (a) describing children's play behaviors in literacy-enriched play centers, (b) determining the effects of play in these settings on children's ability to read play-related environmental print, and (c) understanding the effects of adult mediation and peer interaction on children's literacy play behavior.

However, as our criticism in the preceding section revealed, there are shortcomings in the current research and a number of important issues that remain unresolved or that have yet to be addressed. It is our hope that these issues can serve as guideposts for the next generation of research on the play-literacy interface.

Definitions   More attention needs to be given to the way in which play and literacy are defined. As noted earlier, the common practice has been to define play very loosely in terms of any activity that occurs in a "play" center or in the presence of play materials. Anyone who has observed children interacting in classroom play centers will likely recall exceptions to this premise. While in these play settings, children often engage in goal-directed activities that are closer to work than to play. Indeed, King's (1979) research in a kindergarten classroom revealed that children considered some activities with play materials to be work, rather than play. We hope that future researchers follow the lead of Rowe (1998) and Vedeler (1997) and establish precise criteria for what constitutes play. There is a fairly rich knowledge base to draw upon in crafting these criteria (Christie, 1991; Smith & Vollstedt, 1985).

Whereas there is a need to refine how play is defined, the definition of literacy could use expanding. Most of the studies in this review focus on emergent and conventional forms of reading and writing—what could be termed "school literacy." Even the family literacy studies focused exclusively on educational forms of literacy. It would be desirable for researchers to extend research on the play-literacy interface into broader conceptions of literacy. Hall (2000, p. 190), for example, has connected literacy play with Street's (1995) construct of ideological literacy, "types of literacy that draw their meaning from being situated within cultural values and practices." Hall has developed a strategy in which children engage in "real life" literacy activities that are connected with their ongoing sociodramatic play (e.g., filling out an actual "Planning Application Form" for the local city government in order to set up a garage play center in the classroom).

Theory   The research in this review has been dominated by Piaget's view of play as representation, Vygotsky's emphasis on social interaction and appropriation, and (to a lesser extent) the ecological perspective. We believe that this area of inquiry needs a broader theoretical base.

First, there is a need for an updated, expanded version of the ecological perspective, which places more emphasis on both ends of the spectrum of ecological influences on behavior. More attention needs to be given to both *macrolevel* societal and historical forces that impact play behavior and children's appropriation of literacy and to *microlevel* factors that emphasize individual differences in children's affect, motivation, and individual play styles.

Second, opportunities exist to take fuller advantage of Vygotsky's theory. As noted earlier, researchers have concentrated their attention on Vygotsky's "zone of proximal development" as it pertains to social interaction between children and adults or more competent peers. However, Vygotsky also viewed play *itself* as a zone of proximal development. Vygotsky (1976, p. 552) argued that, "In play a child is always above his average age, above his daily behaviour; in play it is as though he were a head taller than himself." Viewed from this perspective, play is a self-help tool that enables children to achieve higher levels of cognitive functioning (Johnson, Christie, & Yawkey, 1999). Because play activity generates feedback under conditions of less risk, children may acquire the ability to regulate themselves; namely, to correct mistakes and thus re-organize their action and problem-solving schemes to higher levels of performance (Bruner, 1972). It would be interesting, therefore, to investigate if children's solitary play with literacy material does indeed allow them to function at higher levels than in non-play contexts.

Finally, a number of other theories such as narrative theory (Bruner, 1990), collaborative learning theories (Tharp & Gallimore, 1988; Wells & Chang-Wells, 1992), activity theory (Leont'ev, 1978), and cognitive apprenticeship (Rogoff, 1990) have connections with play and literacy that are yet to be exploited. To date, these theories have been underutilized or completely ignored by researchers. Broadening the theoretical base could greatly enrich our understanding of the play-literacy interface.

Methodology While the collection-as-whole featured a nice mix of quantitative and qualitative methodologies, we were struck by the narrow range of qualitative methods employed by the researchers. With two exceptions (Rowe, 1998; Roskos & Neuman, 1993), the qualitative studies utilized a small subset of the available means for analyzing data (constant comparison and computing/tabulating), drawing conclusions (counting and patterns/themes), and verifying those conclusions (checking for bias and weighting evidence). A number of qualitative techniques were rarely, if ever, used:

- Data analysis: ranking/weighting, summarizing/generating themes, and completing matrices
- Drawing conclusions: clustering, making metaphors, splitting variables, subsuming particulars, factoring, noting relations between variables, and finding intervening variables
- Confirming conclusions: making contrasts, checking for outliers, using extreme cases, ruling out spurious relations, replicating a finding, checking out rival explanations, looking for negative evidence, and getting feedback from informants

While it is obvious that not all of these procedures will be appropriate for any given research problem, we do believe that inquiry into the play-literacy interface would benefit from selective use of these underutilized qualitative methods.

Causal Connections Between Play and Development One issue that was not addressed very effectively by this set of studies concerns the impact of literacy play on children's development. Only two studies covered in this review supplied credible evidence about literacy play's developmental impact. Neuman and Roskos (1993) and Vukelich (1994) found that, when children play in literacy-enriched settings with a supportive adult, they learn to read environmental print that is in the play setting. So it does appear that literacy play can improve children's sight recognition of words connected with the play. A third study offered at least the possibility of a link between play and oral language acquisition. Neuman and Gallagher (1994) discovered that their family literacy program, with its emphasis on parental play mediation strategies, resulted in gains in Peabody Picture Vocabulary Test scores. However, the researchers were careful to point out that there was not a clear causal connection between the parental play mediation strategies and these gains in receptive vocabulary.

There is a definite need for further research into causal connections between literacy play and development. Ideally, future studies should feature (a) long-term exposure to literacy play activities, (b) longitudinal designs that can track the effects of interventions over time, and (c) rigorous control over other variables that may impact development. In addition, we hope that future studies will expand the range of dependent variables beyond narrow conceptions of literacy. By spotlighting only literacy, there may be other outcomes of literacy play that we are *not* seeing. For example, what effect does flooding play settings with literacy materials have on structural properties of the play itself? Does this literacy infusion enhance or degrade the quality of children's sociodramatic play? Neuman and Roskos (1992) was the only study in this review that attempted to address this issue. Results were positive, showing the length and complexity of play episodes increased as a result of adding print to play settings. We need to examine how other qualities of play (e.g., narrative structure, social interaction, and imaginativeness) are affected by large infusions of print props. It would also be interesting to see how other areas of development such as oral language development, problem-solving skills, etc. are affected by literacy play intervention strategies.

"Play as Progress" Rhetoric   Sutton-Smith (1995, 1997) has written extensively about the tendency of social science researchers to assume that play is a positive force in child development. He refers to this idealistic view as the "play as progress" rhetoric. He claims, somewhat light-heartedly, "Since the death of Puritanism it has not been easy to find a self-respecting scholar of childhood who would announce that play is of no damn use whatsoever" (1995, pp. 279–280). However, Sutton-Smith also points out the danger of this rhetoric. It can lead researchers to assume that everything about play is good and cause them to overlook or ignore the less positive and sometimes negative aspects of play. And these negative aspects do exist. Children occasionally resort to physical aggression during play and more commonly use verbal and social forms of hostility such as ridicule and exclusion to hurt their playmates. His point is that, in order to get a true picture of play's role in development, researchers have to focus on all facets of play, not just the positive aspects.

We see this "play as progress" rhetoric as dominating the discourse in all of the studies covered in this review. Not one study reported any negative aspects of play's role in literacy learning. Yet, these negative influences may be there, along with the positive influences identified by the researchers. It is possible, for example, that some children may learn misconceptions about literacy during play. It is also possible that some of the social interaction connected with literacy play may be of a negative character. For example, a child might ridicule a peer's use of an emergent form of literacy (e.g., scribble writing) during play.

We are not proposing that researchers make a point of focusing on negative aspects of the play-literacy interface (though this might be an intriguing project). What we do advocate is that researchers be open to other rhetorics of play such as "play as power" (play as means of expressing and gaining power) and "play as frivolity" (play as an optional, non-serious, non-productive activity) and be on the lookout for negative and neutral, as well as positive, aspects and outcomes of playing with literacy.

Conclusion

In retrospect, we learned quite a bit about ourselves through this critical analysis of play/literacy research. While it is difficult to examine and critically analyze one's own research, it is also quite enlightening. We became more aware of our own stance toward science and doing research and of the ways that we have viewed play and literacy. We discovered that we are both "middle-of-the-road" when it comes to the interpretist/positivist dichotomy. This centrist leaning manifests itself in our respect for Miles and Huberman's (1994) guidelines for qualitative research, which emphasize both inductive and deductive approaches to data collection and analysis. We came to realize that we have defined play rather vaguely as any activity that occurs in classroom play centers. In line with the "play as progress" rhetoric, we have tended to focus only on positive aspects of play activity and have not looked for any negative outcomes. Finally, we discovered that we have been closely wedded to "school literacy," focusing on a rather narrow spectrum of literacy promoted in educational settings. While our stance toward scientific inquiry will remain the same, our future research will likely encompass broader, more carefully defined views of play and literacy.

Aside from these self-discoveries, we hope that this critical review will be helpful to others researchers. Credible evidence supports the claim that play can serve literacy in several ways by

- providing settings that promote literacy activity, skills, and strategies;
- serving as a language experience that can build connections between oral and written modes of expression; and
- providing opportunities to teach and learn literacy.

At the same time, our review highlighted a number of limitations and unresolved issues connected with this line of inquiry, including concerns about definitions, theories, research methodology, lack of progress in establishing causal connections with development, and dominance of the "play as progress" rhetoric. We hope that future research will zero in on these concerns and provide even richer, more insightful information about the play-literacy interface.

References

Adler, M. J., & van Doren, C. (1972). *How to read a book.* New York: Simon & Schuster.

Barker, R. (1978). Stream of individual behavior. In R. Barker (Ed.), *Habitats, environments, and human behavior* (pp. 3–16). San Francisco: Jossey-Bass.

Bergen, D., & Mauer, D. (2000). Symbolic play, phonological awareness, and literacy skills at three age levels. In K. Roskos & J. Christie (Eds.), *Play and literacy in early childhood: Research from multiple perspectives* (pp. 45–62). Mahwah, NJ: Erlbaum.

Branscombe, N. A., & Taylor, J. (2000). "It would be as good as Snow White": Play and prosody. In K. Roskos & J. Christie (Eds.), *Play and literacy in early childhood: Research from multiple perspectives* (pp. 169–188). Mahwah, NJ: Erlbaum.

Bronfenbrenner, U. (1995). Developmental ecology through space and time: A future perspective. In P. Moen, G. Elder, & K. Luscher (Eds.), *Examining lives in context* (pp. 619–648). Washington, DC: American Psychological Association.

Brown, G. A., & Armstrong, S. (1984). Explaining and explanations. In E. C. Wragg (Ed.), *Classroom teaching and skills* (pp. 121–223). New York: Nichols Publishing.

Bruner, J. (1972). Nature and uses of immaturity. *American Psychologist, 27* (August), 687–708.

Bruner, J. (1990). *Acts of meaning.* Boston, MA: Harvard University Press.

Christie, J. (1991). Psychological research on play. In J. Christie (Ed.), *Play and early literacy development* (pp. 27–43). Albany, NY: State University of New York Press.

Christie, J., & Enz, B. (1992). The effects of literacy play interventions on preschoolers' play patterns and literacy development. *Early Education and Development, 3,* 205–220.

Christie, J., & Johnsen, E. P. (1983). The role of play in social-intellectual development. *Review of Educational Research, 53,* 93–115.

Christie, J., & Johnsen, E. P. (1987). Preschool play. In J. Block & N. King (Eds.), *School play* (pp. 109–142). New York: Garland.

Christie, J., & Stone, S. (1999). Collaborative literacy activity in print-enriched play centers: Exploring the "zone" in same-age and multi-age groupings. *Journal of Literacy Research, 31,* 109–131.

Clay, M. (1972). *Reading: The patterning of complex behaviour.* London: Heinemann.

Dever, M., & Wishon, P. (1995). Play as a context for literacy learning: A qualitative analysis. *Early Childhood Development and Care, 113,* 31–43.

Dunn, L., Beach, S., & Kontos, S. (1994). Quality of the literacy environment in day care and children's development. *Journal of Research in Childhood Education, 9,* 24–34.

Einarsdottir, J. (1996). Dramatic play and print. *Childhood Education, 72,* 352–357.

Fein, G. (1981). Pretend play in childhood: An integrative review. *Child Development, 52,* 1095–1118.

Fein, G., Ardila-Rey, A., & Groth, L. (2000). The narrative connection: Stories and literacy. In K. Roskos & J. Christie (Eds.), *Play and literacy in early childhood: Research from multiple perspectives* (pp. 27–43). Mahwah, NJ: Erlbaum.

Gandini, L. (1998). Educational and caring spaces. In C. Edwards, L. Gandini, & G. Forman (Eds.), *The hundred languages of children* (pp. 161–178). Greenwich, CT: Ablex.

Gump, P. (1989). Ecological psychology and issues of play. In M. Bloch & A. Pellegrini (Eds.), *The ecological context of children's play* (pp. 35–56). Norwood, NJ: Ablex.

Hall, N. (1987). *The emergence of literacy.* Portsmouth, NH: Heinemann Educational Books.

Hall, N. (2000). Literacy, play, and authentic experience. In K. Roskos & J. Christie (Eds.), *Play and literacy in early childhood: Research from multiple perspectives* (pp. 189–204). Mahwah, NJ: Erlbaum.

Hall, N., May, E., Moores, J., Shearer, J., & Williams, S. (1987). The literate home-corner. In P. Smith (Ed.), *Parents and teachers together* (pp. 134–144). London: Macmillan.

Hodder, I. (2000). The interpretation of documents and material culture. In N. Denzin & Y. Lincoln (Eds.), *Handbook of qualitative research* (pp. 703–716). Thousand Oaks, CA: Sage.

Johnson, J. (2000). Play, literacy, and ecology: Implications for early educational research and practice. In K. Roskos & J. Christie (Eds.), *Play and literacy in early childhood: Research from multiple perspectives* (pp. 139–150). Mahwah, NJ: Erlbaum.

Johnson, J., Christie, J., & Yawkey, T. (1999). *Play and early childhood development* (2nd ed.). New York: Longman.

Jupp, V. (1996). Documents and critical research. In R. Sapsford & V. Jupp (Eds.), *Data collection and analysis* (pp. 299–317). Thousand Oaks, CA: Sage.

Jupp, V., & Norris, C. (1993). Traditions in documentary analysis. In M. Hammersley (Ed.), *Social research: Philosophy, politics and practice* (pp. 46–59). Thousand Oaks, CA: Sage.

Katz, L. (1998). What can we learn from Reggio Emilia? In C. Edwards, L. Gandini, & G. Forman (Eds.), *The hundred languages of children* (pp. 27–48). Greenwich, CT: Ablex.

King, N. (1979). Play: The kindergartners' perspective. *Elementary School Journal, 80,* 81–87.

Leont'ev, A. N. (1978). *Activity, consciousness and personality.* Englewood Cliffs, NJ: Prentice-Hall.

Lubeck, S. (2000, April). *On reassessing the relevance of the child development knowledge base to education: A response.* Paper presented at the Early Education/Child Development SIG, AERA, New Orleans, LA.

Makin, L., Hayden, J., & Diaz, C. (2000). High-quality literacy programs in early childhood classrooms: An Australian case study. *Childhood Education, 76,* 368–373.

Miles, M., & Huberman, A. M. (1994). *Qualitative data analysis: An expanded sourcebook.* Thousand Oaks, CA: Sage.

Morrow, L. (1990). Preparing the classroom environment to promote literacy during play. *Early Childhood Research Quarterly, 5,* 537–544.

Neuman, S. (2000). Social contexts for literacy development: A family literacy program. In K. Roskos & J. Christie (Eds.), *Play and literacy in early childhood: Research from multiple perspectives* (pp. 153–168). Mahwah, NJ: Erlbaum.

Neuman, S., & Gallagher, P. (1994). Joining together in literacy learning: Teenage mothers and children. *Reading Research Quarterly, 29,* 382–401.

Neuman, S., & Roskos, K. (1990). The influence of literacy-enriched play settings on preschoolers' engagement with written language. In S. McCormick & J. Zutell (Eds.), *Literacy theory and research: Analyses from multiple perspectives* (pp. 179–187). Chicago: National Reading Conference.

Neuman, S., & Roskos, K. (1991). Peers as literacy informants: A description of young children's literacy conversations in play. *Early Childhood Research Quarterly, 6,* 233–248.

Neuman, S., & Roskos, K. (1992). Literacy objects as cultural tools: Effects on children's literacy behaviors during play. *Reading Research Quarterly, 27,* 203–223.

Neuman, S., & Roskos, K. (1993). Access to print for children of poverty: Differential effects of adult mediation and literacy-enriched play settings on environmental and functional print tasks. *American Educational Research Journal, 30,* 95–122.

Neuman, S., & Roskos, K. (1997). Literacy knowledge in practice: Contexts of participation for young writers and readers. *Reading Research Quarterly, 32,* 10–32.

Pellegrini, A. (1980). The relationship between kindergartners' play and achievement in pre-reading, language, and writing. *Psychology in the Schools, 17,* 530–535.

Pellegrini, A., & Galda, L. (1993). Ten years after: A reexamination of symbolic play and literacy research. *Reading Research Quarterly, 28,* 163–175.

Pellegrini, A., & Galda, L. (2000). Cognitive development, play, and literacy: Issues of definition and developmental function. In K. Roskos & J. Christie (Eds.), *Play and literacy in early childhood: Research from multiple perspectives* (pp. 63–74). Mahwah, NJ: Erlbaum.

Pellegrini, A., Galda, L., Dresden, J., & Cox, S. (1991). A longitudinal study of the predictive relations among symbolic play, linguistic verbs, and early literacy. *Research in the Teaching of English, 25,* 215–235.

Piaget, J. (1962). *Play, dreams and imitation in childhood.* New York: Norton.

Pickett, L. (1998). Literacy learning during block play. *Journal of Research in Childhood Education, 12,* 225–230.

Rogoff, B. (1990). *Apprenticeship in thinking: Cognitive development in social context.* New York: Oxford University Press.

Roskos K., & Christie J. (Eds.). (2000). *Play and literacy in early childhood: Research from multiple perspectives.* Mahwah, NJ: Erlbaum.

Roskos, K., & Neuman, S. (1993). Descriptive observations of adults' facilitation of literacy in play. *Early Childhood Research Quarterly 8,* 77–97.

Rowe, D. (1998). The literate potentials of book-related dramatic play. *Reading Research Quarterly, 33,* 10–35.

Schrader, C. (1990). Symbolic play as a curricular tool for early literacy development. *Early Childhood Research Quarterly, 5,* 79–103.

Smith, P., & Vollstedt, R. (1985). On defining play: An empirical study of the relationship between play and various play criteria. *Child Development, 56,* 1042–1050.

Sonnenschein, S., Baker, L., Serpell, R., & Schmidt, D. (2000). Reading is a source of entertainment: The importance of the home perspective for children's literacy development. In K. Roskos & J. Christie (Eds.), *Play and literacy in early childhood: Research from multiple perspectives* (pp. 107–124). Mahwah, NJ: Erlbaum.

Spodek, B., & Saracho, O. (Eds.). (1998). *Multiple perspectives on play in early childhood.* Albany, State University of New York Press.

Spradley, J. (1979). *The ethnographic interview.* New York: Holt, Rinehart & Winston.

Street, B. (1995). *Social literacies: Critical approaches to literacy in development, ethnography and education.* London: Longman.

Sutton-Smith, B. (1995). Conclusion: The persuasive rhetorics of play. In A. Pellegrini (Ed.), *The future of play theory: A multidisciplinary inquiry into the contributions of Brian Sutton-Smith* (pp. 275–306). Albany, State University of New York Press.

Sutton-Smith, B. (1997). *The ambiguity of play.* Cambridge, MA: Harvard University Press.

Teale, W., & Sulzby, E. (1986). Emergent literacy as a perspective for examining how young children become writers and readers. In W. Teale & E. Sulzby (Eds.), *Emergent literacy: Writing and reading* (pp. vii–xxv). Norwood, NJ: Ablex.

Tharp, R., & Gallimore, R. (1988). *Rousing minds to life: Teaching, learning and schooling in social context.* New York: Cambridge University Press.

Vedeler, L. (1997). Dramatic play: A format for "literate" language? *British Journal of Educational Psychology, 67,* 153–167.

Vukelich, C. (1991, December). *Learning about the functions of writing: The effects of three play interventions on children's development and knowledge about writing.* Paper presented at the meeting of the National Reading Conference, Palm Springs, CA.

Vukelich, C. (1994). Effects of play interventions on young children's reading of environmental print. *Early Childhood Research Quarterly, 9,* 153–170.

Vygotsky, L. (1976). Play and its role in the mental development of the child. In J. Bruner, A. Jolly, & K. Sylva (Eds.), *Play: Its role in development and evolution* (pp. 537–554). New York: Basic Books.

Vygotsky, L. (1978). *Mind in society: The development of psychological processes.* Cambridge, MA: Harvard University Press.

Walker, C. (1999). Playing a story: Narrative and writing-like feature of scenes of dramatic play. *Reading Research and Instruction, 38,* 401–413.

Weir, R. (1962). *Language in the crib.* The Hague, Netherlands: Mouton.

Wells, G., & Chang-Wells, G. (1992). *Constructing knowledge together: Classrooms as centers of inquiry and literacy.* Portsmouth, NH: Heinemann Educational Books.

Whitehurst, G. J., & Lonigan, C. J. (1998). Child development and emergent literacy. *Child Development, 69,* 848–872.

Wolfgang, C. (1974). An exploration of the relationship between the cognitive area of reading and selected developmental aspects of children's play. *Psychology in the Schools, 11,* 338–343.

Yaden, D., Rowe, D., & MacGillivray, L. (2000). Emergent literacy: A matter (polyphony) of perspectives. In M. Kamil, P. Mosenthal, P. D. Pearson, & R. Barr (Eds.), *Handbook of reading research* (Vol. III, pp. 425–454). Mahwah, NJ: Erlbaum.

Note: Minor changes have been made to this chapter as it was originally published in order to conform with the volume's editorial style. These changes have not altered the meaning of the chapter's content in any way.

APPENDIX A

Coding Matrix

Probes			
1.0 **The problem is...**			
2.0 **Explained by...**			
2.1 direct statement			
2.2 comparison			
2.3 providing a rationale			
2.4 conditional inferring			
2.5 evaluating			
3.0 **The theory is...**			
4.0 **The preferred solution path is...**			
5.0 **The setting is...**			
6.0 **Data are analyzed by...**			
6.1 quantitative statistics			
6.2 classifying/ categorizing			
6.3 ranking/ weighting			
6.4 summarizing/ generating themes			
6.5 computing/ tabulating			
6.6 competing matrices			
7.0 **Conclusions based on...**			
7.1 counting			
7.2 patterns/themes			
7.3 plausibility			

(continued)

(Appendix A continued)

7.4 clustering			
7.5 making metaphors			
7.6 splitting variables			
7.7 subsuming particulars			
7.8 factoring			
7.9 noting relations between variables			
7.10 finding intervening variables			
7.11 building logical chain of evidence			
7.12 making conceptual/ theoretical coherence			
8.0 Conclusions confirmed by...			
8.1 representativeness			
8.2 check for bias			
8.3 triangulating			
8.4 weighting evidence			
8.5 making contrasts			
8.6 checking outliers			
8.7 using extreme cases			
8.8 ruling out spurious relations			
8.9 replicating a finding			
8.10 checking out rival explanations			
8.11 looking for negative evidence			
8.12 getting feedback from informants			

APPENDIX B

Step 3 — It is true?

Author	Agree	Disagree	Uninformed (lacks knowledge relevant to the problem)	soundness		completeness	
				Misinformed a) asserts what is not the case; (b) making assertions contrary to fact; (c) evidences & reasons not good enough in quantity or quality	Illogical (fallacy in reasoning)*non sequitur *inconsistent *reasons poorly from good grounds	Incomplete (not solved all the problems started with)	Suspend Judgment

PLAY IN THE MULTICULTURAL WORLD OF CHILDREN: IMPLICATIONS FOR ADULTS

Barbara Bowman

All young children are predisposed to move their bodies, seek human comfort, exercise their senses, communicate with others, and play. Play, like these other behaviors, arises from the nexus of evolution, individual genes, and particular environments, making it both a biological and a social phenomenon. Although the drive to play is built into the human blueprint, physical and social environments shape children's natural predisposition. The process, of course, can encounter obstacles. For example, children can be too disabled to play—as in the case of profoundly retarded children; environments may be too frightening to permit play—as in the case of children living in danger (Garbarino, Subrow, Kostelny, & Pardo, 1992); and interpersonal relationships can be too unsupportive—as in orphanages (Carlson & Earls, 1997). Nevertheless, most children play, even in the most noxious and depriving circumstances, which indicates that play is an important facet of childhood.

A considerable body of theory and research endorses play both as an aid to development (Erikson, 1950; Freud, 1963; Piaget, 1962); Vygotsky, 1978) and as a method to teach children cultural skills and knowledge (Dewey, 1938; Montessori, 1964; Rousseau, 1762/1911). Play has long been viewed as essential for young children, but in recent years, the priority given to play has become controversial as Americans have become increasingly concerned about children's school achievement. *A Nation at Risk* (National Commission on Excellence in Education, 1983) highlighted for the public the importance of schooling. The report made the connection between education and the future economic and social vitality of the country and subjected schools to considerable pressure to improve children's academic performance. Early childhood programs were not exempt from this pressure. Many programs responded by decreasing the amount of time allotted to play and increasing the time spent on academic-oriented activities, particularly for children at educational risk. Lately, the emphasis on early literacy acquisition has intensified this trend. The push to have all children be accomplished readers by third grade has led many programs to shift time from free play to more direct teaching of the alphabet, phonemic awareness, letter-sound relationships, and beginning reading.

Many early childhood educators see this approach as wrong-headed. In their view, self-directed play is essential for young children, and premature use of didactic methods, as well as a focus on unrelated and abstract bits of information, interferes with children's understanding and interest. They contend that academic goals can be accomplished by enriching play rather than by prematurely forcing children into school-type curricula and methods. This chapter focuses on what we currently know about play that can help early childhood teachers who are concerned about the literacy development of low-income and culturally diverse children. The intent of the chapter is to connect practitioners' questions and concerns with the research and best-practice literature.

What Is Play?

Play is hard to define, and its functions are not always apparent. Part of the difficulty is that play is a mix of physical, emotional, social, and cognitive components that require coordination among neural structures and behavioral systems (Haight & Black, 2001). Play, rather than being a single activity, involves a variety of behaviors, many of which seem to have little in common. Three examples illustrate the difficulty. The first took place on the top of a mountain in eastern Turkey. A young shepherd minding sheep had set a number of small rocks in a pattern around him. I asked him what he was doing, and he smiled and said he was playing with them. Each rock, he said, was a sheep, and he moved them around. He imagined scenarios—perhaps a wolf threatening or a female giving birth—and the herd's reactions and probably also his own. The second example took place in a Montessori program where a suburban 5-year-old American child was washing a table. She was unsmiling, talking to herself, and scrubbing with meticulous attention. She was obviously enacting a previously observed social activity, but we do not know who she imagined herself to be or the context that required her talk. And finally, on a school play yard, a young African American boy was running about, dribbling a basketball, speeding up and slowing down, zigzagging, and feinting. We do not know whether he was pretending to be Michael Jordan or not, but his body movements reflected his understanding of himself playing an adult game.

What draws these examples together as play? Not the content, not the affect, not the outcomes. The boy in Turkey had made a game out of shepherding, a serious responsibility, and his enjoyment of his play was obvious. The 5-year-old washing the table gave no outward signs of joy and invested the task with far more seriousness than it realistically demanded. And the ball dribbler played at an adult's game with the same seriousness of purpose as the table washer, but showed little of the joy of the shepherd. Despite the differences, the children's play shares common elements: it is personal, social, and intelligent. In the above examples, although the imagined content was not evident, the children's affects—pleasure, concentration, purposeful-ness—showed that the activities were personally meaningful. They also demon-strated considerable social knowledge about the common activities in their community and their ability to participate in these. And through their manipulation of objects and themselves, the children showed their ability to untie ideas from ob-jects and imagine alternative ways to view the world and themselves in it.

The research endorses these characteristics of play, On the personal level, play seems to function as a homeostatic mechanism, helping children cope with feelings and thoughts (Erikson, 1950; Piaget, 1962) that they find disturbing, confusing, or both. Presumably, play helps them "make sense" (if only to themselves) of what they know and of what they are trying to know. Play is a form of emotional, social, and cognitive self-regulation, relieving affects and clarifying concepts that arise from their experiences. It is also intensely social. Ethologists and psychologists note that the impetus to play seems to be a vehicle through which animals and children learn the organization and skills of their group. They point out that, in play, animals prac-tice the skills that lead to social competence (Power, 2000; Rogoff, 1990; Vygotsky, 1978). They try out social roles and responsibilities as well as hone skills and con-solidate knowledge about activities that are valued by their community. Play also is implicated in children's intellectual development. By manipulating real-life activities for their own purposes, thus creating nonliteral interpretations of experience, chil-dren learn to untie ideas from their concrete referents and create more abstract con-cepts by which to understand the world and themselves in it.

Inasmuch as children are highly motivated to persist in play activities, they are likely to acquire greater understanding and skill in the tasks that are regularly a part of their play, which may account for the correlation between play and children's in-creasing skill as well as knowledge. Because children play within the context of what they experience in their daily lives, the task of assessing how much of their knowl-edge is attributable to their play as opposed to their other activities is difficult (Power, 2000). However, whether or not play itself teaches, children's enjoyment of play paired with the practice of physical, social, emotional, and intellectual skills of-fers a unique educational opportunity.

Play and Development

In general, children's play follows a developmental sequence. Infants play with their own and their caregivers' bodies. Later, games with repetitive formats, such as peek-a-boo, interest children. Toddlers like locomotive and manipulative play such as pull-push and construction toys, but soon add on roughhousing and chasing games. And finally, during the preschool years, social dramatic play and games with rules occupy children. This sequence, however, is subject to enormous individual and cultural variation and, thus, is difficult to use as a guide to normative age-play correlations.

Dividing play into purposes and sequences makes it easier to think about but does little to clarify what children are doing in a given instance when they play. For instance, when we see children enacting a story like the trolls under the bridge, we wonder whether the primary purpose is to engage with other children, re-create a story, practice confronting fears or fantasizing bravery, understand the physics of a bridge, experience the excitement of leaping out of concealment, please the teacher, or some combination of the above. And how does whatever the child is doing translate into developmental change?

Does play affect neural structures of the brain? Animal studies provide potential models for how this kind of phenomenon might happen. For example, studies showing the increase in cognitive functioning when animals are exposed to complex social and physical environments (Perry, 1995) suggest at least a threshold of stimulation is necessary for optimum development. Does this finding mean that some amount of play is necessary to trigger development? If so, how much play do young children need? Are cognitive or social dangers likely if young children do not enjoy long periods of self-directed play in an enriched environment? What is the ideal balance between self-directed play and play as a vehicle for social knowledge and skills?

Many questions remain about play for which we do not have ready answers, and researchers and practitioners continue to study it. Yet, despite the ambiguities and complexities, we can accept, at least for now, the notion that play is important to children. It has multiple forms, offers opportunities to practice emotional-social, cognitive, and physical skills, and it is associated with personal and social gains. By combining pleasure with activities, play promotes learning.

Play and Culture

Culture exerts a powerful influence on the amount, type, and content of play, making it difficult to identify normative patterns or essential components. Studies of play in diverse cultures indicate that all children play, and on one level, their play is quite similar. During a visit to an African American community, for example, one is apt to see 5-year-old girls jumping double Dutch, and in a middle-class white community, the same age children may be riding bikes. In these examples, the children use the themes and materials from their own communities, but the underlining content— gross motor exercise—is the common element. Thus, using these and other examples, we can say that children's play across cultures is quite similar. They all chase, roughhouse, explore, fantasize, practice, create, play games with rules, and so forth.

Relationships with others play a critical role in children's play. Caregivers, and older children, frame children's exploration of the world; buffer too-stressful experiences; scaffold new learning; stimulate and support communications between children and other people; and guide them into the conventions of the society, including how, when, and what they play.

As an example, think of a toddler playing with a shape toy. He or she starts by trying to force a piece through a hole, whether it fits or not. Imagine three different scenarios. In one, the adults leave the toddler completely alone to figure out for him- or herself how the toy works. In another scene, the adult takes the shaped piece away from the child and puts it into its slot. And in the third scene, the adult lets the toddler try for awhile, but when the child does not get it, the adult turns the child's hand or the toy just a little so the piece goes into its place.

What do children learn in these different scenarios? We may assume the adult behavior has the same meaning, but this assumption is not necessarily true. Meanings are not determined in isolation but by the larger social context, which, depending on the situation, may attribute quite different meanings to the same behavior. In the first example where the child is left alone, he or she may learn either that grown-ups do not care much about this kind of activity or that they value independence. The child may feel successful, or he or she may be frustrated and stop trying. In the second scenario where the adult takes the puzzle piece and demonstrates the solution, the child may learn that he or she is not capable of accomplishing the task or that he or she should look to the adult for guidance and teaching. The child may feel either defeated and ineffective or supported and confident that help is at hand. And in the third example where the child gets a little help, he or she may learn either that adults value this kind of play and will help him or her accomplish what he or she wishes or that the balance between independence and dependence will be mediated by the adult. These examples are, of course, vastly oversimplified, but they bring home both the similarity and diversity in how play is encouraged and valued among different groups.

Outward similarities in play can mask underlying differences in meaning, an alternative understanding of the world (Roopnarine, Johnson, & Hooper, 1994). In most communities, children "play school," but close observation shows that *how* they play is different in authoritarian communities than it is in a freer society where individuality and creativity are valued. Similarly, the age-old "boogie man" found in most cultures is undoubtedly not the same for children who live in communities where adults do not share their fear as he is for children in a superstitious society where adults also are fearful. Similarly, the "boogie man" is certainly not the same for children who live in environments that are dark at night as he is for children who have a nightlight to keep scary things at bay. In addition, cultural variations occur in the amount of time children spend on different types of play. The American pattern of father-son roughhousing is rare in New Delhi, perhaps because of the importance in India of family cooperation throughout the life cycle (Roopnarine, Hossain, Gil, & Brophy, 1994).

The meaning of play is embedded in children's culture, therefore we must be cautious about interpreting it. A number of studies correlate parental encouragement of play with more complex behavior and enhanced cognitive functioning. Mothers' responsiveness, verbal stimulation, positive affect, and object stimulation as well as the absence of restrictedness and negative affect during the preschool years lead to more positive cognitive outcomes, and parent-child play that includes high levels of verbal stimulation correlates with better language development, at least in the United States (Power, 2000). Care must be used in interpreting this observation because other cultures may use different strategies to achieve similar goals.

The reported differences in the play of various social classes also can be misleading. Smilansky (1968) and others found that the sociodramatic play of some immigrant Israeli children was less socially and linguistically complex than that of middle-class Israeli children. The same finding has been reported about low-income children in the United States. Seemingly, middle-class children in Israel and in the United States are more likely to engage in complex verbal play interactions and be more successful in school than are low-income children. However, focusing only on sociodramatic play may detract from other uses of language and communication styles that children may have. For many example, African American children have smaller vocabularies than most middle-class white American children (Bowman, Donovan, & Burns, 2001), yet they have more expressive body language, play complex word games (the "dozens," for instance), or use speech rhythm for communication—talents that go unappreciated if only one context and type of language is considered. Cross-cultural comparisons also may mask differences in community ideas about with whom children should talk as well as where, when, and how that talking should happen. Children from some American Indian tribes, for instance, may be judged language deficient because they speak more slowly than most other Americans. They may also hesitate to speak in the presence of adults, and thus the extent of their verbal knowledge may not be elicited in preschool programs or in comparisons with children from mainstream, middle-class communities.

Erikson (1950) commented, "No ego can develop outside of social processes which offer workable prototypes and roles" (p. 366). Play prepares children for the culture in which they live and reflects that culture. However, as children interact with people from other groups as well as view television and movies portraying other cultures, they try to understand the ideas of other people; they try to make sense of them in the context of their own culture. An example of the stretch this accommodation represents occurred in a village in Ghana where children nightly watched the single television set, which showed American westerns. An informant confided that, as a consequence of these shows, the children called fighting "playing American." As increasing numbers of American children attend programs in culturally diverse settings, they will gather insights—correct or not—into the behavior of others, which will be reflected in their play as they struggle to integrate conflicting ideas and feelings.

Play in Early Childhood Programs

Five psychological perspectives have influenced programs for young children's care and education. First, the maturation-oriented perspective promotes a child-centered approach to pedagogy. Following the lead of philosophers like Jean-Jacques

Rousseau (1762/1911), this approach stressed the orderly unfolding of development. Kohlberg and Mayer (1972) wrote that advocates of this perspective "hold that what comes from within the child is the most important aspect of development; therefore the pedagogical environment should be permissive enough to allow the inner 'good' to unfold" (p. 451). Accordingly, play is highly valued, and the adult role is to interfere as little as possible as children do what is natural. The optimal educational experience is for the child to have the time to develop (Gesell, Ames, & Ilg, 1940).

Second, the behavioral perspective uses a didactic approach to education. It comes from empiricist philosophy and focuses on the responsibility of adults to teach children the common culture, primarily academic skills. This perspective advocates one form or another of direct instruction of content organized in well-structured lessons that transmit what the adult determines the child needs to know, rather than a form in which education follows the interests of the child (Bereiter & Englemann, 1966). This adult-centered approach has often been called "traditional" because it is modeled on schools for older children. Play is disdained as an educational tool; although children may do it, no reason justifies including it in educational programs.

Third, the constructivist perspective follows the lead of John Dewey (1938) and Jean Piaget (1962), who emphasized the need for children to construct knowledge from their experience. Children are thought to have an innate ability to create schemas, or frames of knowledge and action, which they apply as they interact with their environment. If their current constructions prove inadequate, they will reconstruct their thinking to accommodate new information and experience. The constructivist view is child-centered and leads to a progressive form of education in which, instead of teaching children answers to problems, adults encourage children to find answers for themselves. The ideal form of education involves neither instruction nor laissez-faire free play but, rather, an adult structuring the environment so the child can integrate new ideas and concepts into his or her old thinking. The adult provides children with food for thought, or food for play, which fosters children's natural propensity to develop and learn.

Fourth, the psychodynamic perspective, of which Erik Erikson (1950) and Barbara Biber (n.d.; Biber & Franklin, 1968) were proponents, asserts that play is primarily an outlet for emotional expression. Through play, children get control of their affects and social behavior. In this sense, play is self-curative as children relive and rehearse their response to troubling situations or events, achieving mastery over them. Children naturally strive to cope with their inner world, and play offers an opportunity for them to experiment with various balances between fantasy and reality. The adult role is to offer security and support so play does not lead to conflict with the constraints of reality or overwhelm the child with anxiety or fear. This approach also lays the theoretical framework for using play as an intervention for troubled children.

Finally, the sociocultural perspective is based primarily on theories that contend that children learn to construct ideas and ways of thinking essentially through social interaction (Rogoff, 1990; Vygotsky, 1978). Adults stimulate children's learning as they focus children's attention on relevant clues and strategies for solving problems and through their differential response to the child's efforts (called scaffolding). These interactions help children construct their knowledge in a way that gradually comes to resemble that of the adult community in which they live. Ideally, the process of co-construction of knowledge involves a high degree of adult engagement and guidance.

Throughout most of the last century, play was considered an important focus for early education (Biber & Franklin, 1968; Dewey, 1938; Erikson, 1950; Isaacs, 1968; Johnson, 1972; Leeper, Dales, Skipper, & Witherspoon, 1974; Montessori, 1964). In nursery schools, child-directed interactions with materials, peers, and adults (termed "free play") occupied a large segment of the daily program. Teachers structured children's play (and, presumably, their learning) by providing materials (blocks, dress-up clothes, games, toys) and space (housekeeping corners, tables, building areas) as well as time to use them. Children were expected to play freely with materials and equipment, alone and with others.

Nursery schools were popular with upper middle-class families, but they were generally not available for low-income children. In 1965, as the relationship between early experience and later learning gained credibility, the federal government funded Head Start to enroll poor children, many from racial and linguistic minority communities. Of concern was the poor academic trajectory of these children, and the hope was that an earlier start would compensate for the disadvantages they experienced in their families and communities. In most of these new Head Start programs, play still was considered an important, if not the primary, activity.

A few model programs moved sharply away from the play tradition, increasing the amount of preplanned didactic instruction and reducing or eliminating free play (Bereiter & Englemann, 1966). Advocates of these models contended that low-income children did not have time to play in school. Others, later discredited by the genetic scientists, contended that African American children did not learn the same way as white children and, therefore, that their educational programs needed to focus on basic skills rather than on abstract thinking (Jensen, 1973). For these children, self-selected and playful activities were seen as "noneducational," and therefore, not worthy of pedagogical attention.

Although the most didactic-type programs were designed for low-income children, the emphasis on early academic learning began to infiltrate programs for all young children. This practice evoked concern about what was called "push down" curricula. In 1987, the National Association for the Education of Young Children (NAEYC) took a stand in opposition to programs that were heavily laden with direct instruction. NAEYC asserted that play is an essential component of exemplary practice, which they termed "developmentally appropriate" (Bredekamp, 1987). More recently, NAEYC revised its position on appropriate practice, endorsing a more culturally relevant and educationally diverse set of practices. Nevertheless, the organization again went on record in defense of play, saying it supports children's social, emotional, and cognitive development and that child-initiated, teacher-supported play is important in developmentally appropriate practice. Support for this position was found in developmental theory and in correlations between children's play and heightened cognitive performance as well as social competence (Bredekamp & Copple, 1997).

The knowledge base for early childhood education is uncomfortably lean (Eisner, 1985; Fein & Schwartz, 1982; Hatch & Freeman, 1988; Spodek, 1991; Walsh, 1991), and the value of play-based programs has not gone unchallenged. Weikart (1988) criticized developmentally appropriate practices as being too inclusive, without "internal consistency," and unsubstantiated by rigorous research. Jones (1991) found that practitioners often define diametrically opposite practices as being developmentally appropriate. Play-based, developmentally appropriate practice has also been criticized as insensitive to cultural differences, giving too little attention to contextual factors and reflecting only mainstream culture. Families complain that indirect and child-centered teaching programs stressing play deny their children the "information" they need to be successful (Delpit, 1988; Jipson, 1991; Kessler, 1991).

Educators differ on the emphasis that should be put on unstructured play in group settings for all children. These disagreements suggest that there is no single ideal program appropriate for all children and that play, like other variables, needs to respond to program goals and participants' needs and wishes.

Literacy and Play

Writing and reading, like speaking and drawing, are ways of making, interpreting, and communicating meaning. Although children are genetically primed to learn language and to draw, literacy is different. Children have to be taught. Some children need a great deal of instruction and some less, but all children must learn the arbitrary squiggles their language uses and must learn to translate them into sounds, words, and thoughts. The correlation between children's preliteracy knowledge and skills and their success in learning to read and write focused attention on the importance of early childhood for teaching and learning (Snow, Burns, & Griffin, 1998). The timetable for learning literacy skills shows considerable variability from child to child and from community to community; however, the necessary base includes (a) grasp of the language structure and normative vocabulary in the language in which literacy is to be learned; (b) understanding the relationship of oral to written language; and (c) recognition of letters and their sounds. Opportunities to learn these things must match with a child's attentional capabilities, which in turn are influenced by level of maturation, interests, and behavioral expectations. In addition, these opportunities must be consistent with age-related developmental characteristics as these are defined by the child's unique genetic endowment, the environmental contexts in which learning is to occur, and the behavioral expectations of the child's social world.

Literacy is supported by a complex set of attitudes, expectations, feelings, and behaviors (McLane & McNamee, 1990; Snow et al., 1998; Teal & Sulzby, 1986), many of which can be found in children's play. For example, early experience with symbolic relations in which one object is used to stand for another presumably contributes to symbolic sensitivity. Toddlers, for instance, demonstrate their ability to understand iconic representation when they close their eyes to indicate sleep. They also are able to substitute one object for another and use it as if it were the real thing, as indicated when a block becomes a piece of toast during play in the doll corner. Preschoolers bring environmental signs into their play—the McDonald's arches, for example—showing their ability to deal in symbols.

Play can offer ideal experiences for children to integrate literacy into their understanding. Opportunities to use the tools associated with literacy before beginning formal instruction seem to advance children's understanding of the reading-writing process (Gundlach, McLane, Stott, & McNamee, 1982; McLane & McNamee, 1990; Teal & Sulzby, 1986). In play, children talk with others, tell and enact stories, and use literacy tools and, consequently, are likely to learn to read earlier and more easily than children who do not have these type of experiences (Bowman et al., 2001; Snow et al., 1998). Although playing at literacy can confer advantages, it is a mistake to assume that, because children have learned behaviors associated with reading, they also have mastered essential concepts. For example, a child may seem to be reading when, in fact, he or she simply has memorized the words associated with a picture in a book. Or, the child may choose a desired record from a pile, using scratches and other identifiers, rather than the letters, to do so. Thus, children may think they are reading or may pretend to be reading without mastering the core task of literacy: decoding the alphabet into sounds, words, and thoughts. Without more intentional teaching, then, children may not move beyond superficial understanding of literacy.

Print in the environment does not guarantee literacy. Junk mail, notices, TV guides, food, medicines, and cosmetics are ubiquitous, even in the homes of children who have difficulty reading and writing. Instruction alone is insufficient, as indicated by the number of children from various communities who do not learn these skills in school. Literacy, like other learning, is embedded in social relationships. When adults and children focus together on literacy activities using complex ideas and language, children's interest is high and their learning is increased. Learning is enhanced when high-quality cognitive and linguistic interactions occur between children and the adults who are meaningful to them. Children who are most likely to learn to read easily and well have caregivers who are literate and can model the use of print; who endow print activities with both emotional and social meaning as well as offer help, instruction, and reinforcement; and who encourage children to explore and experiment for themselves by providing materials and opportunity. These interactions can be particularly effective when they occur within the context of play.

Learning (including literacy) is less likely to occur when children come from low-literacy families and communities whose belief systems, values, and practices conflict with those of schools (Au & Kawakami, 1991; Heath, 1983; Lubeck, 1994); however, certain programs have successfully taught reading and writing to children such as these. Perhaps the best known of these programs is described by Ashton-Warner (1964), who collected the content for teaching children to read and write from their daily lives and their own vocabulary. Connecting children's home lives to literacy instruction recognizes the importance of prior context knowledge to learning new skills and suggests that family and community are important considerations in effective literacy programs for young children. Play offers ideal ways to bring together what children already know with the skills and knowledge teachers want to instill.

Oral language is at the core of literacy and, generally, predicts the ease with which children will learn to read and write (Snow et al., 1998). An apparent connection happens between sociodramatic play and literacy. In social play, children negotiate a story line (often diffuse, to be sure), manage the players (taking into account social conventions and norms), and move back and forth between reality and fantasy. These experiences feed their understanding of narrative and set the stage for its parallel in reading and writing. Although the association between play behavior and literacy is strong, as in other aspects of play, there is little direct evidence of a causal direction. However, whether children gain an understanding of literacy by playing, whether their literacy play reinforces what they already know, or whether both may occur, play and literacy intertwine.

Does a role for play exist in promoting literacy in early childhood programs? This question earns an unqualified yes. The more significant question is, what kind and how much of a role? The answer to that question must be determined, to a large extent, by program objectives and children's readiness to achieve them. The following observations and suggestions can assist in considering the role of play in programs and how that role can add to the education of culturally diverse children.

Play is a natural ability that children use to manage intrapsychic stress, integrate new knowledge, and control feelings. Consequently, its mental health and cognitive value should not be overlooked. Children in full-day programs need time to refresh themselves with self-selected play. Whether play should be encouraged in part-day programs depends on the goals of the program and whether children can take advantage of the self-curative powers of play at other times during the day.

Play performs a therapeutic function for children who live in home environments that are traumatic or excessively stressful. Providing a safe and supportive place to play can give children the time to work through the problems they confront. Children who are competently working through their feelings about themselves, others, and the world around them are more likely to be interested and able to learn.

Satisfactory interpersonal relationships free children to learn from others. In line with research on parent-child relationships, teachers whose relationships with children are positive, warm, and responsive are most likely to influence how and what children learn. This dynamic applies not only to children's play but also to other learning. Teachers who speak to children in ways that show their regard and interest in children's learning and who provide contingent responses have the greatest effect. Close and supportive relationships can be demonstrated in a variety of ways depending on cultural prototypes. Nevertheless, when well-loved teachers encourage learning, whether in play or didactic lessons, learning is more likely to occur.

Oral language is basic to literacy, and children from different cultural communities have different languages, different ways children and adults relate to one another, and different communication styles and conventions. If a program's goal is to extend and enrich children's speech, teachers must begin by understanding the language framework children already have. Thus, they must speak to children in ways that children understand. The teacher's job is to find a bridge between what children know and what the curriculum is designed to teach. Children can learn multiple languages, styles, and conventions, but when too large a chasm exists between home and school talk—emotionally and linguistically—program effectiveness is compromised (Bowman, 1991). If teachers cannot discover what children already know, they lose valuable learning time and, at worst, they alienate children and their families, decreasing the likelihood of children taking in new patterns of communication. Play offers an excellent opportunity to gain insight into what children already know and a pleasurable way to enrich their speech.

Low-income and linguistic and racial minority families have life experiences quite different from people whose background is more mainstream. They have developed beliefs, values, and behavior patterns that make sense to them and are backed by their experience in the world. Programs seeking to augment or change family patterns must face up to these differences and work for compromise between parents' and programs' goals (Bowman & Stott, 1994). For example, programs wishing to stress informal learning and play-based curricula may select methods that conflict with the preferences of parents who believe that more formal lessons in the basic skills are necessary for school achievement. Programs must confront these kind of differences and either convince parents of the effectiveness of the programs' strategies or incorporate the parents' perspective into their program.

In a world in which literacy is highly valued, children rehearse their understanding by incorporating it into their play and teachers can influence children's play by providing new and challenging experiences. Because children are highly motivated to play and, by playing, practice skills and consolidate knowledge, encouraging play can be a useful strategy to promote learning. Providing similar practice in adult-enforced didactic lessons can be costly in time, enjoyment, and effort for both children and their teachers. For its motivational characteristics alone, teachers should use play to promote voluntary use of what children know. Without an infusion of new stimulation, children can use only what they have already experienced. Programs that seek to extend children's knowledge to include school-related content will need to add this new content to children's programs. The National Research Council's Committee on Early Childhood Pedagogy (Bowman, Donovan, & Burns, 2001) recommended that programs provide a broad, intellectually significant curriculum, one that balances the children's need for information with their need to integrate new ideas into already-formed schemas. One of the best ways to support literacy learning is by offering a literacy-rich environment, which offers children multiple opportunities to participate in literacy activities with adults. Although children can learn to read and write without a great many previous print experiences, they experience much more difficulty in doing so. They learn best when literacy is modeled, expected, enjoyed, and valued in the family and in other early childhood settings. Direct instruction may be the most economical method to accomplish this type of learning; however, teachers must be careful to maintain children's interest and motivation as their students grapple with the new ideas.

Teachers can directly teach by scaffolding children's play. Research on mother-child play suggests that, when adults play with children, play is more complex and verbal. Also, children incorporate the objects available in their environment as themes for their play. When the materials of literacy are provided and their uses demonstrated in their play with adults, children are apt to include these in their spontaneous play. Play that involves using the tools of written language (books, paper, crayons, markers, pens, computers), pretending to be readers and writers, and role-playing story books and children's dictated stories can extend children's understanding of literacy. These activities permit children to experiment with and integrate writing and reading into their way of thinking about the world. Play with literacy artifacts also helps children make personal connections to writing and reading as well as to feel some ownership and control over the roles and materials associated with being literate (McLane & McNamee, 1990).

Teachers must attend to not only the structure for children's play but also its content. Children often must learn new play patterns as well as new skills and knowledge. Although sociodramatic play may be a great medium for enhancing language, simply providing props may not stimulate the desired play. Similarly, children who have not learned to use unstructured time for sociodramatic play may fight, run around aimlessly, or break up things rather than practice language. How children respond to play opportunities depends on their prior playing experience. If teachers want to change or add to their repertoire, they must teach children the new forms and not assume that particular forms are universal and natural for all children. Play can provide a window on children's understanding. Young children often are able to imitate a model without understanding the real meaning of their actions. Play offers an opportunity for observant teachers to assess children's understanding, and to check whether their curriculum is becoming part of children's natural learning system—play.

Many different types of play can be useful for young children. One of the more useful types combines play with more formal content (Gandini & Edwards, 2001; Katz, 1996). This format encourages children's learning by capitalizing on their interest in a particular topic to help them gain new information and represent it in meaningful ways. Drawing and painting are particularly useful methods for combining play and formal content, but so, too, are methods combining literacy activities with the housekeeping corner or with the blocks. For example, a block building labeled by children as a train may be the starting point for taking a pretend trip, presenting a story about trains, bringing examples of tickets to the classroom, and encouraging children to make tickets to use in their play. This combining approach offers teachers the opportunity to ratchet up children's knowledge and skills within the context of a highly motivating activity.

No matter what teaching methods are used, teacher education is essential. The relationship between mothers' education and children's achievement is well established, and a similar connection has been found between teacher-caregiver education in centers and child achievement (Bowman et al., 2001). In centers where teachers have higher levels of both general and professional education, children show more complex interactions with adults and more complex play with peers (Howes & Smith, 1995). Similar findings are reported by Christie (1991), who studied Head Start teachers. He found that teachers with less education did not offer the kind of rich and stimulating conversation necessary to enrich children's thinking and play. This finding suggests that, for children to learn from their play, the teacher must have considerable knowledge of literacy-supporting concepts and behaviors.

The timing of literacy expectations for children are not cut in developmental stone. In the United States, the pendulum has swung back and forth between early emphasis on academic skills and early opportunities for play. Other countries with high standards, like Japan and Sweden, delay reading instruction until later than we do, and their children become competent. However, these countries have less cultural diversity among school children, so children move along a similar learning trajectory. Nevertheless, slowing down formal instruction to make sure that all children have more complex oral language and are highly motivated to engage in literacy activities is likely to be beneficial. This approach might prevent the failures that many children experience when they lack the firm platform on which to build instruction in reading and writing. If so, playful acquisition of literacy skills and knowledge may not only increase children's competence but also promote children's enjoyment of literacy activities.

Conclusions

In summary, how adults structure experiences for children either fosters their drive to learn and to make sense of their learning or stifles their interest and encourages superficial understanding. *Eager to Learn* (Bowman et al., 2001) pointed out that many teaching strategies *can* work, and effective teachers use a range of techniques, including direct instruction and play. Effective teachers also organize the classroom environment and plan ways to pursue educational goals in both child-initiated activities and in teacher-planned and teacher-initiated activities. Further, smaller group size and teacher education correlate with more complex play. The essential message is that play is a powerful tool in the teaching tool kit and the wise teacher is the one who makes good use of it.

References

Ashton-Warner, S. (1964). *Teacher*. New York: Bantam Books.

Au, K. H., & Kawakami, A. J. (1991). Culture and ownership. *Childhood Education, 67*(5), 280–284.

Bereiter, C., & Englemann, S. (1966). *Teaching disadvantaged children in preschool*. Englewood Cliffs, NJ: Prentice-Hall.

Biber, B. (n.d.). *The adaptation of the teaching role*. New York: Bank Street College Publication.

Biber, B., & Franklin, M. (1968). The relevance of developmental and psychodynamic concepts to the education of the preschool child. In M. Almy (Ed.), *Early childhood play* (pp. 21–41). New York: Simon and Schuster.

Bowman, B. (1991). Educating language-minority children: Challenges and opportunities. In S. L. Kagan & K. J. Scott (Eds.), *The care and education of America's young children: Obstacles and opportunities* (pp. 17–19). Chicago: University of Chicago Press.

Bowman, B., Donovan, S., & Burns, M. S. (2001). *Eager to learn.* Washington, DC: National Academy Press.

Bowman, B., & Stott, F. (1994). Understanding development in a cultural context: The challenge for teachers. In B. L. Mallory & R. S. New (Eds.), *Diversity and developmentally appropriate practices: Challenges for early childhood education* (pp. 119–133). New York: Teachers College Press.

Bredekamp, S. (1987). *Developmentally appropriate practices in early childhood programs from birth through age eight.* Washington, DC: National Association for the Education of Young Children.

Bredekamp, S., & Copple, C. (Eds.). (1997). *Developmentally appropriate practice in early childhood programs.* Washington, DC: National Association for the Education of Young Children.

Carlson, M., & Earls, F. (1997). Psychological and neuroendocrinological sequelae of early social deprivation in institutionalized children in Romania. In C. Carte, B. Lederhendler, & B. Kirkpatrick (Eds.), *Integrative neurobiology of affiliation. Annals of the New York Academy of Science, 807,* 419–428.

Christie, J. (1991). Psychological research on play: Connections with early literacy development. In J. Christie (Ed.), *Play and early literacy development* (pp. 27–43). New York: State University of New York Press.

Delpit, L. (1988). The silenced dialogue: Power and pedagogy in educating other people's children. *Harvard Educational Review, 58*(3), 280–298.

Dewey, J. (1938). *Education and experience.* New York: Collier Books.

Eisner, E. (1985). *The educational imagination: On the design and evaluation of school programs.* New York: Macmillan.

Erikson, E. (1950). *Childhood and society.* New York: Norton.

Fein, G., & Schwartz, O. (1982). Developmental theories in early education. In B. Spodek (Ed.), *Handbook on research in early childhood education* (pp. 82–104). New York: Free Press.

Freud, A. (1963). *Psychoanalysis for teachers and parents.* Boston: Beacon Press.

Gandini, L., & Edwards, C. (Eds.). (2001). *Bambini: The Italian approach to infant/toddler care.* New York: Teachers College Press.

Garbarino, J., Subrow, N., Kostelny, K., & Pardo, C. (1992). *Children in danger.* San Francisco: Jossey-Bass.

Gesell, A., Ames, L., & Ilg, F. (1940). The first five years of life. New Haven, CT: Yale Clinic for Child Development.

Gundlach, R., McLane, J., Stott, F., & McNamee, G. (1982). The social foundation of children's early writing development. In M. Farr (Ed.), *Advances in writing research* (Vol. 1, pp. 1–58). Norwood, NJ: Ablex.

Haight, W. L., & Black, J. E. (2001). A comparative approach to play: Cross-species and cross-cultural perspectives of play in development. *Human Development, 4,* 228–234.

Hatch, J. A., & Freeman, E. B. (1988). Kindergarten philosophies and practices: Perspectives of teachers, principals, and supervisors. *Early Childhood Research Quarterly, 3,* 151–166.

Heath, S. (1983). *Ways with words: Life and work in communities and classrooms.* New York: Cambridge University Press.

Howes, C., & Smith, E. (1995). Relations among child care quality, teacher behavior, children's play activities, emotional security, and cognitive activity in child care. *Early Childhood Research Quarterly, 10,* 381–404.

Isaacs, S. (1968). *The nursery years.* New York: Schocken Books.

Jensen, A. (1973). *Educability and group differences.* New York: Harper and Row.

Jipson, J. (1991). Extending the discourse on developmental appropriateness: A developmental perspective. *Early Education and Development, 2*(2), 95–108.

Johnson, H. (1972). *The nursery school.* New York: Agathon Press.

Jones, E. (1991). Do ECE people really agree? Or are we just agreeable? *Young Children, 46*(4), 59–61.

Katz, L. (1996). Interview with Lilian Katz on The Project Approach. *Scholastic early childhood today* (pp. 43–44). New York: Scholastic.

Kessler, S. (1991). Alternate perspectives on early childhood education. *Early Childhood Research Quarterly, 6,* 183–197.

Kohlberg, L., & Mayer, R. (1972). Development as the aim of education. *Harvard Educational Review, 42*(4), 449–469.

Leeper, S., Dales, R., Skipper, D., & Witherspoon, R. (1974). *Good schools for young children.* London: MacMillan.

Lubeck, S. (1994). The politics of developmentally appropriate practice: Exploring issues of culture, class, and curriculum. In B. Mallory & R. New (Eds.), *Diversity and developmentally appropriate practices* (pp. 17–43). New York: Teachers College Press.

McLane, J., & McNamee, G. (1990). *Early literacy.* Cambridge, MA: Harvard University Press.

Montessori, M. (1964). *The Montessori method.* New York: Schocken Books.

National Commission on Excellence in Education. (1983). *A nation at risk: The imperative for educational reform.* Washington, DC: Government Printing Office.

Perry, B. (1995). Incubated in terror: Neurodevelopmental factors in the "cycle of violence." In J. Osofsky (Ed.), *Children, youth and violence: Searching for solutions.* New York: Guilford.

Piaget, J. (1962). *Play, dreams and imitation in childhood.* New York: Norton.

Power, T. G. (2000). *Play and exploration in children and animals.* Mahwah, NJ: Erlbaum.

Rogoff, B. (1990). *Apprenticeship in thinking: Cognitive development in social context.* New York: Oxford University Press.

Roopnarine, J., Hossain, Z., Gil, P., & Brophy, H. (1994). Play in the East Indian context. In J. Roopnarine, J. Johnson, & F. Hooper (Eds.), *Children's play in diverse cultures* (pp. 9–30). Albany, NY: State University of New York Press.

Roopnarine, J., Johnson, J., & Hooper, F. (Eds.). (1994). *Children's play in diverse cultures.* Albany: State University of New York Press.

Rousseau, J. (1911). *Emile* (B. Foxley, Trans.). New York: Everyman's Library (Original work published 1762)

Smilansky, S. (1968). *The effects of sociodramatic play on disadvantaged preschool children.* Glenview, IL: Scott Foresman.

Snow, C., Burns, S., & Griffin, P. (Eds.). (1998). *Preventing reading difficulties in young children.* Washington, DC: National Academy Press.

Spodek, B. (1991). Reconceptualizing early childhood education: A commentary. *Early Education and Development, 2*(2), 161–167.

Teal, W., & Sulzby, E. (Eds.). (1986). *Emergent literacy: Writing and reading.* Norwood, NJ: Ablex.

Vygotsky. L. S. (1978). *Mind in society.* Cambridge, MA: Harvard University Press.

Walsh, D. J. (1991). Extending the discourse on developmental appropriateness: A developmental perspective. *Early Education and Development, 2*(2), 109–119.

Weikart, D. (1988). Quality in early education. In C. Warger (Ed.), *A resource guide to public school early childhood programs.* Alexandria, VA: Association for Supervision and Curriculum Development.

9

REVISITING SHARED MEANING: LOOKING THROUGH THE LENS OF CULTURE AND LINKING SHARED PRETEND PLAY THROUGH PROTO-NARRATIVE DEVELOPMENT TO EMERGENT LITERACY

Carollee Howes and Alison Gallwey Wishard

Imagine watching Maria and Elena[1] in the front room of their tiny bungalow in one of the poorer neighborhoods of Venice, California. Three-year-old cousins, only 8 months apart in age, Maria and Elena are pretending to wash their "babies." Forbidden to play with water, they have reluctantly agreed with the suggestion of their 14-year-old aunt, Tia Janie, that the "babies" could go into an upturned stool and be swished around instead of being put into the real bathtub. After the bath, the "babies" are carefully wrapped in blankets borrowed from a much younger sister and then, in parallel fashion, cradled in arms and rocked to sleep. The children use few words to enact this play. There is no script such as "You be the mommy and I'll be the sister and we will . . ."; instead, the children use nonverbal actions to share the meaning of the pretend play. By careful observation we, the observers, can ascertain

---

[1]Pseudonyms are used for children and programs throughout this chapter.

that the play indeed has a script (washing the babies), and roles (baby washer, dryer, and rocker) are enacted and exchanged by means of actions. A scholar interested in the emergence of shared meaning within social pretend play among peers (Farver, 1992; Howe, Rinaldi, Jennings, & Petrakos, 2002; Howes, 1985, 1992) might note that the children have communicated the symbolic meaning of their play through jointly constructed actions.

Now imagine observing this interaction as a researcher who is attempting to understand culture as integrated constellations of practices (Rogoff, 2002). A researcher in this capacity would want to know that Maria and Elena are the first and second daughters of sisters newly migrated from Oaxaca, Mexico, and that Tia Janie is Elena's big sister, who was born in Mexico and is newly migrated to Venice to help her aunt and mother care for the two younger children. Maria and Elena live with their mother and aunts, father and uncle, Janie, and two of Maria's father's brothers in a two-bedroom bungalow. All of the adults work—Elena's mom as a housekeeper, both fathers and Maria's mom as janitors, and Maria's uncles as day laborers. At any time of the day or night, some of the adults are sleeping and some are working. A researcher might also want to know that previous research in rural Mexican towns similar to Janie's birthplace has documented that children play pretend with peers, cousins, neighbors, and their mothers in the context of everyday life activities such as laundry (Farver & Howes, 1993). This researcher would also find it important to understand that Maria's and Elena's mothers are distressed because they worry that the younger girls have no freedom to go outside to play "as children should" in this strange and violent neighborhood in Venice (Garza Mourino, Rosenblatt, & Howes, 2001).

Now imagine stepping into the scene and asking Maria and Elena to tell the "story" of what they are doing. They might, especially if you provided some scaffolding (e.g., "What happened first when you washed babies?"), be able to begin the narrative at the beginning (e.g., "We are washing babies"), continue with a salient middle part (e.g., "Tia said, 'No water'"), and end with the end (e.g., "They are sleeping"). A scholar interested in the development and emergence of narratives and their link to emergent literacy (Heath, 1982, 1983; Imbens-Bailey & Snow, 1997; Snow, 1983) might focus on how jointly constructed narratives are a marker of the development of shared meaning and speculate that Maria and Elena are beginning to understand both the elements of a story and the significance of storytelling as defined by their specific cultural community.

Now finally, imagine being a teacher who observes a similar episode of baby-washing pretend play within the classroom. If you have been reading the National Association for the Education of Young Children's journal, *Young Children*, attending workshops sponsored by your local school district, or reading advice to parents in popular magazines, you might have a variety of strategies available. You could engage the children in a conversation about their play and redirect them to labeling babies and washtubs with appropriate signs of letters. You might have the children tell the washing babies story, make their own book by illustrating the transcription of the story, and then practice reading the story at home to Tia Janie. You might find a commercial book that shows and tells a story of children taking baths, read it with the girls, and talk with them about their pretend baby washing. Or you might "simply" note that Maria and Elena have acted out a complex pretend-play sequence and think about ways that you might help them move from a script in action to verbally negotiated scripts and roles in shared pretend and narrative. In this chapter, we will argue that this last strategy must be included in the teacher's "tool box" if children are to develop literacy. We suggest that a direct pathway to children's literacy forms through the development of shared meaning. We will further argue that only by examining shared meaning through the lens of cultural practices will we be able to link shared meaning to emergent literacy.

Sharing Meaning in Social Pretend Play

This chapter is a joint construction among researchers with a shared passion for understanding cultural practices but with divergent scholarly experiences and interests in shared meanings. Through the 1970s and 1980s, one of this chapter's authors, Carollee Howes, enacted a research agenda based on observations similar to the first of the imaginings that opened the chapter, shared meaning in social pretend play. This research program was nourished by two sets of experiences. The first set of experiences came from the field: an excellent early childhood teacher training program at the University of Delaware lab school followed by working with toddlers inside a Guatemalan orphanage and then working as a child-care teacher in an African American community. From these experiences, she came to value pretend play as an important activity of childhood and to understand that culture and shared meaning intersect. The second set of formative experiences occurred in graduate school, assisting a dynamic group of young researchers, including Ned Mueller, Jeff Brenner (Brenner & Mueller, 1982; Mueller & Brenner, 1977), and Deborah Lowe Vandell (Vandell, Wilson, & Buchanan, 1980), who used naturalistic observation to examine how very young children jointly construct social interactions.

We came to understand the developmental process of shared meaning. The toddlers who came together daily for 10 months in our research lab used actions to communicate meaning. Over time, and with numerous repetitions, meanings such as the "under the curtain game" became shared by the group of 2-year-olds (Brenner & Mueller, 1982). To play the "under the curtain game," the partners needed to understand the initiation (Child A goes under the curtain, turns to establish mutual gaze with the partner, drops the curtain to obscure mutual gaze, often accompanied by a giggle), the next turn required by the partner (Child B moves toward the curtain making a noise or a giggle), the response by the initiator (Child A lifts curtain again to establish mutual gaze, turns, and runs), and, finally, the action reversal (Child B lifts curtain, establishes mutual gaze, and runs in the same direction as Child A). To continue the game, either Child A circles to the curtain and repeats the actions or Child B, in a more sophisticated move, reverses and returns to the curtain so the children end up on either side of the curtain. Shared meaning in the peer play of toddlers, also called complementary and reciprocal play, requires not only mutual understanding of the goals and sequence of behaviors within an action sequence but also the social skills to reverse the actions of the partner while establishing mutual gaze (Howes, 1988).

To engage in social pretend play, children must incorporate pretend play into shared meaning (Howes, Unger, & Seidner, 1989). Pretend play is a category of play during which objects, actions, people, places, or other aspects of the here and now are transformed or treated nonliterally. To develop shared fantasy or shared pretend play, the children who are play partners must integrate their emerging understandings of pretend and their emerging social interaction skills. Social pretend play is easier to achieve when a more knowledgeable partner—a mother, a teacher, an older sibling— is the partner of the toddler or young preschooler (Dunn & Dale, 1984; Dunn & Hughes, 2001; Dunn & Shatz, 1989; Forys & McClune-Nicolich, 1984; Howes et al., 1989; Youngblade & Dunn, 1995). The more experienced partner can help the play along by scaffolding the pretending (e.g., "Are you pretending to be the Mommy?"), the social interaction (e.g., "If the baby cries what will the mommy do?"), or both. However, a series of cross-sectional and longitudinal studies with same-age children who had long histories of interaction with one another find that, by age 2 years, children can engage in cooperative social pretend play with an implicit script and roles, and, by age 3 years, they can engage in more complex social pretend play with elaborated verbal scripts as well as role assignment and negotiation (Forys & McClune-Nicolich, 1984; Howes & Matheson, 1992; Howes et al., 1989).

Sharing Meaning in Proto-Narratives

Pulling from ecocultural and sociocultural theory that places children's development within shared social interactions mediated through language, Alison Wishard has been seeking to understand how language provides content, structure, and meaning to social interactions and, thus, to children's developmental outcomes. This research interest emerged from experiences in the field in the 1990s and from subsequent graduate work in applied developmental psychology. Her experiences include her own challenges in understanding how to share meaning with others in a second language in a new culture while working in a Chilean orphanage for preschool-age children and then working as an assistant preschool teacher in an ethnically and linguistically diverse university community.

Children's earliest narratives, sometimes called "proto-narratives," are very short stories, sometimes only two utterances long, about routine experiences that are produced by children who are just learning to use talk to share meaning. Preschool children's proto-narratives and narratives are not actually individual productions; rather, they are collaborative undertakings co-constructed by two or more participants in an effort to interpret and anticipate experiences together. Similar to social pretend play, proto-narratives are easier for very young children to produce when their partner is more knowledgeable about narratives. When toddlers are engaged with an adult or older child, they can rely on extensive scaffolding and prompts from their more advanced conversational partners both in terms of the technical structure of their narratives and in terms of content orientation (Gleason & Melzi, 1997; Imbens-Bailey & Snow, 1997; Ochs & Capps, 2001; Snow & Imbens-Bailey, 1997). For these reasons, research on proto-narratives is almost exclusively placed within the context of adult-child talk. However, in the preschool context, when literacy props are placed within creative play activity centers (such as dress-up or coloring table), then oral narratives, with the assistance of the teacher, begin to transform into more formal written narratives.

Social Pretend Play Links to Proto-Narrative and to Emergent Literacy

Both social pretend play and proto-narratives are opportunities for children to share meaning with a partner. Cooperative social pretend play can be enacted without any verbal exchanges, but this type of social pretend play, with its implicit script and, certainly, with its complex social pretend play that requires the verbal negotiation of a script and differentiated roles, provides opportunities for children to jointly construct narratives. Narrative development, rather than language development in general, is directly linked to later literacy development (Snow & Tabors, 1993). Narratives, especially fully developed ones that follow a standard high-point structure, including referential content, or key events and characters, and affective evaluations (Labov & Waletzky, 1976), are consistent in structure with written stories and help children move toward reading comprehension.

An older literature suggests that experiences in social pretend play are important facilitators of talk that is shaped not only to assist in the comprehension of the listener but also to persuade the partner to take on the other's point of view (Connolly & Doyle, 1984; de Lorimier, Doyle, & Tessier, 1995; Doyle & Connolly, 1989; Doyle, Doehring, Tessier, de Lorimier, & Shapiro, 1992; Dunn & Dale, 1984; Farver, 1992; Howe et al., 2002). In particular, Doyle's studies of the complex and lengthy negotiations that precede and interrupt social pretend play suggest that complex social pretend play might be considered a special case of dueling narratives and their eventual resolution in the play script or in the abandonment of the social pretend play for parallel pretending (de Lorimier et al., 1995; Doyle & Connolly, 1989; Doyle et al., 1992).

Narrative production has found its way into the "to do list" of early childhood teachers. The example of asking Maria and Elena to tell the washing babies story, make their own book by illustrating the transcription of the story, and then practice reading the story at home to Tia Janie comes from applying research linking narratives to literacy (Christian, Morrison, & Bryant, 1998; Lonigan, Burgess, & Anthony, 2000. The one extant research report that we have found suggests that narratives do occur within preschool classrooms (Stone, 1992). It also suggests that teacher-directed narrative production requires that an interested adult be available for a quiet and somewhat intimate interaction with individual or small groups of children (Stone, 1992).

Early childhood classrooms are busy places with many more children than adults. One adult for every eight children is considered optimal. This structure does not lend itself to quiet, leisurely, and intimate child-adult interactions. Our experiences observing in otherwise excellent classrooms suggest that much of preliteracy activity occurs in large groups that are dominated by teacher-led activities such as reading to the group and asking questions to which teachers know the answers rather than permeated with interactions related to joint construction of narratives (Wishard, Shivers, Howes, & Ritchie, 2003).

If social pretend play presents an alternative pathway to shared meaning and construction of story structure, then that social pretend play may be easier to implement in early childhood classrooms than teacher-directed emergent literacy activities. Let us be clear. We are not arguing that teachers should stop engaging children in formal narratives, in storybook construction, or in understanding letter-sound correspondence. All of these activities are tied to emergent literacy (Lonigan et al.,). We are suggesting instead that proto-narrative construction and social pretend play among peers be considered important tools in children's developing emergent literacy.

Proto-Narratives, Social Pretend Play, and Culture: Where to Find Complex Shared Pretend and Peer-Constructed Narratives

Considering the social nature of narrative interactions, children's unique interactions with their social world shapes how they interpret and react to their daily experiences, including the method and manner in which they engage in narrative and social pretend-play interactions. Cross-cultural work on narratives and social pretend play suggests that these interactions appear in many very different cultural communities but that they take different forms in different cultural groups (Haight, Wang, Fung, Williams, & Mintz, 1999).

In this section of this chapter, we look through the lens of culture to find social pretend play. We begin by reviewing the basic developmental literature on variations in the contexts that frame the development of both proto-narrative and social pretend play. We then move to the context of early childhood classrooms. We describe data collected over a 20-year period in Los Angeles early childhood programs that suggest that complex social pretend play is disappearing from the everyday life of children in these programs. We then present several case exemplars of particular cultural communities within Los Angeles early childhood programs where we found children engaging in peer-generated shared meaning. We conclude the chapter by describing new work locating social pretend play among family-cluster caregiving in Mexican migrant communities.

Play at Home

Play at home includes both social pretend play and narrative production.

Social pretend play. Haight and colleagues (Haight, 1999; Haight, Masiello, Dickson, Huckely, & Black, 1994; Haight & Miller, 1992; Haight, Parke, & Black, 1997; Haight et al., 1999;) review the development of social pretend play within homes across several cultural communities and conclude that pretending universally includes objects as well as partners and varies in a number of dimensions. In middle-class, Euro-American homes, social pretend play primarily develops within mother-child interaction (Dunn & Dale, 1984). Mothers often enter into pretend play with children (Farver & Howes, 1993), using it as a means for socialization around home and caregiving themes (e.g., "Let's feed the babies, they must be hungry") as well as the enhancement of communication skills. Parents provide children with the materials of play—toy miniatures (Haight et al., 1999)—and many mothers and grandmothers, including the first author of this chapter, have a toy replica kitchen in the "real" kitchen all ready for pretend-play opportunities.

Narratives. Proto-narrative construction, as researched in middle-class American homes, relies on maternal scaffolding and prompts in terms of not only the technical structure of their narratives but also the content orientation, highlighting the collaborative process of co-constructing meaning with the primary caregivers in their lives (Imbens-Bailey & Snow, 1997; Ochs & Capps, 2001; Snow & Imbens-Bailey, 1997). Within this home context, the more traditional high-point narratives, including key events and evaluation, occur almost exclusively in routine and scripted activities such as mealtime (Eisenberg, 1985; Lucariello & Nelson, 1987). Routine, scripted activities are thought to afford young children more cognitive flexibility and a predictable cultural framework that provides a context in which children learn to individuate and to evaluate their experiences as they narrate (Daiute & Nelson, 1997).

Social Pretend Play Disappears from Early Childhood Classrooms

Using both cross-sectional and longitudinal designs, one of this chapter's authors (Carollee Howes) has been gathering data on social pretend play during free play in community-based child-care centers in Los Angeles from 1982 through 2002. We selected the three most comparable studies with data collected at 10-year intervals (Howes, 1988; Howes & Matheson, 1992; Howes & Shivers, 2003). The children who participated in these studies, consistent with the child population of Los Angeles, have been predominantly Latino (45% to 60%) and African American (20% to 25%), with a small percentage of Asian American children and the remainder White children. The children in these studies were all enrolled full time in full-day, center-based child care, including both subsidized care and tuition-based care. Although the overlap between particular programs and classrooms sampled across the three studies is not exact, a substantial proportion of the child-care centers in all three studies were the same. In all three of the studies, complementary and reciprocal play or shared meaning with no pretend play and cooperative social pretend play (enactment of pretend without script or role negotiation) were time sampled. In the two most recent of the studies, complex social pretend play with script, role negotiation, or both was coded. Table 9.1 presents the proportion of each of these play forms in each study for infants, toddlers, and preschoolers. The proportion of social pretend play decreases over time. This decrease is consistent with anecdotal reports that early child-care programs are providing relatively little unstructured time for children to play.

Somewhat alarmed by these data, we set out to find exemplars of places where children construct narratives and play. We were particularly interested in the cultural practices associated with children's sharing meaning. In all three of these cases, we used a mixed methodology approach, participant observation, naturalistic observation, and child assessment. We found that these mixed methods were necessary to describe cultural practices and to describe shared meaning in a manner consistent with the existing literature.

The first of these cases comes from a study of narrative production, the second two from a larger study of child-care programs identified as working well for the families and geographic communities they served (Howes, 2003; Wishard et al., 2003). Although all of the programs provided excellent quality child care, the approaches of two programs to social pretend play were particularly interesting.

Infant-Toddler Child Care and Narrative Production

One of this chapter's authors (Alison Wishard) conducted a study of the development of narratives in a small (20 children from 2 months to 3 years) infant-toddler child-care center. The center serves low-income families who are monolingual Spanish

Table 9.1 Children's Social Pretend Play in Los Angeles Child Care Centers 1980s–2000

Type of Play and Age of Children	Percentage of Observation Period		
	Howes, 1988	Howes & Matheson, 1992	Howes & Shivers, 2003
Complementary and reciprocal play			
16–17 months	.04	.06	—
18–35 months	.18	.13	.03
36–47 months	.22	.19	.06
48–53 months	.24	.26	.06
Cooperative social pretend			
18–35 months	.09	.05	.02
36–47 months	.21	.16	.04
48–53 months	.41	.21	.09
Complex social pretend			
36–47 months	—	.07	.00
48–53 months	—	.12	.02

speakers and newly migrated from Mexico. The children enter the program well before they have developed language fluency in either language. Their parents prefer that the child-care experience be conducted in English, and although their teachers are by-in-large Spanish-English bilingual, they, too, believe that children need to learn to speak English by speaking English in child care. The parents note that their children are more talkative at home (in Spanish) than they are at child care. The children tend to use English with teachers and Spanish among themselves. Consequently, they are sharing meaning with peers in a different language than the one they are using to share meaning with adults.

Children within the 18- to 36-month range in the program were observed, using time sampling to describe the activity settings, participants, and language used in proto-narratives while video recordings and later transcriptions captured the complexity of the proto-narratives. Recall that the bulk of the literature on proto-narratives suggests that they occur in routine activities with adults. In contrast to our expectations, 20% of the time children were observed engaging in narrative interactions with peers independent of adult-child interactions, primarily while the child participants were playing within creative play centers such as the sandbox or housekeeping corner. About half of the remaining observed narrative interactions occurred within small groups of children and one adult. Children would often engage in narrative interactions with one another while the adult would provide minimal to substantial scaffolding with varying success.

Imagine Lucia and Pedro pretending to make tacos while at the play dough table. The two children begin to role out the tortillas, place different colored play dough inside, and fold the taco, exchanging simple explanatory comments in Spanish while demonstrating each step of the taco-making process to the other. The teacher, also sitting at the table with Lucia and Pedro, makes suggestions, in English, of different ingredients to put in the tacos. The children repeat her comment in English and then return to their shared on-line explanation of taco making in Spanish, incorporating the teacher's suggested new ingredient with referents in both Spanish and English.

Although adult–child narratives tended to be produced in English, with adults occasionally assisting in Spanish, the peer–peer narratives tended to be produced in Spanish. Although in the above example the teacher mostly monitored, providing only minimal scaffolding and allowing the children to control the narrative in their more proficient Spanish language, in many examples of adult–child narratives, the teacher's scaffolding and use of English become so pervasive that the child or children get pushed out of the narrative.

The older literature on sharing meaning noted that, for very young children, coordinating activity with a peer partner and emerging manipulation of symbols was a daunting task (Howes, 1988). In light of this observation, it is even more remarkable that the toddlers in this child-care program were sharing meaning and language code switching. If the overarching goal of early childhood programs is to enhance children's literacy and if narrative development is associated with literacy development, perhaps providing a preschool environment that promoted talk and play without also trying to introduce a second language would be sufficient.

Social Pretend Play on the Playground and Not in the Classroom: An African American Academy in Los Angeles   Children begin at the African American Academy soon after their second birthdays and can remain through elementary school. The director, a professor of early childhood development at a local community college, fiercely expects all of the children to learn basic academic skills, particularly reading and math, from the earliest ages. This setting is a school, not a play program. Inside the school, the day is very structured for all age groups: children sit in groups of 8 to 12, receive direct instruction in academic skills, and repeatedly practice identifying letters and vowel sounds as well as producing cursive writing. Teachers are very affectionate, verbally and physically, with the children. The emotional climate is warm and supportive. Everyone, teachers and children, are well behaved. The program lasts for a long day. Children arrive between 7 and 8 a.m. and stay until 5 or 6 p.m. The school provides home-cooked meals. Because the school is in California, children can go outside daily for relatively long breaks from their inside activities. The outside playground comprises a maze of play structures and materials that support social pretend play and a more open space for large muscle activity. Teachers go outside with the children and often enter into the play, making suggestions for expanding the fantasy. Our time-sampled observations indicated that the 3-year-olds in this program were spending 18% of their time in cooperative social pretend play, even though their only chance to play was when they were outside.

Often, the early childhood field frames learning basic academic skills and playing as dichotomous activities. The director of this program was adamant that she was not running a program where children learned by playing. However, our observation suggests that one approach does not necessarily exclude the other. The practices of this program kept learning inside and playing outside. We can see the inside practices of learning and the outside practices of playing as enactment (a) of African American women's long history of caring in the best way possible for all the children (Collins, 1990) and (b) of storytelling within everyday activities (Heath, 1982). Inside, the children were being prepared for school. Outside, the children were learning to tell a good story in the context of social pretend play.

Social Pretend Play and Sibling Caregiving Within a Child-Care Center: A School District Full-Day, Child-Care Center in a Multiethnic Neighborhood   A full-day, child-care program in a multiethnic neighborhood supported by the school district serves 120 children and their families, beginning when the children are 2 years old and continuing with after-school programs until they are 12 or 13 years old. The main building, located directly across an alley from a public elementary school, contains three large classrooms surrounded by an even larger asphalt yard.

The catchment area for the child-care center and elementary school includes primarily Spanish-speaking and Chinese-speaking children. Two of the classrooms within the center are filled with Spanish-speaking children and teacher aides. The other classroom has Chinese-speaking children and teacher aides. The long-term language practice in this program, like the program in the previous section, is for children to learn English. However, two important differences are that the children in this program have established language fluency in Spanish or English before they enter the program and that children are not expected to be English fluent until they are nearly 5 years old. The program's teachers use English, Spanish, or Chinese rather randomly with the children. Our observations suggest that the language used was primarily a function of the fluency of the adult and the age of the child. Some of the adults were monolingual Spanish or Chinese speakers, rarely speaking to anyone in English. Others, more often teachers than teacher aides, tended to be primarily English fluent, rarely speaking in Spanish or Chinese. The older children tended to be spoken to in English and the younger ones in their home language. This practice effectively meant that younger children tended to engage with teacher aides.

A second relevant practice in this program was that younger siblings were always enrolled in the same classroom as their siblings. Therefore, in the Spanish-speaking classroom, the program replicated, to a degree, sibling caregiving practices typical of rural Mexico (Velez-Ibanez, 1996). Children, particularly the girls, tended to play in mixed age groups that incorporated younger siblings.

Social pretend play in this program was not particularly frequent, about 6% of the observation period on the average. We re-analyzed our data to locate activities and participants associated with social pretend play. Adults in this program, unlike the African American Academy program teachers, rarely appeared in the same time frame as social pretend play. Our field notes suggest that they were erratic in their appearance on the playground and, when outside, tended to organize and direct games with rules (e.g., setting up an obstacle course and monitoring children's turn taking on the equipment). Instead, almost all the social pretend play tended to occur when older Spanish-speaking girls organized younger children into pretend-play games. Older boys and Chinese-speaking children tended not to play pretend. The social pretend play in the mixed age groups was constructed in a mix of Spanish and English talk. Therefore, in this program, the nurturing of social pretend play was the responsibility of older Spanish-speaking girls. In this setting, the program practices of family grouping and of expecting younger children to use their home language while in school were associated with encouraging social pretend play.

Within Family Cluster Caregiving in a Latino Neighborhood: Back to Maria and Elena   We began this chapter with a description of Maria and Elena playing. These children are part of a longitudinal study of the children of migrant Mexican mothers moving from rural Oaxaca to Los Angeles and giving birth soon after. The study of these children and their mothers began before the children were born and has continued to follow the children until they enter kindergarten. We regularly visit the children in their homes, even if someone other-than-their-mother is regularly caring for them in that setting. We have extensive clinical interviews with the mothers, asking about their experiences of being cared for, of caring for children, and of migration. As is typical of Mexican migrant families, most of the mothers were part of an extended family cluster within which income and household responsibilities were shared. As women within these households, the mothers were responsible for giving and receiving material and social support. This support took several forms, including mutual responsibilities for rent, purchasing food, cooking, child care, and sending part of the income received from working to family members who do not physically live with them (e.g., to a mother caring for one of the children across the border).

During the first 3 years of their lives, most children did have regular access to age-mates. Almost three quarters of the children had another child, a cousin or sibling, within 2 years of their age in their household. About one quarter of the children had an older sibling or cousin who was expected by caregiving adults to take care of the younger child. Although most of the mothers worked outside the home, two thirds of the children did not attend either a child-care center or licensed child-care home.

When children did have regular access to age-mates, we observed their interaction, sometimes at home, other times in child care. By age 3 years, only 10% of the children had ever been observed in social pretend play, either cooperative or complex, at home or in child care. The average time spent in social pretend play was zero. The children who did pretend were similar to Maria and Elena; they had an age-mate living in their household, they experienced sibling caregiving, and their mothers were well integrated into a family cluster. Research conducted in rural Mexico (Farver & Howes, 1993) suggests that children do pretend, indeed, using the same measures as we used. Farver (Farver & Howes, 1993) reports similar frequencies of social pretend in Mexican and Euro-American samples. However, cultural practices suggest that pretending occurs outside of the home, with older children who are responsible for the toddlers. When the contextual circumstances of the Los Angeles children were most similar to these, they, too, pretended.

Summary

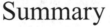

We have made two arguments in this chapter: (1) the construction of narratives (or proto-narratives) and social pretend play with peers are, for young children, experiences that can be important for emergent literacy and (2) whenever meaning is shared, in narratives or in social pretend play, community cultural practices must be considered. We implore early childhood educators to reemphasize shared meaning in the lives of children. At times, the best role for the teacher in this process is to monitor, rather than to interrupt and scaffold, children's play or communication. This approach is inconsistent with current pressures for the teacher to be actively helping children to engage with books and written material.

An important role of the teacher, as our examples of places where children do construct narratives and play pretend illustrate, is to be aware of community cultural practices around shared meaning. Teachers need to be aware of and to be creative in carrying out responsive programs, which is not an easy task. For example, in one of the many programs in which we have spent time, a well-meaning community college teacher taught Central American Mayan immigrant teachers to play pretend with children. As Gaskin's (1999) work sensitively illustrates, children's pretend play is not supported by adults in Mayan communities. Instead, social pretend play occurs almost exclusively in mixed age groups of children playing outside of the realm of adults (Gaskin, 1999). Social pretend play (fortunately, briefly) then became an activity center in the program in which adults instructed children how to play pretend using didactic instruction (e.g., "Hold the baby this way. Now, put the bottle in the doll's mouth.").

As our examples of shared meaning illustrate, community cultural practices around language use, around the meaning of play and work, and around who participates in play are all important to consider as we put shared meaning back into early childhood education.

References

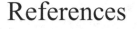

Brenner, J., & Mueller, E. (1982). Shared meaning in boy toddler peer relations. *Child Development, 53,* 380–391.

Christian, K., Morrison, F. J., & Bryant, F. B. (1998). Predicting kindergarten academic skills: Interactions among child care, maternal education, and family literacy environments. *Early Childhood Research Quarterly, 13,* 501–521.

Collins, P. H. (1990). *Black feminist thought: Knowledge, consciousness, and the politics of empowerment.* New York: Routledge.

Connolly, J., & Doyle, A. (1984). Relation of social fantasy play to social competence in preschoolers. *Developmental Psychology, 20,* 797–806.

Daiute, C. N., & Nelson, K. (1997). Making sense of the sense-making function of narrative evaluation. *Journal of Narrative and Life History, 7,* 207–215.

de Lorimier, S., Doyle, A. -B., & Tessier, O. (1995). Social coordination during pretend play: Comparison of nonpretend play and effects on expressive content. *Merrill-Palmer Quarterly, 41,* 497–516.

Doyle, A. -B., & Connolly, J. (1989). Negotiation and enactment in social pretend play relations to social acceptance and social cognition. *Early Childhood Research Quarterly, 4,* 289–302.

Doyle, A. B., Doehring, P., Tessier, O., de Lorimier, S., & Shapiro, S. (1992). Transitions in children's play: A sequential analysis of states preceding and following social pretense. *Developmental Psychology, 28,* 137–144.

Dunn, J., & Dale, N. (1984). I a Daddy: 2-year-olds collaboration in joint pretend with a sibling and with a mother. In I. Bretherton (Ed.), *Symbolic play* (pp. 131–158). New York: Academic Press.

Dunn, J., & Hughes, C. (2001). "I got some swords and you're dead!": Violent fantasy, antisocial behavior, friendship, and moral sensibility in young children. *Child Development, 72,* 491–505.

Dunn, J. S., & Shatz, M. (1989). Becoming a conversationalist despite or because of having an older sibling. *Child Development, 60,* 399–410.

Eisenberg, A. (1985). Learning to describe past experiences in conversation. *Discourse Processes, 8,* 177–204.

Farver, J. (1992). Communicating shared meaning in social pretend play. *Early Childhood Research Quarterly, 7*, 501–516.

Farver, J. M., & Howes, C. (1993). Cultural differences in American and Mexican mother-child pretend play. *Merrill Palmer Quarterly, 30*, 344–358.

Forys, S., & McClune-Nicolich, L. (1984). Shared pretend sociodramic play at three years of age. In I. Bretherton (Ed.), *Symbolic play* (pp. 159–193). New York: Academic Press.

Garza Mourino, R., Rosenblatt, S., & Howes, C. (2001, April). *How did you end up here? Collaborative ways of listening to Mexican immigrant mothers as they contemplate their lives.* Paper presented at the Society for Research in Child Development, Minneapolis, MN.

Gaskin, S. (1999). Children's daily lives in a Mayan village: A case study of culturally constructed roles and activities. In A. Goncu (Ed.), *Children's engagement in the world: A socio-cultural perspective* (pp. 25–61). New York: Cambridge University Press.

Gleason, J. B., & Melzi, G. (1997). The mutual construction of narratives by mothers and children: Cross-cultural observations. *Journal of Narrative and Life History, 7*, 217–222.

Haight, W. L. (1999). The pragmatics of caregiver-child pretending at home: Understanding culturally specific socialization practices. In A. Goncu (Ed.), *Children's engagement in the world* (pp. 128–147). New York: Cambridge University Press.

Haight, W. L., Masiello, T., Dickson, L., Huckely, E., & Black, J. E. (1994). The everyday contexts and social functions of mother-child pretend play in the home. *Merrill-Palmer Quarterly, 40,* 509–522.

Haight, W. L., & Miller, P. (1992). The development of everyday pretend play: A longitudinal study of mothers' participation. *Merrill-Palmer Quarterly, 38,* 331–349.

Haight, W. L., Parke, R. D., & Black, J. E. (1997). Mothers' and fathers' beliefs about and spontaneous participation in their toddlers' pretend play. *Merrill-Palmer Quarterly, (43)*, 271–290.

Haight, W. L., Wang, X. -L., Fung, H. H., Williams, K., & Mintz, J. (1999). Universal, developmental, and variable aspects of young children's play: A cross-cultural comparison of pretending at home. *Child Development, 70*, 1477–1488.

Heath, S. B. (1982). What no bedtime story means: Narrative skills at home and school. *Language in Society, 11*, 49–76.

Heath, S. B. (1983). *Ways with words.* New York: Cambridge University Press.

Howe, N., Rinaldi, C. M., Jennings, M., & Petrakos, H. (2002). "No! The lambs can stay out because they got cozies": Constructive and destructive sibling conflict, pretend play, and social understanding. *Child Development, 73,* 1460–1473.

Howes, C. (1985). Sharing fantasy social pretend play in toddlers. *Child Development, 56*, 1253–1258.

Howes, C. (1988). Peer interaction in young children. *Monograph of the Society for Research in Child Development, 53*(1, Serial No. 217).

Howes, C. (with Unger, O. A., & Matheson, C. C.). (1992). *The collaborative construction of pretend: Social pretend play functions.* New York: State University of New York Press.

Howes, C. (2003). *Child care practices: Ethnic variations in the enactment of quality.* Manuscript in preparation.

Howes, C., & Matheson, C. C. (1992). Sequences in the development of competent play with peers: Social and social pretend play. *Developmental Psychology, 28,* 961–974.

Howes, C., & Shivers, E. M. (2003). *New relationships.* Los Angeles: University of California at Los Angeles.

Howes, C., Unger, O., & Seidner, L. (1989). Social pretend play in toddlers: Social pretend play forms and parallels with solitary pretense. *Child Development, 60,* 132.

Howes, C., & Wishard, A. (2003). *Why no pretending: Influences of Latino migration, family clusters, work and child care, and emotional climate.* Manuscript in preparation.

Imbens-Bailey, A. L., & Snow, C. E. (1997). Making meaning in parent-child interaction: A pragmatic approach. In C. M. A. McCabe (Ed.), *The problem of meaning: Behavioral and cognitive perspectives* (pp. 261–295). New York: Elsevier Science.

Labov, W., & Waletzky, J. (1976). Narrative analysis: Oral versions of personal experience. In J. Help (Ed.), *Essays on the verbal and visual arts* (pp. 12–44). Seattle: University of Washington Press.

Lonigan, C. J., Burgess, S. R., & Anthony, J. L. (2000). Development of emergent literacy and early reading skills in preschool children: Evidence from a latent-variable longitudinal study. *Developmental Psychology, 36,* 596–613.

Lucariello, J., & Nelson, K. (1987). Remembering and planning talk between mothers and children. *Discourse Processes, 10,* 219–235.

Mueller, E., & Brenner, J. (1977). The origins of social skills and interaction among playgroup toddlers. *Child Development, 48,* 854–861.

Ochs, E. C., & Capps, L. (2001). *Living narrative: Creating lives in everyday storytelling.* Cambridge, MA: Harvard University Press.

Rogoff, B. (2002). *The cultural nature of human development.* New York: Oxford University Press.

Snow, C. E. (1983). Literacy and language: Relationships during the preschool years. *Harvard Educational Review, 53,* 165–189.

Snow, C. E., & Imbens-Bailey, A. (1997). Beyond Labov and Waletzy: The antecedents of narrative discourse. *Journal of Narrative and Life History, 7,* 197–207.

Snow, C. E., & Tabors, P. O. (1993). Language skills that relate to literacy development. In B. S. Spodek, (Ed.), *Handbook of early childhood research* (pp. 249–261). New York: Teachers College Press.

Stone, P. S. (1992). "You know what?" Conversational narratives of preschool children. *Early Childhood Research Quarterly, 7,* 367–382.

Vandell, D. L., Wilson, K., & Buchanan, N. (1980). Peer interaction in the first year of life. *Child Development, 51,* 481–488.

Velez-Ibanez, C. (1996). *Border visions.* Tucson: University of Arizona.

Wishard, A. (2003). *Bilingual narratives in preschool: A situated perspective of meaning making.* Manuscript submitted for publication.

Wishard, A., Shivers, E., Howes, C., & Ritchie, S. (2003). Child care program and teacher practices: Associations with quality and children's experiences. *Early Childhood Research Quarterly, 18,* 65–103.

Youngblade, L. M., & Dunn, J. (1995). Individual differences in young children's pretend play with mother and siblings: Links to relationships and understanding of other people's feelings and beliefs. *Child Development, 66,* 1472–1492.

PLAY AND SCHOOL
READINESS

Sue Bredekamp

In Evelyn Delgado's Head Start classroom in Philadelphia, the dramatic play area has been turned into a doctor's office (HeadsUp! Reading, 2002). Six or seven children dress up in white coats and play with more or less realistic props such as stethoscopes, "medicines," plastic syringes, prescription pads, and other medical implements. Several books about visiting the doctor are also available. Evelyn enters the play, and the children designate her the patient as they swarm around her on the floor. She nervously says, "What's wrong with me, doctor?" and the children start listing her various symptoms, diagnosing a fever, and giving her medicine for her eyes. When Evelyn becomes fearful, one of the children gives her a telephone to call her Mom. "Mommy, please come," she cries into the phone. "There's a whole bunch of doctors and I'm afraid." One of the little girls quickly takes on the role of Evelyn's mother. She picks up the book, *Go to the Doctor* (Berenstein & Berenstein, 1981) and begins to "read" it to Evelyn to calm her fears. The little girl points to one of the pictures and says, "He's not afraid because he's the big brother."

Evelyn Delgado is a masterful early childhood educator. In her teaching, she puts into practice what research says about the potential positive effects of preschool children's play on readiness for school. Sociodramatic play provides an excellent

159

context for children to develop and practice many of the important skills and behaviors that contribute to later success in school and life (Bergen, 2002; Fromberg, 1999; Smilansky & Sheftaya, 1990). The purpose of this chapter is to describe some of the key research findings that demonstrate the relationship between school readiness and preschool play. The chapter begins with definitions of both school readiness and play. Next and perhaps most important, the chapter describes the teacher's role in ensuring that play is used effectively to promote school readiness. As the scene in Evelyn Delgado's classroom shows, play does not automatically result in positive learning experiences for children; teachers have several essential roles to play themselves. Then, the chapter explores the relationship between children's dramatic play and the development of key school readiness skills—self-regulation, higher order social skills, language, and early literacy skills such as symbolic representation and print awareness. Finally, the chapter concludes with a discussion of motivation in relation to play and school readiness.

Defining Terms:
School Readiness and Play

The terms *school readiness* and *play* represent complex constructs that have been defined and used in various ways, sometimes leading to miscommunication and misinterpretation. The main problem with each of these terms is that, at times, they are defined very broadly and, at other times, quite narrowly. Therefore, any discussion of these constructs must begin with explication of how these terms will be used in this context.

School Readiness

The concept of school readiness first reached national prominence in 1990 when the president and 50 governors established the National Education Goals Panel, identifying Goal 1 as "By the year 2000 all children will start school ready to learn." Subsequently, the Goals Panel (National Education Goals Panel, 1991) defined the construct of "ready to learn" as consisting of five dimensions: language use, cognition and general knowledge, physical health and well-being, social and emotional development, and approaches to learning. More recently, the Head Start Bureau (2001) expanded on the construct when it promulgated a Child Outcomes Framework delineating the expectations for children on leaving Head Start. The Head Start Child Outcomes Framework lists eight dimensions of school readiness with numerous indicators or examples provided to further describe each dimension: language development, literacy, mathematics, science, creative arts, social and emotional development, approaches to learning, and physical health and development. Unlike the Goals Panel definition, the Head Start framework uses terminology more aligned with the academic subjects of elementary school.

Kindergarten teachers also have been asked to report which factors are very important or essential for kindergarten readiness. In one survey by the U.S. Department of Education (National Center for Education Statistics, 1999), more than 75% of teachers considered it very important or essential that children be physically healthy, rested, and nourished; enthusiastic and curious in approaching new activities; and able to communicate needs, wants, and thoughts verbally in their home language. In addition, 51%–75% of teachers reported that taking turns and sharing, not disrupting class, being sensitive to other children's feelings, and following directions are very important or essential. Finishing tasks, knowing the English language, and sitting still and paying attention were reported as being important or very important by 26%–50% of teachers. Most interesting, fewer than 26% of kindergarten teachers in this survey reported that it is essential or very important for entering kindergarten children to count to 20, have good problem-solving skills, use a pencil or paintbrush, or know letters of the alphabet. Clearly, these survey results show that kindergarten teachers believe that children's language abilities, their eagerness to learn, and their overall ability to regulate their own behavior in group settings (including following rules set by the teacher and getting along with peers) are the key determinants of readiness. Teachers no doubt assume that, given these preexisting conditions, they can teach children specific skills but that, in the absence of these factors, teaching becomes quite difficult.

Contrary to the opinions of many of these kindergarten teachers, however, research shows that children who enter kindergarten with certain kinds of knowledge and skill in early literacy such as recognizing letters, phonological awareness, and overall language ability are more likely to succeed in learning to read later on (Snow, Burns, & Griffin, 1998; Whitehurst & Lonigan, 1998). Probably more important, children who are severely lacking in these areas are more likely to experience difficulties in learning to read (Snow et al., 1998).

School readiness matters because achievement gaps continue to persist between children from low-income families and their middle-class counterparts as well as among children from diverse linguistic and cultural groups (Coley, 2002). Because these gaps are evident as early as kindergarten entry (Lee & Burkam, 2002; West, Denton, & Germino-Hausken, 2000), addressing these inequities during the preschool years is necessary.

Extensive research reviews (Bowman, Donovan, & Burns, 2001; FAN: The Child Mental Health Foundations and Agencies Network, 2000; Shonkoff & Phillips, 2000; Snow et al., 1998) have contributed a great deal to what is now known about the kinds of skills and knowledge that constitute school readiness. Given this broad knowledge base, it becomes essential to use a multidimensional definition of school readiness that in effect encompasses all aspects rated by the kindergarten teachers and more. For the purposes of this chapter, however, that definition will be limited to those dimensions of school readiness on which play seems to have the greatest potential effect: self-regulation, social skills, language, and early literacy skills such as print awareness and symbolic representation.

Play

The term *play* is one of the most frequently used but most loosely defined terms in the early childhood lexicon. Because so many general, bromidic statements about play appear frequently in early childhood literature, a great deal of misunderstanding surrounds the concept (see DeVries, Zan, Hildebrandt, Edmiaston, & Sales, 2002, pp. 6–10). In fact, if advocates for play in early childhood used the term less often but under more clearly delimited conditions, they would strengthen their case.

This chapter works from a relatively narrow definition of play. The kind of play that appears to be most effective in developing the school readiness abilities listed previously is *sociodramatic play* (Smilansky, 1968) about which a great deal has been written in the literature. This type of play, also called dramatic, imaginative, or pretend play, can occur with peers, adults, or both. Characteristics of sociodramatic play include make-believe that involves roles, objects, and situations; persists for at least 10 minutes; and includes language and social interaction. The social dimension distinguishes sociodramatic play from dramatic play because children can and do pretend during solitary play. Sociodramatic play may also occur in combination with constructive play in early childhood classrooms, for example, when a group of children build a car with blocks and then pretend that they are a family taking a trip.

Much of the current research on sociodramatic play derives from a Vygotskian theoretical base (Berk & Winsler, 1995; Bodrova & Leong, 1998). Vygotsky (1933/1966) saw play as the leading behavior in children's development, "the preeminent educational activity of early childhood" (Berk & Winsler, 1995, p. 57). In Vygotsky's theory, during play, children behave beyond their current level of independent mastery. This type of play is characterized by several elements. First, the play must include an imaginary situation such as the doctor's office in Evelyn's classroom. Second, the players have assigned roles with implicit rules for acting each part. As the classroom scene showed, the children playing the role of doctor knew that their role was to be in charge, providing the diagnosis and treatment, not asking What's wrong with me? like a patient would; similarly, the girl playing the mother took on the parental role of reading to her child. And finally, language must be involved (Bodrova & Leong, 1998).

Dramatic play first emerges during late toddlerhood when children begin using objects for imaginary purposes and "playing tea party" or other situations with adults or older children (Haight & Miller, 1993). If this type of play is supported during the preschool years, then by age 4 or 5, children can become quite skilled as players, engaging in the kind of play that includes all the elements listed above. Bodrova and Leong (2003) identify this type of play as "mature play" to distinguish it from the "immature play" in which many children engage, even as preschoolers and kindergartners, because they have not learned more sophisticated play skills. Immature play is repetitive and unimaginative and does not benefit children the same way mature play does. As Bodrova and Leong (2003) wisely point out, "when parents or school administrators propose replacing play in an early childhood classroom with more academic activities they are prompted by the fact that the play they see in these classrooms is actually happening at an immature level" (p. 14).

Vygotsky's view of play is one in which the individual renounces his or her own needs and desires to conform to the rules of the play situation. Anyone who has observed children engaged in dramatic play has seen that, at times, they will step out of their roles to renegotiate (e.g., "Now you be the patient. I want to be the doctor."). But if children cease to conform to the roles assigned (that is, break the implicit rules), the play inevitably breaks down. In other words, from Vygotsky's perspective, play actually sets limits on children's behavior (Berk & Winsler, 1995; Bodrova & Leong, 1998). This perspective is a different view of play than that denoted by the oft-used phrase, "free play." As Berk and Winsler state so eloquently, "Free play is not really 'free' since renouncing impulsive action—that is, not doing just what one wants to do at the moment—is the route to satisfying, pleasurable make-believe" (1995, p. 56). And, as research is beginning to demonstrate more and more, play is at least in part the route to school readiness.

The Teacher's Role in Promoting Sociodramatic Play

Like virtually every other aspect of development, mature play does not happen naturally or occur automatically as children get older. Rather, children must learn how to engage in satisfying sociodramatic play, which means that adults or more capable peers must take responsibility for assisting them in this learning.

Several researchers have described various teacher roles with respect to supporting children's play (Christie & Enz, 1992; Roskos & Neuman, 1993; Schrader, 1989, 1990). The most basic framework of this kind asserts that teachers play three key roles: observer, stage manager, and co-player. The observer role is obvious and similar to that played in other areas of the early childhood classroom. In the case of play, teachers must observe carefully to determine whether, when, how, and with whom to intervene. The roles of stage manager and co-player are particularly important to ensure that mature sociodramatic play develops and is sustained and that individual children who may need additional support to become more skilled players receive it. As stage manager, teachers can help provide a "theme" for the play that organizes it around a set of common experiences or knowledge, and they can provide time, space, and props to enhance the play (Schrader, 1990). The theme may arise from a shared experience such as a curriculum topic, a visit to the class by a doctor, or a trip to a nearby grocery store. As co-player, the teacher carefully involves him- or herself in the play, scaffolding language, and intervening to appropriately support and extend the play. In this context, the most helpful teacher support involves, not directly instructing or explaining, but rather, modeling, demonstrating, guiding as well as possibly elaborating and extending children's language by engaging in one-to-one conversation (Berk & Winsler, 1995). This role is crucial when children "get stuck" in immature play, repeatedly playing the same thing or simply imitating superhero or monster play. But adults must be careful not to be too intrusive in children's play. If adults begin to take over, children will inevitably desist (Jones & Reynolds, 1992).

With key terms defined, the chapter now examines the relationship between play and school readiness. Each of the research studies described here clearly shows that the role of the adult is key to ensuring that children's involvement in play produces the desired school readiness results, a finding that has important implications for early childhood teacher education and professional development.

The Relationship Between Play and School Readiness Factors

A growing body of research connects Vygotskian-type sociodramatic play to particular skills and abilities that relate to later success in school and life. Key studies described here demonstrate how mature, teacher-supported sociodramatic play promotes desired learning and developmental outcomes in preschool children.

Self-Regulation

A recent review of child development and neurobiology research concluded that "the growth of self-regulation is a cornerstone of early childhood development that cuts across all domains of behavior" and that "development may be viewed as an increasing capacity for self-regulation, not so much in the specifics of individual behaviors but in the child's ability to function more independently in personal and social contexts" (Shonkoff & Phillips, 2000, p. 26). Thus, the prestigious scientists of the National Research Council concurred with the kindergarten teachers surveyed by the U.S. Department of Education about the importance of self-regulation for healthy development and learning. In the broadest sense, self-regulation is the ability to control one's own emotions, behaviors, and thinking processes.

Operating from a Vygotskian theoretical perspective, Bodrova and Leong (2001) developed a preschool-kindergarten curriculum model, Tools of the Mind, within which sociodramatic play has a central place. The model focuses on the teacher's role in developing mature play among young children. Preschoolers spend 40 to 50 minutes per day in sustained sociodramatic play, and teachers are trained in special instructional strategies, including strategies to introduce imaginary situations and props (that move from more realistic to less realistic to encourage symbolic thought) as well as strategies to expand the roles children take on.

One of the core elements of Tools of the Mind that is designed to promote mature play is the use of "play plans." The plan is a written description of what the child plans to do during play, including the situation, roles, and props. Over time, the teacher encourages two or more children to plan together, an activity that enables the children, either themselves or with the teacher's help, to defuse potential social conflicts in advance. A key element of these plans is that they are on paper. Children draw or write their plans, using their own writing approximations that become more conventional over time (a process called "scaffolded writing"), thus integrating early literacy skill development in the program. In the Tools of the Mind classrooms, play plans increased the level of self-regulation, both cognitive and social, and yielded less fighting and arguing among the children as well as more on-task behavior (Bodrova & Leong, 2001). Research in Tools of the Mind classrooms confirms the theory that mature play is not "free play" but, rather, contributes to children's impulse control and self-regulation, key aspects of school readiness. The Tools of the Mind curriculum approach also had significant positive effects on early literacy skills, which are described later in the chapter.

Elias and Berk (2002) also tested Vygotsky's theory of play and self-regulation. In a short-term longitudinal design, they observed 51 middle-income 3- and 4-year-olds in their preschools. The study involved naturalistic observations of total dramatic play, complex sociodramatic play, and solitary dramatic play as well as of self-regulation during clean-up and circle time. They found a positive relationship between the amount of time a child spent in complex sociodramatic play and that child's self-regulation during clean-up (but not the child's self-regulation during circle time). No relationship was found between total time a child spent in dramatic play and his or her self-regulation, and a negative relationship was found between a child's solitary dramatic play and his or her self-regulation. The relationship between complex sociodramatic play and self-regulation during clean-up was particularly strong for highly impulsive children. The researchers hypothesized that clean-up time requires greater levels of self-regulation than circle time because, during circle time, each child is clearly under the teacher's supervision and is constrained by the norms of the group, whereas during clean-up time, each child must function more independently.

Ironically, preschools are becoming more school-like in an attempt to prepare children for the self-regulatory expectations of school when research shows that play during the years before school is effective in developing the self-regulatory capacities of preschool children. But a qualifier must be added to this conclusion on self-regulation: Only mature sociodramatic play supported by trained teachers is effective.

Social Skills

Perhaps not surprising, research supports a strong relationship between sociodramatic play and social competence (Fromberg, 1999). Congruent with the findings on self-regulation, during pretend play, social behavior among preschoolers is more mature, cooperative, and reciprocal, and children remain engaged longer than in other classroom situations (Connolly & Doyle, 1984; Connolly, Doyle, & Reznick, 1988). Children who engage in sociodramatic play are better able to take the perspective of others and are seen as more intellectually and socially competent by their teachers (Burns & Brainerd, 1979; Connolly & Doyle, 1984).

Involvement in sociodramatic play not only reflects children's social ability but also contributes to social competence (Berk & Winsler, 1995). A large-scale observational study of early childhood programs (Layzer, Goodson, & Moss, 1993) provided some insights into what goes on in early childhood classrooms. The study described experiences of 4-year-old children from low-income families in three types of programs: Head Start, child-care centers, and prekindergartens funded by Chapter I. The sample included 199 randomly selected programs from five areas of the country. Observers spent 1 week in each classroom and collected a wealth of data to provide a rich picture of "life in preschool" as the study was called. The researchers examined two outcome measures related to school readiness: (a) engagement in activities with goals and (b) use of higher-level social strategies such as initiating and sustaining cooperative social activities, taking turns, or working with others on joint projects. They found that children engaged in activities with goals approximately 40% of the time, whereas about 25% of children's interactions involved higher-level social strategies.

The relevance of these findings is that each of these types of child behavior occurred under different classroom conditions. Goal-directed tasks were more likely to occur during teacher-planned, teacher-directed activities, whereas higher-level social strategies were more likely to occur during sociodramatic play or informal, active play with peers. Apparently, children develop different, but equally important, school readiness abilities from their experiences in the diverse contexts of an early childhood classroom. One disturbing finding of the study was that, in classrooms with more highly qualified teachers (those with baccalaureate degrees), children spent more time on activities with goals, indicating that these better-trained teachers were not prepared to use the context of play to support the development of sophisticated social skills, self-regulation, and other school readiness abilities. Another disturbing finding is that one-on-one conversational interactions were relatively rare. Much of teacher talk was devoted to directives and administering routines, demonstrating that many preschools are marked by too many missed opportunities for learning.

Language

All the different ways of defining school readiness agree on one dimension of the definition: the importance of language. Language is a strong predictor of reading success, but language also relates to cognitive and social development in general (Dickinson & Tabors, 2001; Snow et al., 1998). One of the major characteristics of mature pretend play is the use of language, so it should come as no surprise that a strong relationship exists between pretend play and language development. During sociodramatic play, children often take on the roles of adults and, therefore, emulate the more sophisticated language of adults (Anderson, 1986); similarly, when children play out specific roles in pretend contexts, they adapt their speech style and emulate the scripts common to those settings. Different contexts such as the doctor's office, a space shuttle launch, a restaurant, or taking care of a baby at home require different language, and children learn to adjust their language to the demands of the situation.

One study (Levy, Schaefer, & Phelps, 1986) of 28 3- and 4-year-olds in a child-care center found that sociodramatic play can be valuable in improving the language scores of boys. Before the teacher's intervention, only girls participated in sustained sociodramatic play. The teachers engaged all of the children by organizing play around a shared set of experiences (a theme); providing time, space, and props to enhance the play; and intervening to support and extend involvement—especially that of males—in the play, thus enhancing their language development.

One of the most impressive recent studies from which we can learn about play and language is the Home School Study of Language and Literacy Development (Dickinson & Tabors, 2001). This longitudinal study of the effects of language and literacy environments on a group of 74 children from low-income homes began when the children were 3 years old. Dickinson and Tabors (2001) report effects through kindergarten, although children have since been followed into middle school where effects are still being found. Researchers conducted home visits all 3 years and observed and recorded parent-child interactions during play and reading. Then, they conducted observations and audiotaping of both children and teachers during a preschool visit each year. They obtained language data from "group meeting times, large-group book reading, small teacher-led groups, free play, mealtimes, and transition times" (Snow, Tabors, & Dickinson, 2001, p. 9). During the kindergarten year, children were administered a battery of measures called the SHELL-K, which includes the following components: narrative production, picture description, definitions, superordinates (e.g., What are tables and chairs?), story comprehension, emergent literacy (including letter recognition, writing concepts, story and print concepts), and receptive vocabulary.

The findings of this study are rich and have numerous implications for teachers and parents. Of particular interest to the current discussion are the findings related to free play (Dickinson, 2001). Note that, although Dickinson refers to this play as "free play," it was actually mature, sociodramatic, rule-bound play, which, as discussed above, is not truly "free." The free play time during preschool was most beneficial for long-term language growth in classrooms that were rich with varied vocabulary. Researchers found "consistent links between kindergarten measures and the total number of words and the variety of words that children used during free play" (Dickinson, 2001, p. 251). Researchers also found that how teachers talked with children in varying contexts matters. During group times, the quantity of interesting and varying words teachers used seems to be what makes the difference for children. But during pretend play, the most effective teachers were those who were selective in their choice of words and were reciprocal in conversation.

In addition, the study found that children performed better in kindergarten if, during play, their preschool teachers limited their own talking and gave children more opportunity to talk. Effective preschool teachers listened to children, then spoke about the topic of their play, using rare and varied words related to the theme of the play. Children's kindergarten outcomes were less positive in situations where the teachers did more explaining during play than extending of children's own conversations. The researchers explained that what tended to happen was that teachers stepped in to resolve problems or enforce rules, which led to lengthy explanations that the children undoubtedly tuned out. This finding is the opposite of the study's finding related to group times where explanatory talk was beneficial. In short, preschool children benefit when teachers engage them in one-on-one extended conversation during pretend play, using rare words in context to extend children's vocabulary.

The major findings of this study point to the important role of play in the development of school readiness, especially literacy-related language skills (Dickinson, 2001):

- Across all 3 years of the study, the data showed associations between the amount of time children engaged in pretending and their performance on outcome measures in kindergarten.

- Pretend play provides opportunities to talk with other children and across all 3 years, the amount of time spent talking to other children was related to positive outcomes.

- Children benefited from talk with other children and teachers that involved varied vocabulary and interesting intellectual content.

- Children benefited when teachers engaged them in sustained conversation with several turns for each to listen and speak. (pp. 253–254)

Important to note is that the Home School Study found specific kinds of adult language that varies by context to be beneficial for children's development. In other words, what constitutes effective teacher talk with children varies depending on whether the context is group time, story time, mealtime, or pretend play. And the researchers caution that all of these contexts provide important learning opportunities. The findings are not suggesting that pretend play replace group time or other more structured teaching situations; rather, the researchers are imploring that those situations do not replace pretend play time, which, as this longitudinal study shows, provides powerful benefits for school readiness when effectively supported by teachers.

American preschools are now enrolling increasing numbers of children whose home language is not English. In fact, almost one third of Head Start children speak a language other than English at home. The realities of so many second-language learners means that preschools have a special responsibility to help children acquire English while also maintaining their home language. However, sociodramatic play, which is a desired activity of preschool children, can also be very challenging for second-language learners because the linguistic demands of pretend play are so high. Often, other children do not include second-language learners in pretend play or, at least, not until late in the year. Tabors (1997) describes the approach that is used by the Language Acquisition Preschool at the University of Kansas to ameliorate this situation and engage second-language learners in pretend play. Rather than leave the situation entirely up to the children, which is too often done in preschool, the teachers use a strategy called "scripted dramatic play." In this strategy, the teachers introduce the props and roles for the play, giving background information in discussion and introducing new vocabulary and routines as part of the script related to the play situation. This strategy provides second-language learners with opportunities for verbal communication in meaningful contexts during situations where they are motivated to participate in play with other children.

Early Literacy Skills

A great deal of attention is now focused on the need for preschools to prepare children with early literacy skills that will increase the likelihood of later success in reading. With the emphasis on literacy, many preschool teachers feel pressured to limit or even eliminate sociodramatic play and increase group time during which teachers instruct the whole group in letters and sounds. The previous description of the Home School Study has shown that teacher-supported dramatic play can have a positive effect on children's literacy-related language skills at kindergarten.

Earlier, this chapter described the Tools of the Mind curriculum approach and its use of written play plans (Bodrova & Leong, 2001). An additional element of the approach that supports the use of play plans is scaffolded writing, a technique invented for the project. In this technique, the teacher helps a child plan his or her play by drawing a line to stand for each word the child says. The child repeats the message, and then writes on the lines, attempting to represent the words with letters and symbols. Over time, as children develop more understanding of letter-sound relationships, the amount of support provided by the teacher diminishes. In Tools of the Mind classrooms where children spent 50–60 minutes of a 2½-hour program using play plans and scaffolded writing techniques based on Vygotsky's theory, children scored significantly higher than control group children on literacy skills in both preschool and kindergarten. Preschool measures included the following: letter recognition, sound-to-symbol correspondence, comprehension of pattern in a text, understanding of the symbolic function of a printed word, and separating of a printed word into letters (Bodrova & Leong, 2001).

The teacher's role in using sociodramatic play as a context to support literacy is critical. Several researchers (Morrow, 1990; Neuman & Roskos, 1992, 1993; Roskos & Neuman, 1993, 2001; Vukelich, 1994) have found that the physical environment of the classroom has a powerful effect on children's literacy behaviors. Simply by providing writing tools in dramatic play areas, children's writing increases. But here again, when the teacher provides a thematic organization for the play (such as veterinarian's office) and props, more literacy experiences result and more reading occurs. When the teacher participates and offers suggestions, scaffolding children's engagement, children participate more.

Davidson (1996) and Owocki (1999) describe the many ways that play can support literacy learning. Play provides a context within which children read and write for real purposes. By putting writing tools and appropriate books in play settings, children engage with these materials in meaningful ways. Dramatic play also provides practice in constructing narrative, or relating events or stories, similar to the process used in writing and helpful in understanding what is read (Fromberg, 1999).

Play is also related to the important capacity of symbolic representation, the ability to separate thought from objects and actions. Oral language is a symbol system, and written language is a more complex symbol system. In both instances, an agreed-on set of abstract symbols is used to represent or stand for something else. Dramatic play also requires use of symbols. Children use words, actions, and props to stand for or symbolize what they are imagining. The ability to symbolically represent objects in thought is developmental (Corrigan, 1987). Toddlers require the real object (such as a toy telephone) to pretend, whereas by age 2 years, children can use a less realistic prop such as a block to stand for a phone. Preschoolers can imagine the object without the prop. Vygotsky believed that play serves as vital preparation for later abstract and imaginative thought by helping children separate meaning from concrete objects and action; that is, acquire the capacity for symbolic representation (Berk & Winsler, 1995).

Play and Motivation

Having seen the importance of play for self-regulation, social skills, language, and early literacy, let us return to Evelyn Delgado's Head Start classroom. Today, the dramatic play area of Evelyn's class is an eye doctor's office. In the play area is a large eye chart filled with varying-size alphabet letters, notepads, eye patches, and numerous pairs of old eyeglass frames that several of the children are wearing. At first, Evelyn plays the role of patient again. Two children hold the chart while the doctor points to the letters. Evelyn covers one eye and hesitantly says, "Doctor, I can't see very well. Is that an *R*?" After examining the chart, the doctor replies impatiently, "No, it's a *K*!" Although not much research supports the role of dramatic play in acquiring alphabet knowledge or phonological awareness (two important predictors of reading in first grade), Evelyn's creative teaching demonstrates how easily instruction related to these topics can be incorporated in a play situation that also promotes other important school readiness skills.

But why use pretend play as the context for teaching and learning when group time or worksheets might also be effective? One answer to this question is that preschool children are highly motivated to engage in pretend play. Play is such a pleasurable activity for young children, in fact, that there is no need to coerce or cajole them to participate as there often is in other types of teacher-directed activity.

One interesting study (Wiltz & Klein, 2001) actually asked preschool children in high- and low-quality child-care centers their preferences with respect to their experiences in those centers. The quality of the centers was assessed independently by the researchers based on classroom observations using the Early Childhood Environment Rating Scale (ECERS). Researchers observed and interviewed 122 children about their likes and dislikes as well as their understanding of events and procedures at school (about which their perceptions were highly accurate). Not surprisingly, play (broadly defined by the children) was the favorite activity of 98% of the children across all classrooms, even children in low-quality classrooms where opportunities to play were more limited and teacher-controlled. Children in high-quality classrooms expressed a greater desire specifically for dramatic play than did children in low-quality classrooms where the environments were more impoverished.

When asked what they do not like about school, responses were more varied. Nearly one third of the children reported meanness by teachers or peers. Nap time and time-out were other aspects of school disliked by some children. But circle time was also actively disliked, less often by children in high-quality centers (8%) than by children in low-quality centers (25%) where the circle time lasted 30 to 40 minutes and involved rote memorization of calendar, letters, and numbers. Even in high-quality classrooms where circle time was more interesting and engaging, many children reported disliking it primarily because it takes too long. As one little boy, Don, said, "Well, I don't really like . . . you know, like sit in circle and listen . . . I don't like that part (because) I think it's too long for me. I'd rather be playing" (Wiltz & Klein, 2001, p. 225).

Considerable evidence exists that pretend play during preschool is associated with development of important school readiness behaviors such as self-regulation, social skills, language, and early literacy skills (Bodrova & Leong, 2001; Connolly & Doyle; 1984; Dickinson, 2001; Neuman & Roskos, 1992, 1993). Evidence also exists that the preschool years are a unique period of the life span during which the capacity to engage in dramatic play gradually develops if modeled and supported by adults and peers (Haight & Miller, 1993). This kind of play seems to reach its peak by kindergarten and then gradually wanes as school-age children's play becomes dominated by games with rules. In other words, preschool is the optimum time for sociodramatic play to support children's development. And children are highly motivated to engage in play. But all play is not equal, and children are not natural players. The most valuable play is mature play involving imaginary situations, roles, implicit rules for behavior, and extended language interaction.

For children to benefit fully from play, teachers must take their own roles seriously. Early childhood educators cannot wander around classrooms operating on the vague assumption that children learn through play while, at the same time, lamenting the challenges to play coming from parents and administrators. Instead, teachers must recognize play as one of the key teaching and learning contexts in the early childhood classroom, must acquire skills themselves in research-based effective teaching strategies such as scaffolding language to use during play, and must incorporate play along with other more directive teaching throughout the preschool day.

References

Anderson, E. S. (1986). The acquisition of register variation by Anglo-American children. In B. B. Schieffelin & E. Ochs. (Eds.), *Language socialization across cultures*. New York: Cambridge University Press.

Berenstein, S., & Berenstein, J. (1981). *The Berenstein bears go to the doctor*. New York: Random House.

Bergen, D. (2002). The role of pretend play in children's cognitive development. *Early Childhood Research and Practice, 4*(1). Retrieved March 19, 2003, from http://ecrp.uiuc. edu/v4n2/bergen.html.

Berk, L. E., & Winsler, A. (1995). *Scaffolding children's learning: Vygotsky and early childhood education*. Washington, DC: National Association for the Education of Young Children.

Bodrova, E., & Leong, D. J. (1998). Adult influences on play: The Vygotskian approach. In D. P. Fromberg & D. Bergen (Eds.), *Play from birth to twelve and beyond: Contexts, perspectives and meanings* (pp. 277–288). New York: Garland Press.

Bodrova, E., & Leong, D. J. (2001). *The Tools of the Mind project: A case study of implementing the Vygotskian approach in American early childhood and primary classrooms*. Geneva, Switzerland: International Bureau of Education, UNESCO.

Bodrova, E., & Leong, D. J. (2003). Chopsticks and counting chips: Do play and the foundational skills need to compete for the teachers' attention in an early childhood classroom? *Young Children, 58*(3), 10–17.

Bowman, B. T., Donovan, M. S., & Burns, M. S. (Eds.). (2001). *Eager to learn: Educating our preschoolers*. Washington, DC: National Academy Press.

Burns, S. M., & Brainerd, C. J. (1979). Effects of constructive and dramatic play on perspective taking in very young children. *Developmental Psychology, 15,* 512–521.

Christie, J. F., & Enz, B. J. (1992). The effects of literacy play interventions on preschoolers' play patterns and literacy development. *Early Education and Development, 3,* 205–220.

Coley, R. J. (2002). *An uneven start: Indicators of inequality in school readiness Policy Information Report*. Princeton, NJ: Educational Testing Service.

Connolly, J. A., & Doyle, A. (1984). Relations of social fantasy play to social competence in preschoolers. *Developmental Psychology, 20,* 797–806.

Connolly, J. A., Doyle, A., & Reznick, E. (1988). Social pretend play and social interaction in preschoolers. *Journal of Applied Developmental Psychology, 9,* 301–313.

Corrigan, R. (1987). A developmental sequence of actor-object pretend play in young children. *Merrill-Palmer Quarterly, 33,* 87–106.

Davidson, J. (1996). *Emergent literacy and dramatic play in early education*. Albany, NY: Delmar.

DeVries, R., Zan, B., Hildebrandt, C., Edmiaston, R., & Sales, C. (2002). *Developing constructivist early childhood curriculum: Practical principles and activities*. New York: Teachers College Press.

Dickinson, D. (2001). Large-group and free-play times: Conversational settings supporting language and literacy development. In D. Dickinson & P. Tabors (Eds.), *Beginning literacy with language: Young children learning at home and school* (pp. 223–256). Baltimore: Paul H. Brookes.

Dickinson, D., & Tabors, P. (Eds.). (2001). *Beginning literacy with language: Young children learning at home and school*. Baltimore: Paul H. Brookes.

Elias, C. L., & Berk, L. E. (2002). Self-regulation in young children: Is there a role for sociodramatic play? *Early Childhood Research Quarterly, 17*(2), 216–238.

FAN: The Child Mental Health Foundations and Agencies Network. (2000). *A good beginning: Sending America's children to school with the social and emotional competence they need to succeed*. (Available from the National Institute of Mental Health, Bethesda, MD).

Fromberg, D. (1999). A review of research on play. In C. Seefeldt (Ed.), *The early childhood curriculum: Current findings in theory and practice* (3rd ed., pp. 27–53). New York: Teachers College Press.

Haight, W. L., & Miller, P. J. (1993). *Pretending at home: Early development in a sociocultural context*. Albany: State University of New York Press.

Head Start Bureau. (2001). *The Head Start path to positive child outcomes*. Washington, DC: Department of Health and Human Services.

HeadsUp! Reading. (2002). *Shows 11(Playing) & 14 (Learning the Code)*. Alexandria, VA: National Head Start Association.

Jones, B., & Reynolds, G. (1992). *The play's the thing: Teachers' roles in children's play*. New York: Teachers College Press.

Layzer, J. I., Goodson, B. D., & Moss, M. (1993). *Life in preschool: Volume one of an observational study of early childhood programs for disadvantaged four-year-olds*. Cambridge, MA: Abt Associates.

Lee, V. E., & Burkam, D. T. (2002). *Inequality at the starting gate: Social background differences in achievement as children begin school*. Washington, DC: Economic Policy Institute.

Levy, A. K., Schaefer, L., & Phelps P. C. (1986). Increasing preschool effectiveness: Enhancing the language abilities of 3- and 4-year-old children through planned sociodramatic play. *Early Childhood Research Quarterly, 1*(2), 133–140.

Morrow, L. M. (1990). Preparing the classroom environment to promote literacy during play. *Early Childhood Research Quarterly, 5*(4), 537–554.

National Center for Education Statistics. (1999). *Digest of education statistics, 1998*. Washington, DC: Department of Education.

National Education Goals Panel. (1991). *The Goal 1 Technical Planning Subgroup report on school readiness*. Washington, DC: Author.

Neuman, S., & Roskos, K. (1992). Literacy objects as cultural tools: Effects on children's literacy behaviors in play. *Reading Research Quarterly, 27,* 202–225.

Neuman, S., & Roskos, K. (1993). Access to print for children of poverty: Differential effects of adult mediation and literacy-enriched play settings on environmental and functional print tasks. *American Educational Research Journal, 30,* 95–122.

Owocki, G. (1999). *Literacy through play*. Portsmouth, NH: Heinemann.

Roskos, K., & Neuman, S. B. (1993). Descriptive observations of adults' facilitation of literacy in play. *Early Childhood Research Quarterly, 8,* 77–97.

Roskos, K., & Neuman, S. B. (2001). Environment and its influences for early literacy teaching and learning. In S. B. Neuman & D. K. Dickinson (Eds.), *Handbook of early literacy research* (pp. 281–294). New York: Guilford Press.

Schrader, C. T. (1989). Written language use within the context of young children's symbolic play. *Early Childhood Research Quarterly, 4*(2), 225–244.

Schrader, C. T. (1990). Symbolic play as a curricular tool for early literacy development. *Early Childhood Research Quarterly, 5*(1), 79–103.

Shonkoff, J. P., & Phillips, D. A. (Eds.). (2000). *From neurons to neighborhoods: The science of early childhood development*. Washington, DC: National Academy Press.

Smilansky, S. (1968). *The effects of sociodramatic play on disadvantaged children*. New York: Wiley.

Smilansky, S., & Sheftaya, L. (1990). *Facilitating play: A medium for promoting cognitive, socioemotional, and academic development in young children*. Gaithersburg, MD: Psycho-social & Educational Publications.

Snow, C., Burns, S., & Griffin, P. (Eds.). (1998). *Preventing reading difficulties in young children*. Washington, DC: National Academy Press.

Snow, C., Tabors, P., & Dickinson, D. (2001). Language development in the preschool years. In D. Dickinson & P. Tabors (Eds.), *Beginning literacy with language: Young children learning at home and school* (pp. 1–26). Baltimore: Paul H. Brookes.

Tabors, P. (1997). *One child, two languages: A guide for educators of children learning English as a second language*. Baltimore: Paul H. Brookes.

Vukelich, C. (1994). Effects of play interventions on young children's reading of environmental print. *Early Childhood Research Quarterly*, 9, 153–170.

Vygotsky, L. (1966). Play and its role in the mental development of the child. *Soviet Psychology, 12*(6), 62–76. (Original work published 1933)

West, J., Denton, K., & Germino-Hausken, E. (2000). *America's kindergartners: Findings from the Early Childhood Longitudinal Study, Kindergarten Class of 1998–99, Fall 1998*. Washington, DC: National Center for Education Statistics, U.S. Department of Education.

Whitehurst, G., & Lonigan, C. (1998). Child development and emergent literacy. *Child Development,69*(3), 848–872.

Wiltz, N. W., & Klein, E. L. (2001). "What do you do in child care?" Children's perceptions of high and low quality classrooms. *Early Childhood Research Quarterly, 16*(2), 209–236.

ENCOURAGING SCHOOL READINESS THROUGH GUIDED PRETEND GAMES

Dorothy G. Singer and Jerome L. Singer

[P]lay should be recognized as the central activity of childhood. . . . A child who is not free to play will struggle with independence later in life. Educators who think [that] equipping children with academic skills earlier and earlier will make them independent may be misguided.
— Sally Jenkinson (Jenkinson, 2002, p. 130)

Despite the warnings of Jenkinson in the United Kingdom and numerous child development experts in the United States, many educators are refashioning their early childhood curricula to include academic skills. This phenomenon has set off a heated debate among scholars about the value of play for preschool-aged children. However, as this new emphasis on phonics replaces attention to other areas of young children's experience and development, we have been surprised to see little outcry from professionals and parents.

Extensive empirical research, reviewed and described elsewhere in this volume, has demonstrated that play provides a rich context for children's learning. Guided by a teacher, child-care provider, or parent, play can contribute to emerging literacy by motivating a child to learn the skills that are prerequisites for success in kindergarten and during the early elementary school years. This chapter describes five studies, carried out from 1998 to 2003, that were designed to help parents and caregivers encourage school readiness by guiding preschool children's pretend play.

We were influenced by the following: the pioneer work of Sarah Smilansky (1968) in Israel, who used play techniques with poor immigrant children; Ernest Boyer's survey of kindergarten teachers' views about children's lack of preparedness for school (Boyer, 1991); and the recommendations of the National Association for the Education of Young Children (NAEYC) concerning the importance of play in a preschool curriculum (Bowman, Donovan, & Burns, 2000).

Our strategy called for the application of a growing body of knowledge about the motivational significance of pretend play in the cognitive, emotional, and social development of children between the ages of 2 and 5 years (D. G. Singer & J. L. Singer, 1990). Although efforts such as these had proven reasonably successful in earlier studies with middle-class children, we specifically targeted our intervention research efforts toward children who were being raised in inner-city families with low incomes. Researchers had regularly reported that children living in these circumstances had a low level of school readiness and that parents were minimally involved in their children's play. The goals of our project were to (a) arouse in parents and other caregivers an awareness and interest in introducing make-believe play to their children and (b) provide parents with written materials and videotapes that demonstrated how make-believe play could incorporate school readiness content and skills.

Learning Through Play—Studies I and II

Learning Through Play is the first of three projects comprising our five studies. This project involved parents of children who were enrolled in Head Start programs and municipally sponsored child-care centers that served low-income families in New Haven, Connecticut, and the surrounding area (Study I) and, ultimately, also included child-care centers in Atlanta and Los Angeles in Study II.

Study I—The First Year of the Learning Through Play Project

For Study I, we prepared assessment and observational procedures to establish children's baseline levels relevant to school readiness skills and their play behaviors. Our sample of 103 children attending five centers was divided into an Experiment group, whose parents received the play training, and a Control group, whose parents did not receive the training. The 50 boys and 53 girls in the study included 33 European American children, 33 African American children, 18 Latino children, 4 Asian American children, and 12 children of mixed or unspecified backgrounds. Less than half of the parents (47) were married; in 35 instances, a single parent or another single relative reared the children. Parents received a small payment for participation in the study. All participants signed agreements describing the study and ensuring the anonymity of children and parents.

We developed printed manuals and a videotape demonstrating how parents could play pretend games involving school readiness concepts with their children. A professional producer, Harvey Bellin, president of the Media Group of Connecticut, Inc., and his crew filmed the games with children from schools that were not part of the study. Members of his staff did all the editing of the various videotapes and the written manuals used for all projects described in this chapter. Adults who were at the educational level of our target readers reviewed all texts for clarity and comprehensibility. The manuals presented the goals of the games, gave directions for playing them, identified concepts for parents to stress with their children, and listed relevant books and other resources. (In later studies, we added a brief discussion of young children's developmental stages to the manual.) Finally, the booklet described additional games that parents could use in the future.

We adapted games from *Make-Believe: Games and Activities to Foster Imaginative Play in Young Children* (D. G. Singer & J. L. Singer, 1985), including "Restaurant," "Bus to the Zoo," "Submarine to the Ocean Floor," and "Springtime." The Restaurant game involves pretending to go a restaurant to celebrate a child's birthday. The game emphasizes vocabulary, colors, shapes, counting, and manners. The parent offers suggestions to the children as they play and can play along with them the first few times until they get the idea of the game. The children assume the roles of chef, waiter, birthday child, and guests and can decide to include stuffed animals for some of the roles. In the pretend game, children set the table with paper place mats that they have decorated with various shapes and colors. The birthday child and the guests order food from the waiter, who pretends to write the order on a pad. The chef "cooks," the waiter "serves," and the interaction provides many opportunities for the birthday child and the guests to practice good manners (e.g., "Thank you," "May I?," "Excuse me," "You are welcome"). Finally, the birthday child can count the candles on his or her play dough birthday cake. When the waiter brings the bill, the child counts out pretend money, pays the bill, and leaves the restaurant. Then the roles are reversed, with the birthday child becoming the waiter.

The Bus to the Zoo game offers children practice in using language as they name the library and other neighborhood landmarks to help a lost monkey find his way back to the zoo. The Submarine game, about going down into the ocean depths to find a buried treasure, involves counting, colors, shapes, and the use of small motor skills (cutting with a scissors and drawing with pencils and crayons). Springtime focuses on the seasons. Children pretend to plant seeds and watch flowers grow, learn how the sun and rain help plants grow, count, and practice large motor movements as they pretend to be birds flying into the garden. The games require only simple props—large cardboard boxes for the bus as well as the submarine and paper to represent the grass and sun. Children imagine the birds, the animals in the zoo, the ocean, the fish, the jewels in the treasure box, and other objects, creatures, and settings that the games require.

Before we began to train parents, we assessed each child individually on a School Readiness Test that we developed based on cognitive and social knowledge as well as skills selected from the games, including vocabulary, colors, numbers, shapes, names of the seasons, an understanding of manners, and the ability to describe concepts (e.g., the purpose of a library). In addition, trained assistants used an Observation Checklist and a 5-point scale on two occasions to rate the children's imagination, positive emotions, persistence, and constructive social behaviors (e.g., cooperation, helping, sharing with peers).

We trained the parents in the evening when they came to pick up their children from child care. We supplied dinner for all, and child care for the children. Parents enjoyed these training sessions, which gave them an opportunity to meet other parents and to share some of their concerns. A facilitator explained the purpose of the training and then used the video to illustrate how to play Restaurant, Bus to the Zoo, and the other games. We asked parents to play the games with their children each day over a 2-week period and to keep a record of the games they played, how long they played each game, and the children's as well as their own reactions to the games.

At the end of the 2-week period, we invited the parents to attend focus groups where they could tell us about their experiences with the games and give us suggestions about the study. Parents suggested that we develop games about feelings and about going to the store. In the next study, we did devise a game about emotions, and we incorporated a game about going to the store into a later study. Parents voiced the idea, now a staple of many parenting books, of playing the games during regular routines. While bathing a child, for example, they could play the Submarine game by pretending fish were in the tub and treasure was below the water. They could play the Restaurant game at mealtime. As children set the table, they could count the silverware or napkins, or name the colors of the dishes and the shapes of various objects on the table. We felt that these ideas would offer parents more opportunities to be in a playful mode with their children, and would allow learning through play to take place naturally during a typical day.

Results—Study I

Children took the School Readiness Test for a second time after we had trained the Experiment-group parents and had asked them to play the games with their children for 2 weeks. The Experiment-group children attained a statistically significant higher total score on the School Readiness Test than the Control-group children. The children in the Experiment group also achieved higher scores than the children in the Control group on the subtests of vocabulary, knowledge of colors, general information, nature information, and knowledge of good manners; these gains were also statistically significant. Improvement in vocabulary was especially important because vocabulary and language usage correlate best with general intelligence and have been shown to be particularly relevant to school readiness (J. L. Singer, D. G. Singer & Bellin, 1998). The observations made by our assistants indicated that children's imaginativeness was significantly correlated with positive emotionality, cooperation, and persistence. Imaginativeness was related to the School Readiness Test scores but was only marginally statistically significant.

We then trained the parents in the Control group and asked them to follow the same procedures that the parents and children in the Experiment group had followed. After repeating the 2-week regimen, the children in the Control group, like the children in the first Experiment group, demonstrated gains when the pre- and posttests were compared.

In the first study, child-care and Head Start teachers were purposely blind to our experimental procedures and did not get the play training the parents had received. We found that the children in the study were not playing the games in school that they played at home. In fact, the observers reported that teachers did not take advantage of free-play periods to interject any basic skills into the children's play. We realized that we should offer play training to teachers and to parents, especially because the children were with their teachers for most of their waking weekday hours.

Study II—The Second Year of the Learning Through Play Project

Study II, our second year of the Learning Through Play project, focused on improving the videotape and printed training materials by considering parental feedback and our own evaluation of the effectiveness of the training materials. We sought to determine whether training not only parents but also teachers in the games would yield stronger effects for the children than training either parents or teachers. We also decided to produce videotapes of two new games: the "Mirror" game, which dealt with feelings by having the child in the tape talk about what made him or her feel happy, sad, or angry, and the "Counting" game in which children learned the notion of one-to-one correspondence by using hand puppets made of socks to pick up and count actual objects. The Springtime game became a "Camping" game that not only involved learning about the seasons but also introduced new vocabulary words, colors, and standards of politeness.

We extended our study to child-care centers in Atlanta and Los Angeles. Our research design now involved four groups: (a) parent training only; (b) teacher training only; (c) training for parents and teachers; and (d) control group of parents and teachers (which also would be trained only after concluding observations and testing of the children in all four groups during the actual experiment). With minor refinements, our procedures were the same as those in the first study—obtaining informed consent from parents, observing and testing children in the participating centers, conducting the appropriate training for each group, testing and observing the children 2 weeks after completion of the training, and offering workshops for the adult participants for training and feedback.

Participants in Study II included 107 children, about equally divided between boys and girls. The sample was composed mainly of inner-city children, 81% of whom were non-White (predominantly African American, with just a few Latino, Asian, or mixed ethnicity). Slightly more than half of the parents were unmarried. Two thirds of fathers and mothers worked at clerical, manual, semiskilled, or unskilled jobs.

Research assistants with backgrounds in developmental psychology were placed in charge of each phase of the study in Atlanta and Los Angeles. They came to Yale for training, and members of our staff made periodic visits to be sure that the study was carried out with similar training and testing procedures in all locations.

Results—Study II

As in the first study, the vocabulary gains of children in the three Experiment groups as measured on the School Readiness Test were statistically significant. These groups of children also made sizable gains in information, animal identification, and recognition of emotion. Unfortunately—at least from a research perspective—the Control-group child-care center held an intensive training session in counting and matching numbers for its teachers during the same period in which our Experiment groups were undergoing training. (We found out about this training only at the completion of our study.) This teacher training resulted in sizable improvements in the counting scores of Control-group children and meant that we could not include counting in our analysis of School Readiness Test results. Interestingly, assistants using the observation checklist noted that the children in the three Experiment groups became more cooperative over the course of the project while the Control-group children became less cooperative. We were gratified to find that, at all four sites, children in the Experiment groups gained knowledge and skills in most of the cognitive and social variables we measured, especially in vocabulary (J. L. Singer, D. G. Singer, Bellin, & Schweder, 1999; J. L. Singer, D. G. Singer, & Schweder, 2004).

Parents and teachers in the Experiment groups reported that children's courtesy was improving. Parents and teachers found the videotape and manual useful and easy to follow. Children could play the make-believe games using objects and materials available at home or in the classroom; no extra expense was required. Parents played modified versions of many of the games in the car with their children—for example, counting, identifying colors, and naming places they passed on the way to school. Parents kept a daily log and reported spending an average of 15–20 minutes a day playing the games; in some instances, older siblings joined in the fun. The Restaurant game was by far the favorite game of all participants in all sites, children and adults alike.

Circle of Make-Believe—
Studies III and IV

Because of the modest success of our first two studies, we planned to test our make-believe play manuals and videotape in many more sites around the country. Just as we had completed our first two studies—and 10 years after the Boyer (1991) report—the Department of Education released a study of 19,000 children in 940 public and private school kindergarten programs (West, Denton, & Germino-Hausken, 2000; Zill & West, 2001). Researchers had conducted telephone interviews with the children's parents or guardians and analyzed questionnaires completed by their kindergarten teachers. They had also observed the children directly.

The researchers found that more than one third (34%) of the kindergarteners had difficulty recognizing letters. More than 7 in 10 (71%) had difficulty understanding the beginnings of sounds. Teachers reported a range of limitations in children's social skills. Some children argued, fought, and had difficulty making friends. Some children had difficulty paying attention or persisting at a task; they showed limited eagerness to learn. The kindergarteners who experienced difficulties in social relationships and who were less eager to learn tended to be the children of single parents who had less than a high school education. In general, kindergarteners who were older and whose mothers had a college education performed at higher levels in reading, mathematics, and general knowledge than younger children whose mothers had a lower level of education (Zill & West, 2001). The study findings showed that the lack of school readiness identified by Boyer a decade earlier was still a grave problem. More than ever, we felt driven to find effective ways to help parents and teachers of inner-city preschoolers prepare them for successful learning.

Our next project, called the Circle of Make-Believe, was conducted over a 2-year period (Studies III and IV). During the first year of the project, before we prepared the videotape and manual for this next phase of our research, we conducted a telephone survey with 58 parents, home child-care providers, and teachers of preschoolers from low-income families. To be sure that we were on the right track, we asked respondents what "ready-to-learn" skills they considered most important for their children. Respondents said that cognitive skills (knowledge of letters and numbers) and social skills (cooperation, dealing with emotions) were their highest priorities.

Study III—The First Year of the Circle of Make-Believe Project

During the first year (Study III) of the Circle of Make-Believe project, we tested a prototype of the video and manual with 118 children from low-income families. We used five games: two games that had been developed previously—Restaurant and Counting—and three new games—"Where Is My Kitten?" (which dealt with spatial relationships such as in front of, in back of, on top of, under, near, and far), "Nature Island" (which encouraged identifying letters of the alphabet, vocabulary growth, and taking turns), and "Grumbles Makes Friends" (which emphasized feelings, the process of making friends, cooperation, taking turns, and politeness).

Study III included 43 parents, 35 home-care providers, as well as 40 child-care and Head Start teachers, all of whom received the training materials and carried out guided play with the children in the study. All adults completed a Record of Children's Play form and a Feedback Information form; they also provided data on their own education, play training courses they may have taken, marital status, and employment. They completed a Play Skills form on which they rated the children's imagination, social skills (sharing, taking turns, and cooperation), persistence (ability to stay with a goal or task), and positive emotions both before and after their training. Finally, the adult participants used a Readiness Skills form to rate the children's ability to recognize numbers, letters, colors, and shapes and to compare manifestations of independence (self-help) before and after the training.

At the end of the study, all adults attended a focus group session to give us additional feedback on their experiences with the materials and to share their attitudes about the training of the children. The purpose of Study III (and later, of Study IV) was to assess how useful our materials would be for parents and for teachers who were not given the kind of training we had done in the Learning Through Play studies. We hypothesized that the materials would be so clear and self-explanatory that anyone, anywhere would be able to play these make-believe games with children.

Results—Study III

Study participants played the games in the Circle of Make-Believe project an average of 20 to 30 minutes a day. Home child-care providers and teachers played the games the longest, averaging 30 minutes per session of play. All participants rated the materials highly. They described the video as very useful, with the average rating being 4.17 (out of 5), and gave the manuals, on average, a rating of 4.30. The program successfully engaged the preschoolers. According to the parent-teacher reports, most of the children responded positively to the games. Although the children played the games on their own at home and in the home-care settings, they did not play the games on their own as much in the center-based settings. This difference may be because of centers' more structured routines, which allow less time for free play in general.

Parents, home child-care providers, and teachers in child-care centers recorded children's improvements on the Play Skills forms; parents reported the most significant rates of enhancement on all skills rated, especially imagination and positive emotions such as smiling and laughing (Bellin, Singer, Singer, & Plaskon, 2000). Data from the Readiness Skills forms suggest that, after play training, children's recognition of shapes and numbers improved; their recognition of letters improved least. Again, parents reported the most changes (compared to home-care providers and child-care center teachers) for all variables rated.

As in the two previous studies, participants reported that they enjoyed all of the games. The Restaurant game remained the favorite, and it was played the most.

Study IV—The Second Year of the Circle of Make-Believe Project

During the second year of the project, we wanted to answer the following questions. Do parents and other caregivers from low-income families perceive the Circle of Make-Believe program to be beneficial? Would they want to use it in their homes or in their school settings? Are parents and other caregivers from diverse communities able to use the program without any prior training? How do 3–5-year-old children from low-income families respond to these games? Do they want to play them? Are they able to play them? After the children learn the games, do they play them on their own? Do adults find any changes in the children as a result of playing these games?

To prepare for this study, we added two new games to the series (D. G. Singer & J. L. Singer, 2001). Our materials now consisted of seven learning games on one video and a larger, more comprehensive manual. The games included the popular games of Restaurant and Counting; three other previously used games, Nature Island, Where is My Kitten?, and Grumbles Makes Friends; and the two new games, "Store," which had been suggested by parents in the previous studies, and "Make a Story," which emphasized imagination, expressive language, colors, shapes, and sizes. The Store game introduced new vocabulary and the sequence of shopping (selecting merchandise to buy, asking for the price, paying for the goods). The game provided opportunities for good manners, choosing objects that were labeled with various letters of the alphabet, and counting pretend money to pay for the purchases. We added an introduction to the manual that explained our rationale for developing these games and their relationship to school readiness skills. We also reduced the amount of text in the instructions for each game to make them more user friendly and easier to reference while playing the games.

We tested the material in eight locations in the states of Alabama, California, Connecticut, Maryland, Minnesota, Ohio, Wisconsin, and Wyoming. Participants were 105 low-income parents, home child-care providers, and teachers in child-care and Head Start centers, all of whom completed the forms about the children in the study. We used the same assessment procedures as in Study III—an Information form for background data on the adult participants and Record of Children's Play, Feedback Information, and two Child Rating forms (one for Play Skills and one for School Readiness Skills).

Results—Study IV

The answer to our questions about the benefits of the Circle of Make-Believe program and whether parents and caregivers could use the program without training was clearly, yes. The revised videotape and manual alone were sufficient to teach these adults how to use guided imaginative play to help children learn the skills necessary for kindergarten entry. Moreover, we found no consistent differences in outcomes across the different sites. All participants agreed that the materials were self-explanatory and easy to use. Adults kept daily records, playing the games with the children, on average, slightly more than six times per week over the 2-week play period. The majority of participants, adults and children, played the games for an average of 30 minutes each time they played. Home child-care providers tended to play for longer periods than parents or teachers, possibly because they have a less fixed routine in their settings and because most of the participating parents were at work.

All adult participants reported that the video was useful; the average rating was 4.33 out of a possible 5. They rated the manual even higher; the average score was 4.46. The ratings adults made with respect to children's enjoyment of the games averaged 4.24; home child-care providers rated children's enthusiasm for the games most highly. Comments on the Feedback Information forms attested to the fact that the children not only liked the games but also wanted to continue to play them. Home child-care providers reported more frequently than parents or center-based child-care providers that children played the games on their own. Using a rating scale ranging from 1, Never playing the games, to 5, Very often, home child-care providers averaged 3.84 (which was approximately Often on the scale) whereas parents averaged 3.00 (which was equal to Sometimes on the scale). Overall, 95 participants (90% of the adults) reported scores of 3 or higher.

The data from the Play Skills forms indicated that children improved on every variable—imagination, social skills, persistence, positive emotions, and independence—between the pre- and posttests. Positive emotions increased the most, a finding that validates other studies demonstrating that children evidence more positive emotionality when they play (D. G. Singer & J. L. Singer, 1990). We found similarly positive changes with respect to other variables. Results for the Readiness Skills measure for recognition of numbers, letters, colors, and shapes indicated that all scores were higher on the posttest scores than on the pretest scores, with number recognition receiving the highest change score. Children in the home-care settings exhibited especially strong gains in the Readiness Skills measures. This finding may be attributable to the longer time these caregivers spent playing with the children.

According to the adult participants, the children's three favorite games were Restaurant, Store, and Counting. Children enjoyed using the pretend money that was supplied in the materials section of the manual in Restaurant and Store games and enjoyed using the hand puppets in Counting.

The Lost Puppy—Study V

Our fifth study built on recent research that indicates that precursors to literacy start well before school entry. Grover J. Whitehurst, director of the U.S. Department of Education Institute of Education Sciences, has identified two broad categories of emergent literacy skills—the "Inside-Out Domain" and the "Outside-In Domain."

The first domain, the Inside-Out Domain, refers to children's knowledge of the skills that are necessary for translating written text into spoken words. These elements include the following: (a) phonological sensitivity—the ability to detect and manipulate the sound structure of oral language, letters, sounds, the links between letters and sounds, and how letters in written language correspond to speech sounds at the level of phonemes; (b) print knowledge—how to hold a book, understanding that English text runs from top to bottom and from left to right across the page, and the ability to name letters of the alphabet; and (c) emergent writing—pretending to write, learning to write one's name, and using crayons and other writing instruments to draw and, later, to write letters.

The second domain, the Outside-In Domain, includes children's understanding of information outside the printed words they are trying to read—for example, meanings of words (vocabulary), comprehension that is based on knowledge of the world, and understanding of narrative and story structure (Whitehurst, 2001).

Following up on Whitehurst's theory of domains and our earlier research on readiness skills, we decided to develop materials that would address some of the problems that children face with respect to the development of language and literacy skills. As before, we planned to prepare an imaginative game, but this game would highlight language and emergent literacy skills. We would present the domains identified by Whitehurst in a pretend game that featured print knowledge—for example, parts of a book (front and back cover); the concepts of author and title; understanding that English runs from top to bottom and from left to right; and book vocabulary (e.g., *library, borrow* [as in to borrow a book from the library], *librarian, author*, and *title*). We also wanted the children to learn to name letters of the alphabet, practice writing their name, and understand narrative and story structure. We did not want to teach children to read or emphasize phonics, but we did want children to become familiar with books and know that words on a printed page have special meanings.

Our study involved preparing a 10-minute videotape of a game, "The Lost Puppy," and a printed manual for parents and other caregivers to use with 4-year-old children. The story involves a puppy who gets lost. He cannot find his way home. To help the puppy come home, the children need to find a book that will tell them what to do. The (pretend) book, *The Puppy is Found*, is in the library. To get to the library, the children must take a trip in a "car" (a large cardboard box). On the way to the library, they obey the traffic lights (learning the colors and what they mean) and count the number of traffic lights en route.

After the adult has demonstrated the game, one child plays the puppy and another plays the librarian. In the "library" (a table set up with cards for the children to fill out and some books on display), the children obtain their own "library card," write their name on it (if they can) or their initials, and then take the book home. The "librarian" reads the book to the children and helps them learn the title of the book, the author of the book, and lets them know they can "borrow" the book and then return it. The children point to the author, title, and after the teacher demonstrates, the children point to how they read the book from left to right and from top to bottom. As the game is played, the adult has ample opportunity to emphasize the goals in the manual and practice the vocabulary, letter naming, and the other elements involved in learning about books.

The puppy's owner is found when the children guess and point to the correct letter on a sheet of alphabet letters that we provided in the manual. The parent or teacher knows the correct name. One child (the one who plays the puppy) also knows the correct name of the owner. The puppy makes a whiny sound if the letter of the guessed name is incorrect and a happy puppy sound when the correct letter is guessed. For fun, this child wears a puppy mask made out of a paper plate. Once the children learn the correct name of the owner, the puppy goes home. The participants in Study V, the Lost Puppy project, were 57 children enrolled in inner-city child-care settings in New Haven, Connecticut. The group consisted of predominantly African American and Latino children. On average, the children were slightly less than 4 years old; about the same number of boys and girls were in the study. Before we began the study, we conducted telephone interviews with the parents and with home child-care providers to establish baseline data with respect to children's emergent literacy knowledge and to obtain background information about the parents and children. We asked about library use, ownership of a library card, visits to the library, whether children were read to regularly, and how active the parent was while reading to the child (e.g., pointing to words and pictures, using funny voices, explaining the story), where books were kept in the home, and whether children pretended to read. We conducted the same survey at the end of the study to identify any changes as a result of our intervention.

The children were then randomly divided into Experiment and Control groups. Parents and home child-care providers in the Experiment groups kept records of the play periods with the children. At the end of the study, after the parents and teachers in the Experiment group had played the Lost Puppy game for 2 weeks, they filled out a Feedback Information form similar to those used in our previous studies. Parents and home child-care providers attended a feedback session during which they offered us comments and suggestions for future literacy-type games. We carried out the same procedures with the Control group after we collected data for the Experiment group.

Results—Study V

Children of Experiment-group parents showed significant changes in their ability to identify the meaning of the words *author* and *title* as well as a strong trend toward being able describe what was meant by the term *borrow* (from the library). Children of Experiment-group parents also identified more letters of the alphabet than those of parents in the Control group. Home child-care providers in the Experiment group showed an increased recognition of the importance of pointing to words while reading to children. Compared to children in the Control group, children from the Experiment group who were in home child-care settings showed significant increases in using crayons, identifying letters of the alphabet, writing their own names, and defining vocabulary words. Both parents and home child-care providers in the Experiment group increased their appreciation of the importance of reading books to their children.

Parents and home child-care providers in the Experiment group found the materials useful and engaging. Through playing this imaginative game, children increased their print knowledge, alphabet recognition, as well as knowledge and use of the library. Experiment-group children in the parent and home child-care groups continued to play the game on their own, showing much evidence of pretending to read books. Once parents and child-care providers in the Control group were exposed to the project materials and process, then children in the Control group made similar gains.

We believe that emergent literacy skills can be taught within a playful setting using pretend games. Rather than omit play from preschool, we urge administrators to consider guided play as an exciting, effective strategy for motivating children, their parents, and teachers to appreciate the importance of language and books.

References

Bellin, H. F., Singer, J. L., Singer, D. G., & Plaskon, S. L. (2000). *Circle of make-believe.* Prepared for United States Department of Education Early Childhood Institute. Unpublished manuscript, Yale University, New Haven, CT.

Bowman, B., Donovan, M. S., & Burns, M. S. (Eds.). (2000). *Eager to learn: Educating our preschoolers.* Washington, DC: National Academy Press.

Boyer, E. L. (1991). *Ready to learn: A mandate for the nation.* Princeton, NJ: The Carnegie Foundation for the Advancement of Teaching.

Jenkinson, S. (2002). *The genius of play.* Stroud, Gloucestershire, England: Hawthorn Press.

Singer, D. G., & Singer, J. L. (1985). *Make-believe: Games and activities to foster imaginative play in young children.* Glenview IL: Scot, Foresman.

Singer, D. G., & Singer, J. L. (1990). *The house of make-believe.* Cambridge, MA: Harvard University Press.

Singer, D. G., & Singer, J. L. (2001). *Make-believe: Games and activities for imaginative play.* Washington, DC: Magination Press.

Singer, J. L., Singer, D. G., & Bellin, H. F. (1998). *Parenting through play for school readiness: Report, year one.* Prepared for United States Department of Education Early Childhood Institute. Unpublished manuscript, Yale University, New Haven, CT.

Singer, J. L., Singer, D. G., Bellin, H. F., & Schweder, A. E. (1999). *Parenting through play for school readiness: Report, year two.* Prepared for United States Department of Education Early Childhood Institute. Unpublished manuscript, Yale University, New Haven, CT.

Singer, J. L., Singer, D. G., & Schweder, A. E. (2004). Enhancing preschoolers' school readiness through imaginative play with parents and teachers. In R. Clements & L. Fiorentino (Eds.), *The child's right to play: A global approach.* Westport, CT: Greenwood Publishing.

Smilansky, S. (1968). *The effects of sociodramatic play on disadvantaged children.* New York: Wiley.

West, J., Denton, K., & Germino-Hausken, E. (2000). *America's kindergartners: Findings from the early childhood longitudinal study, kindergarten class of 1998–99, fall 1998.* NCES 2000-070 (Revised). Washington, DC: U.S. Department of Education, National Center for Education Statistics.

Whitehurst, G. J. (2001, July 26). *Cognitive development.* Address at the White House Summit on Early Childhood Development, Washington, DC. Retrieved from From White House Summit on Early Childhood Cognitive Development http://www.ed.gov/pressreleases/07-2001/07262001_whitehurst.html

Zill, N., & West, J. (2001). *Entering kindergarten: Findings from the condition of education 2000.* NCES 2001-035. Washington, DC: U.S. Department of Education, Office of Educational Research and Improvement.

AFTERWORD

The contributors to this volume provide relatively consistent points of view concerning the nature of children's play and how that play—especially through its narrative, pretense, and sociodramatic features—can contribute to children's enjoyment and motivation to learn as well as to their cognitive, emotional, and social readiness for school. Each chapter of this volume includes a considerable body of empirical research supporting these conclusions. We can say with confidence that, with relatively small investments in time and expense, parents, teachers, and home child-care providers can learn to help young children increase their skill in imaginative play. Along with the pleasure this type of play affords children can come a readiness to read and to count and, even more important, curiosity and motivation to learn that can last a lifetime.

List of Contributors

Sandra J. Bishop-Josef is assistant director of the Yale Center in Child Development and Social Policy.

Barbara T. Bowman is past president and co-founder of the Erikson Institute, Chicago. She now teaches courses in early childhood education and administration and supervises practice teachers at the Institute.

Sue Bredekamp is the director of research at the Council for Professional Recognition in Washington, D. C., and is a consultant to RISE Learning Solutions, a distance learning organization in Cincinnati, OH.

James Christie is a professor of curriculum and instruction at Arizona State University. He is also president of The Association for the Study of Play (2002–2003).

Carollee Howes is a professor of psychological studies in education and is the division head in the Department of Education at the University of California–Los Angeles, Graduate School of Education and Information Studies.

Sharon Lynn Kagan is the Virginia and Leonard Marx Professor of Early Childhood and Family Policy as well as co-director of the National Center for Children and Families at Teachers College, Columbia University, and is professor adjunct at Yale University's Child Study Center.

Amy Lowenstein is a research assistant at the National Center for Children and Families at Teachers College, Columbia University.

Mawiyah A. Lythcott is a research associate at the University of Maryland–College Park.

Kathleen Roskos is a professor in the Department of Education and Allied Studies at John Carroll University, University Heights, OH.

Marilyn Segal is dean emeritus and director of professional development at the Mailman Segal Institute for Early Childhood Studies (formerly the Family Center) of Nova Southeastern University, Fort Lauderdale, FL. She is also founder and chair emeritus of the A. L. Mailman Family Foundation in White Plains, NY.

Dorothy G. Singer is senior research scientist at the Department of Psychology and Child Study Center, Yale University. She also is co-director of the Yale University Family Television Research and Consultation Center and is a fellow at Morse College.

Jerome L. Singer is a professor of psychology and child study at Yale University and is co-director of the Yale University Family Television Research and Consultation Center.

Ross A. Thompson is Professor of Psychology at the University of California–Davis, where he is a core faculty member of the Developmental Psychology Program.

Brian Vandenberg is a professor of psychology at the University of Missouri–St Louis.

Alison Gallwey Wishard is a doctoral student in applied developmental psychology at the University of California–Los Angeles, in the Graduate School of Education and Information Studies.

Edward F. Zigler is a Sterling Professor of Psychology, emeritus, at Yale University and founder and director of Yale's Center in Child Development and Social Policy.

Index